Cinematic Storytell

This book presents a new, story-based approach to cinematic coverage and storytelling in film and video. It breaks from the conventional idea that shots are the fundamental unit of filmmaking, instead exploring the specifics of determining coverage. Keyframes in patterns are introduced, delivering scripted material in a context-rich presentation that supports the storytelling.

All the analysis, interpretation, and creative decision making is done first, with shots derived as the very last step. Scripted material is divided into six categories with associated patterns. Like cinematic building blocks, these can freely stack up and interconnect, supporting creativity and avoiding rigid formulas. This approach enables filmmakers to tap into the film "language" that audiences already understand and put it to practical use, helping the audience to feel the storytelling deeply. Dozens of film examples are provided throughout, plus conceptual and camera diagrams to contextualize the methods presented, and exercises are provided to reinforce concepts. Emphasis is placed on supporting performance and story meaning through a cinematic context. With all the concepts and decision-making options described and shown in examples, a scripted scene is analyzed and developed through an eight-step process, illustrated with storyboard, camera diagrams, and ultimately shot list descriptions.

The book is ideal for filmmaking students interested in directing and cinematography, as well as aspiring and early-career filmmakers, cinematographers, and directors.

Thomas Robotham teaches screenwriting, filmmaking, and cinematography. He is currently Affiliated Faculty at Emerson College, and Director of Photography (DP) in the International Cinematographers Guild. He holds a patent in light-emitting diode (LED) lighting for film and video. Thomas has also worked as Creative Director (advertising) and as a fine artist (sculpture). www.robotham.com

Cinematic Storytelling

A Comprehensive Guide for
Directors and Cinematographers

Thomas Robotham

Routledge
Taylor & Francis Group

LONDON AND NEW YORK

First published 2022
by Routledge
2 Park Square, Milton Park, Abingdon, Oxon OX14 4RN

and by Routledge
605 Third Avenue, New York, NY 10158

Routledge is an imprint of the Taylor & Francis Group, an informa business

© 2022 Thomas Robotham

British Library Cataloguing-in-Publication Data
A catalogue record for this book is available from the British Library

Library of Congress Cataloging-in-Publication Data
Names: Robotham, Thomas, author.
Title: Cinematic storytelling : a comprehensive guide for directors and
    cinematographers / Thomas Robotham.
Description: Abingdon, Oxon ; New York, NY : Routledge, 2021. |
    Includes bibliographical references and index.
Identifiers: LCCN 2021001900 (print) | LCCN 2021001901 (ebook) |
    ISBN 9780367531423 (hardback) | ISBN 9780367531430
    (paperback) | ISBN 9781003080657 (ebook)
Subjects: LCSH: Cinematography. | Motion pictures—Production and
    direction.
Classification: LCC TR850 .R625 2021 (print) | LCC TR850 (ebook) |
    DDC 777—dc23
LC record available at https://lccn.loc.gov/2021001900
LC ebook record available at https://lccn.loc.gov/2021001901

ISBN: 978-0-367-53142-3 (hbk)
ISBN: 978-0-367-53143-0 (pbk)
ISBN: 978-1-003-08065-7 (ebk)

DOI: 10.4324/9781003080657

Typeset in Bembo
by Apex CoVantage, LLC

This book is dedicated to all my
students – past, present, and future.

Contents

Preface

There are many books and resources for directors *or* cinematographers. But very little is written about what they work on together – the central area where they overlap and collaborate. That is in the planning of coverage – the choices of imagery to present the entire story.

Directors are responsible for the storytelling in all its manifestations. Cinematographers are responsible for the pictures, in both aesthetic and technical dimensions. Coverage falls into an overlapping zone of responsibilities – cinematic storytelling. That is the sole focus of this book.

This book presents a new, story-based approach to cinematic storytelling in film and video. We focus on how the audience feels and grasps the storytelling through the film "language" they already know. We link that to the mechanisms that will produce the physical and emotional responses that the filmmakers want the audience to feel. Dozens of examples are presented, along with conceptual and camera diagrams.

The book is intended to give filmmakers a shared framework for understanding coverage in storytelling terms. The concepts apply to stories of any length, from short films to feature films to long-form, multi-episode stories.

I've taught filmmaking to undergraduates and adult career-changers. What I have found is that – regardless of age or experience – deciding what to shoot is the hardest part. It can be an amorphous and confounding challenge without some framework for thinking about it clearly and creatively. That's what I hope to provide.

This is not just an issue for students. Except at the level of expert filmmakers, it can actually be quite hit-or-miss. Ideally, the story and the imagery create a whole that is bigger than the sum of its parts. How many shows – regardless of their budget – reach that high bar? Many productions fall short. That's a shame, because great ideas and deep feeling get lost before they reach the audience. Tremendous amounts of work go unrewarded when the cinematic storytelling falls short.

Other filmmaking professionals, beyond directors and cinematographers, have a stake in the cinematic storytelling. Producers have the ultimate interest in making the most of the script and in how their filmmaking team works together. Having a language for ephemeral and abstract concepts can help make creative discussions productive. Editors need to understand the components of cinematic storytelling to open up creative opportunities in the editorial shaping of coverage. Actors may want insights on how camera usage can be supportive of performance.

This book is written for anyone who wants to be a filmmaker or wants to understand some of the things that filmmakers do at a fundamental level, to orient and inform the audience and shape their experience at a subconscious level.

One more thing: None of this book is "the Truth" with a capital T. These ideas do not replace the art and craft of filmmaking with something shiny and new. This book is just a way to talk about a complex creative task, breaking it down into ideas and processes. It is describing and systematizing what many film professionals already know at a gut level. The way you use a camera affects how the audience engages with, responds to, and feels the storytelling.

I hope you find this book useful in your quest to make movies that entertain us, make us think, and above all, make us feel deeply.

Acknowledgements

This book would not be possible without the help of many people. I would like to thank Sheni Kruger, Claire Margerison, Sarah Pickles, and all the helpful professionals at Focal Press. I would like to thank the readers of preliminary drafts for their incredibly useful comments, plus Kate Fornadel and staff for invaluable help in production. Thanks to all of the film professionals I have learned from, especially the gaffers and camera assistants who taught me so much while getting so little credit. Appreciation goes out to my colleagues at all of the places where I have taught over the years, for helping me kick around the ideas in this book. Thanks to my excellent classmates and to Professors Jean Stawarz, James Lane, James Macak, and Linda Reisman, from whom I learned so much about storytelling while earning my MFA at Emerson College. I'd like to respectfully acknowledge all the filmmakers, in every role, who have inspired me over the years. I look at the examples in this book and I feel the compelling reality they create, the performances so vivid and moving (even in still images). There is so much craft, heart, and intelligence clearly in evidence both in front of and behind the camera. It was hard to choose examples from all the films that have taught me so much. I would especially like to thank my life partner, Mary Ellen Schloss, for her superb editing and tireless help; our son James for his insightful ideas; and our son Christopher for joining in family discussions of these concepts over the years. You have all challenged me to communicate ideas with clarity and coherence. I could not have done this without all of you.

Table of illustrations

Chapter 6

Chapter 7

Chapter 8

Chapter 9

Chapter 1

What is cinematic storytelling?

The pictures help us feel the story

Cinematic storytelling means putting the moving pictures to use, helping the audience feel the story. This means trusting the imagery to carry story weight. Fundamentally, it means the camera is serving the story.

The moving images are not simply there to record performances but also to present them to the audience in a way that clarifies and deepens their meaning. The pictures do not exist on their own, like a flashy sideshow or visual decoration. The pictures present story information and the movie conventions help us understand it. Their job is to help communicate the story and to help us, the audience, feel the unique and special nature of the story.

The cinematic storytelling for every movie is unique in its own way. It's not like baking a cake, where one recipe works each and every time. Effective cinematic storytelling is never the same thing twice. A cinematic approach could be very plain for a quiet, character-based story. It might be very flashy in support of a stylized thriller. We will need to dig deep below the surface in order to find the commonalities that unite all of the different ways that cinematic storytelling works to support the story and helps the audience to really feel its impact.

This book is about making thoughtful, story-centered creative choices to suit the material at hand. The goal is to help you think about and make choices that are firmly anchored in the scripted storytelling. If the choices are formulaic, they will come across as mechanical. If the decision making is isolated from story needs, the results will be arbitrary and lack emotional depth. If copied from other movies, it will feel derivative and lack its own emotional fingerprint. These are pitfalls that a story-centered approach can help filmmakers avoid.

Each motion picture can and should be unique to the scripted storytelling, deeply felt and thoughtfully presented. With a creative process that is story-centered, you can make highly individual choices that will feel coherent, cohesive, and emotionally resonant with the storytelling.

DOI: 10.4324/9781003080657-1

A cinematic approach through keyframes – not shots

The general standard for going from script to screen is to start with making a shot list. That is almost the last thing we will do, discussed in the final chapters. The shot is not the fundamental unit of this approach. It is the end product.

The fundamental unit for us is the frame. We will take a **keyframe** approach in laying out a detailed and deep analysis of how moving pictures serve the storytelling. A keyframe is a representative frame, and its qualities connect the script to the images. Patterns of keyframes deliver the movie conventions that the audience understands, without conscious thought, in their assembly of the story and its possible meanings.

We will investigate keyframes and patterns, their connection to audience comprehension, and their foundational connections to the script. With these ideas in hand, your creative process will be rooted in the script, "growing" imagery that fully supports your individual story.

Cinematic storytelling exists for every form, length, and budget

Although the examples in this book are almost exclusively from feature films, I see little difference between feature films, short films, or multi-episode long-form series in terms of the cinematic storytelling. All have similar problems and opportunities at the level of cinematic choice. Everything in this book should be applicable to all forms and lengths of narrative storytelling using motion picture cameras of any type or cost.

Great movies exist at every length and every budget. Most aren't perfect or flawless. They don't have to be. They do have to be compelling, engaging, and satisfying. A confident hand at cinematic storytelling will bring you a long way toward those goals.

Not every filmmaker needs to be a genius. By tightly integrating the visual presentation with the script, we can make sure that the story and characters found in the script will feel vivid on the screen. That's cinematic storytelling. It takes effort and creative courage, not genius, so it is within the grasp of most of us who love movies enough to want to make them.

Going beyond formulas or easy solutions

You can find lots of explanations of famous shots in famous movies. We may want to "borrow" those, hoping they will have the same beneficial result in our own work. That ignores the facts – different script, different creative contributors, different budgets, etc. Borrowing shots is like borrowing precisely tailored clothes. Or like taking the wheel off someone's car and trying to install it on a different make and model. They won't fit. You can utilize underlying concepts and approaches. They will, by necessity, result in different shots. That is good. They will custom-fit your movie, not someone else's.

It is easy to be distracted by technical tools, thinking they might provide answers. Cameras and lenses are a lot of fun. Add all the specialized mounts and gizmos, and you could spend forever thinking about them and not the storytelling. But if you postpone the fun of playing with high-quality toys, you can solidify the purpose behind making the images. Then, all these wonderful devices stop being toys and instead become creative tools for the execution of story-based decisions.

Throughout this book, we will look at many examples – not to find a cookbook formula but to find the underlying factors that make the presentation story-centered. We can find common approaches in a vast range of movies, indicating that coming up with unique cinematic storytelling isn't "secret knowledge," just something that needs study and practice. These fundamentals exist across the vast range of films, but you need to train yourself to see them.

Consider this – we don't need to invent new letters to express ourselves with different words. We don't need to invent words to communicate new or complicated ideas; we just choose the right words to convey meaning. We don't need to invent new notes to make a new melody. We take the underlying fundamentals and reapply them in new ways and new configurations to arrive at unique results.

Let's start with a few examples from actual movies, to point out some of the ways that the visual presentation contributes to the audience's visceral understanding of the story. We'll see how cinematic choices help us feel the progression of the story and enrich our understanding of character actions and relationships.

Clear presentation that informs and orients

Cinematic storytelling helps the audience respond to the storytelling and feel its emotional significance. The audience doesn't need to know how that works, but filmmakers do.

Our first example shows how the focus of the storytelling is clearly indicated through the progression of framings. In the movie *Cast Away*[1] (Figure 1.1, Figure 1.2), a family holiday dinner includes several plot points. This scene delivers the story event that sends our protagonist, Chuck, on his fateful journey. How do the framings and their progressions shape our understanding?

The scene starts with a wide frame of a holiday dinner. This introduces us to the main table and orients us to the activity – the big family dinner. Old folks sit at one end of the table, younger folks at the other, with main characters Chuck and Kelly in the middle. At first, we see groups, emphasizing the social nature of the situation. The first significant story point is when Chuck is asked about marriage plans. Chuck and Kelly have had a bet about that. Their brief dialogue has Chuck framed over the shoulder (OTS in shot terminology) of Kelly, and Kelly is shown OTS Chuck, keeping each in the other's frame of reference. (A list of some standard shot abbreviations is at the end of this chapter's Summary.)

Two things have happened. One is that by reducing the number of subjects in frame, we (the audience) understand that the center of the storytelling is now between them, not the larger group. The second is that, with the pattern of reciprocal, mirror-image framing, we know that Chuck and Kelly

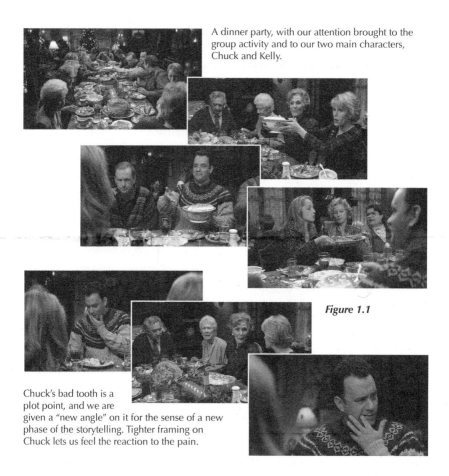

A dinner party, with our attention brought to the group activity and to our two main characters, Chuck and Kelly.

Figure 1.1

Chuck's bad tooth is a plot point, and we are given a "new angle" on it for the sense of a new phase of the storytelling. Tighter framing on Chuck lets us feel the reaction to the pain.

are talking to each other, sharing mutual attention. This might not seem like a big deal, but it is.

Movies are filled with interpersonal interactions and dialogue. The basic pattern of reciprocal shot pairs will occur many times in many movies. The variations in the way they occur will be a major force in helping the audience feel the emotional flow of these interactions.

The next plot point is Chuck's wince over the pain of a bad tooth. Two things make this stand out so that we give it proper notice. One is the different angle on the old folks, which signals us that the prior flow has been interrupted and the story has gone in a new direction. The second is the first close-up (CU) of Chuck checking the tooth, OTS Kelly. These two visual cues, of change in a pattern and of closer focus on Chuck's reaction, give us a context for registering story progress and significance.

Immediately after the focus on his tooth, Chuck's beeper alerts him to a demand from work. The frame shifts from Chuck's CU to the beeper in his

Figure 1.2

Chuck's work beeper catches his attention, then Kelly's. The tighter frame on Kelly now matches that on Chuck, letting us feel the importance of her reaction.

This non-verbal exchange feels like silent dialogue centered on their interaction, leaving out the family. We can feel that this hits Kelly harder, with the small push-in on her reaction.

hand, like a magnet drawn to the object with story significance. We instantly register Kelly's gaze toward the beeper, and how it intrudes on the happy scene. We don't have to think about it – we see the intensity of her look, and we see the beeper and know that was the focus of her attention. These are simple mechanics in terms of shots, but they are critical to following the story.

A small, almost unnoticeable push-in on Kelly shows us how this new situation impacts Kelly's emotional state. Her disappointment makes sense because this is her family. Her potential future husband just let work interrupt Christmas dinner. We get the feeling that he's done this kind of thing before. This push-in on Kelly is intercut with Chuck and Kelly's pair of CU framings. Even though no words are spoken in the moment, we instantly recognize the silent conversation between them through the pattern we associate with dialogue. Interpersonal interaction does not need spoken words – the pattern of shots tells us that they are communicating non-verbally.

The entire movie hinges on our understanding of the very simple chain of events. The emotional consequences of Chuck's actions, which feel like a minor disappointment in the moment, become life-changing for both characters.

Notice how the framing encompasses the entire social situation at the start, then the subset of social groups engaged with our main characters, and then the mutual connection between them as a couple. This progression tells us something fundamental: **What is in the picture has story significance, and what is out of the picture no longer does.** We know this, subconsciously, as movie-watchers. Now we need to make it part of our conscious focus as movie makers.

The framing provides clear presentation of the story movement within the scene, from a broader social situation to the specific actions and reactions of our main characters. This gives us a clear chain of cause and effect (C&E as our abbreviation), from the toothache to the work interruption.

A big part of our understanding of movies comes from understanding people and social situations, and so we need to become consciously aware of how we do that, through what we see and hear. The clear focus on facial expressions lets us connect with the character's inner state – thoughts, feelings, and intentions. We can tell that the main characters are sharing these inner states and feelings through their mutual attention. The cinematic storytelling capitalizes on our ability to know and understand people and their behaviors.

We learn so much about their relationship from the way the scene is presented. That helps us share the feelings of Chuck being put on the spot. We can relate to Kelly, whose relationship is made fair game over dinner. Two very clear demonstrations of Chuck's current life trajectory are brought to our attention. He postpones important life actions (fixing his tooth) for the sake of his work. He will put everything with emotional significance, this dinner and the love of his life, on the back burner in favor of work. The clarity of the dinner scene sets up all of this.

The way the dinner is presented is conventional but highly effective. Much of what is considered "conventional" coverage can be understood in the story progression from the general to particular, wider to tighter. We go from the broader situation to the specific reactions of the main characters. We will see these concepts flexibly employed in a wide range of ways to suit the specifics of different stories and filmmakers.

We will also see examples of storytelling that don't fit the conventional mold but are comprehensible just the same because our attention is shaped, and our understanding is informed, by the cinematic storytelling.

Including us in a character's subjective attention

The next example showcases the basic filmmaking conventions that let us know what captures a character's attention, propelling their subjective experience into the center of story significance. In the movie *Midsommar*[2] (Figure 1.3), the main character is introduced through her strong emotional reaction to a disturbing email from her sister.

Dani is seen from the front, slightly above her eyeline, in keeping with seeing over the top of her laptop computer. She is upset and intent on her screen. We get closer to her as we get progressively closer framings of an email list, the specific message, and then the word "goodbye" that so alarms her.

The first shot of the laptop is easy to understand as her point of view (POV). The close-up (CU) and extreme close-up (ECU) of the screen are representing the focus of her attention – not necessarily all that she sees, but all that occupies her attention.

Movies allow us to enter into and share the subjective experiences of a character. It is done through their focused gaze, followed by the presentation of the subject of their attention. I refer to this as the ***Look/See*** pattern, because it is understood by the audience not as an isolated shot or frame but as a relationship between a character's subjective experience and our sharing of their attention and interest.

The Look/See pattern is the simplest of all clear and obvious patterns in filmmaking. It lets us comprehend story significance in terms of a character's inner motivations. Motion picture stories are usually centered on character experience. This pattern lets us enter and share that subjective experience, not just observe from the sidelines. This is at the root of the dialogue pattern we've seen in the prior example, known conventionally as ***shot-and-reverse***. The shot-and-reverse pattern is actually reciprocal Look/See patterns, indicating shared, mutual attention and interaction between two subjects. In the baseline Look/See pattern, the subject of the character's attention does not look back.

The more distant framing of Dani at her desk cools down the intensity and gives us some space to observe how she reacts. The next few frames show a clear chain of cause and effect (C&E), with her picking up her phone, scrolling to a choice, thinking twice, then committing and dialing Christian, whose name we see in close-up (CU).

We enter the next phase of the scene with her pivoting in her chair, giving us a new framing. For an instant she adjusts her hair and demeanor, clarifying that this is a boyfriend. Then she asks for support but is met with distance and judgment. We see this situation impinging on her with the camera pushing into a tighter CU.

This scene is all about the inner state of the character, Dani. Her subjective attention – her focused gaze – directs us to material with story

Figure 1.3

We connect with Dani's response to a disturbing email. From her look, we see the laptop. Then the intensity ramps up. We get closer to her and the word that is so upsetting.

We observe her reactions and reaching for the phone. She thinks twice, then makes the call.
The CU on the phone tells us the call is to Christian. She pivots, facing a new direction for this new phase. We get closer to her as the intensity and intimacy increase and her inner state becomes the focus of the storytelling.

significance. The ramping up, down, and up again of the emotional intensity is tracked by how close we are – filled with her emotions – or through a cooling distance that gives us a chance to observe and assess her reactions in light of what little we already know or anticipate. Her misgivings about the phone call are proven true and give us the initial insight into her relationship with Christian – which is central to the entire movie.

Shifting perspective and physicality

Movies can make us feel things physically, not just emotionally. Consider how images of a roller coaster ride give us strong sensations in our bodies, as if we were there. This sensation is called kinesthesia. Films are uniquely able to convey physical sensations as part of the storytelling. Movies that deliver powerful physical feelings are among the most successful at drawing large audiences – even when characterization or plot development is weak. In the service of strong characters and a good story, kinesthesia can be wonderfully evocative, conveying subjective experiences and the resulting emotions.

In the movie *Gravity*[3] (Figure 1.4), novice astronaut Ryan Stone is repairing a circuit board on a satellite when a catastrophic hail of debris blows apart the space shuttle. Strapped to a remote arm, she is sent spinning off into space. We feel the panic-inducing spin and tumble of her body in our own bodies as we watch.

It is as if the character functions as our avatar in the movie-world, transmitting their physical sensations to us in our chairs. That observational, informational, full-body framing of the character allows us to see and feel their bodily sensations vicariously. This is also true for watching sports or dance performance. We can feel in our own bodies the motions and actions of the participants on screen.

The next phase begins with the camera drawn to Stone's tether – it must be disconnected before she is lost in space or burns up in the atmosphere. This gives us a clear example of action-scene C&E. The tether will kill her; she must conquer panic and follow orders, no matter how terrifying it is to be shot into the void. We feel this sense of being cut off through observing her rapid tumble into the distance, until she is just a tiny dot in the vastness.

We go into a third phase, aligned with her subjective experience, watching the earth, sun, and stars spinning around her. After that sense of shared subjective experience, we can easily relate to her fear and the sense of barely keeping emotions in check.

We get closer to her until we are visibly inside her helmet, looking out. When the framing goes to the earth spinning past her, we have entered into sharing the character's POV through a Look/See pattern in a continuous shot. We see her wide-eyed gaze and then see the earth spinning past, attaching us to her subjective experience in a powerful way. We have gone

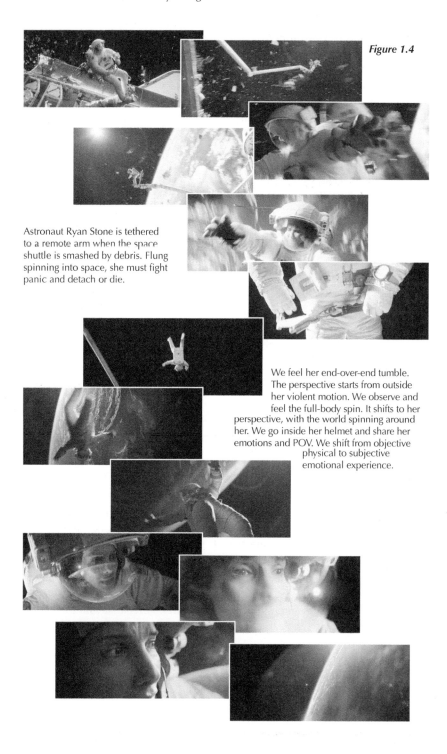

Figure 1.4

Astronaut Ryan Stone is tethered to a remote arm when the space shuttle is smashed by debris. Flung spinning into space, she must fight panic and detach or die.

We feel her end-over-end tumble. The perspective starts from outside her violent motion. We observe and feel the full-body spin. It shifts to her perspective, with the world spinning around her. We go inside her helmet and share her emotions and POV. We shift from objective physical to subjective emotional experience.

from observing through full-body framing, to connecting with her emotions through access to her expression, to seeing what she sees, putting us fully inside her subjective experience.

With so many levels of one character's experience presented to us, we have no trouble understanding that this is Stone's story and that her experience is central. We feel her physical sensations, we connect with her emotions, and we feel the subjective sense of being lost in space. We grasp the physical and emotional C&E relationships through the images.

In this example, a disastrous crash results in a visceral, kinetic, physical experience. **We observe, participate, and emotionally connect.** Our perspective shifts fluidly from a position that feels independent of the character to one that is fully dependent upon and mediated by the character experience. It's like we are brought up and down through levels of meaning, and we emerge with an understanding of what we've seen as a synthesis of all those levels.

This is all without any conscious thought on our part, and without interfering with the ongoing flow of story progress. We can feel the difference between having some stable vantage point outside of Stone's experience and a vantage point that we share with her. That shift from objective to subjective perspective is a huge part of movies. Physical peril is felt in our bodies when we see the whole body of the character tumbling and flying off into the distance. Emotional response is felt through her expression. We simply feel it in the audience. How to make that happen is something filmmakers need to know.

Story information is delivered in a way that orients us to what is important, moment to moment as the story unfolds, and gives us understanding of the objective and subjective character experience. In the chapter on Character Action patterns, I will discuss perspective and proximity in a concrete way that relates to the storytelling.

Dynamism in dialogue

Our next example demonstrates how the seemingly simple patterns associated with dialogue can give us a dynamic sense of story progression through adjustments and modulations. The presentation of dialogue – interaction between characters – is the one filmmaking pattern that most film lovers will easily recognize. Frames with one character speaking (and reacting) are interspersed with similar frames of the other character in the dialogue. That pair of mirror-image framings are so ingrained in all of us who've watched movies for years that we can recognize them without even thinking about it – the Look/See pattern that shows us a single character and their active attention. What they see does not look back. When this is reciprocated, it creates the standard shot-and-reverse dual character sharing of mutual attention. Now we are past the single-character action and into dual-character interaction. Each looks and each sees.

The frames at the end of our first example, from the *Cast Away* dinner, are immediately recognizable because of that pattern of shot pairs. This next example, from *The Incredibles*[4] (Figure 1.5), gives us a rapid-fire group of variations on this basic two-shot pattern of frames that we all understand represents dialogue. This provides shaping of the scene into phases that house the major dramatic beats that signal progression of the story.

This scene opens on the character Helen (Elastigirl) crying. The camera follows her reaching for tissues from the character Edna. We then follow Edna, and we see what's called stacking in depth, where we can connect with Edna's expressions in the foreground while understanding that Helen can't see this – we are in a privileged position of sharing both emotional displays. Edna turns and we get the first pairing of frames OTS of the foreground character. The OTS framing does two things at once. The main function is to connect with the character whose face we see, letting us read their emotions and reactions. But also, by looking over the foreground character's shoulder, we participate with them in this shared context.

Edna does not like the weakness that Helen is showing and comedically seeks to stiffen her spine. She leaps on the table and whacks Helen with rolled up papers. We then observe them both, clearly seeing their relative positions from a side angle. A wide frame from the side shows Edna leaning in, visually pushing Helen to the edge. Then we return to the reciprocal OTS frames in this new position while Edna reminds Helen that she is strong, she is Elastigirl, and she can solve her own problems through action.

Edna moves to the other end of the table and the framing adjusts to sustain her place in the frame. We can feel that Edna is in charge in this whole scene because the camera follows her, not Helen. The character who is followed, or whose movements demand reframing to accommodate their actions, is felt as the center of story agency and dynamics in the moment. **The character who controls the frame tends to have story agency.** This feeling is on the subconscious level for most of the audience. We just feel the energy and it infuses Edna as the character whose actions drive the shifts in framing. Helen, given a literal slap in the face, a good talking-to, and then a little space, rises up and stands tall (spine stiffened!). The scene ends with more concentrated focus on Edna, who relishes the positive results of her coaching.

Two characters talk. We observe from the sidelines at points, but mostly we are totally engaged in the interaction – each character is the subject of the other's attention in a reciprocal Look/See pattern of subjective attention. Dialogue is reciprocal subjective attention, and we recognize that story importance centers on what happens between them. It sounds simple.

If applied mechanically, without regard for the potential of all possible variations, it can be boring and lifeless. When tied to the arc and dramatic "beats" (central moments of story progression), the fluidly flexible dialogue

Figure 1.5

Edna offers sympathy. Next, she reminds Helen that she is a superhero and calls for action. Helen's spine is stiffened, and Edna is pleased with herself.

pattern can be an exciting form of presentation. It informs us that the story-telling is now centered on mutual attention and social interaction. It shapes the scene and orients us to changing contextual cues as it progresses.

The Look/See component brings us into character subjective experience. The mutual Look/See of the dialogue shot-and-reverse pair brings us into the shared subjective experience of social interaction.

In our chapters on Dialogue patterns, we will discuss the variety of ways that Dialogue coverage stems from, and leads back to, the story. We will go further in the chapters on Movement and on Scene Shaping.

Summary

We all love movies and know how to watch them. We have lots of sub-conscious knowledge that we can bring to our conscious awareness. We can be vicariously engaged in the storyworld and in the lives of the charac-ters. We can even be in their shoes, seeing what they see and feeling what they feel. Cinematic storytelling plays a role in that, carrying weight in the storytelling.

The framing shows us what is important and leaves out what is not. It helps us to experience a range of perspectives on the story. Our understand-ing is informed and oriented through a shorthand of movie conventions we've all learned.

Our lifetimes of watching movies make the effects of cinematic choice invis-ible or subconscious. Our job as filmmakers is to become conscious and self-aware of how cinematic choices generate impact and amplify the emotions of the story. This includes becoming aware of how the images clearly present information, and how to align audience experience with character experience.

- Cinematic presentation puts the images in the service of the storytell-ing, carrying weight in the storytelling.
- The images provide information in context, to help us feel the signifi-cance and meaning in actions and performances.
- What is in the frame draws our attention to what is important, and what is out of the picture is no longer significant in that moment.
- Dependence on character perspective creates subjective experience where we are in their shoes and feel what they feel, sometimes even seeing what they see.
- The range of storytelling perspective includes opportunities for physi-cality and audience mirroring of the character's movements; the com-prehension of social interaction information; and access to expressions and the inner state of characters.
- The basic pattern of dialogue – characters talking in reciprocal frames – offers great variability that can shape scenes to show story progress.
- The character who controls the frame has story agency.

Our goal is to make story-centered – not mechanical – decisions about the imagery. We seek to maintain connection to the script and capitalize on cinematic opportunities.

Fundamentals of visual storytelling exist, and we can see them operating through a vast range of different stories and storytelling approaches. The creative freedom is vast. With full awareness of how cinematic storytelling works, any script can have its story tracked and supported. This means that you can put it to use in your own stories, with your own approach and vision.

Common shot list abbreviations

All of the following are in relationship to character framing.

LS – long shot, typically full body. MED or Med – medium shot, typically hips or waist up. MCU – medium close-up, typically upper body. CU – close-up, typically head and shoulders or bust framing. ECU – extreme close-up, typically just face or isolated detail. OTS – over-the-shoulder, referring to using the back of a character's head, neck, and shoulders as a foreground framing device in the shot of another character or action.

What you can do . . .

Watch a scene from any movie you know well. Turn the sound off. Now watch it again and ask:

- Can you follow the general outline of the scene just by following the pictures?
- Was there a moment when something critical happened, and if so, how were the pictures helping to set that up?
- Were you given an observational vantage point at any time that clarified who was there and what they were doing?
- Were you given a vantage point that let you feel like a participant in the scene, looking over the shoulders of characters as it played out?
- Were there any pairs of matched shots that instantly let you know that two characters were engaged in dialogue, whether spoken or non-verbal?
- Did you ever see a character's focused gaze, followed by what you understood to be their POV on the focus of their attention?
- How did any or all of these elements contribute to your sense of what was happening in the story and what it might mean?

Notes

1 *Cast Away.* Directed by Robert Zemeckis, Cinematography by Don Burgess. Twentieth Century Fox, Dreamworks, released 2000. DVD: Twentieth Century Fox Home Entertainment (2001, USA). Start time: 00:14:06.

2 *Midsommar*. Directed by Ari Aster, Cinematography by Pawel Pogorzelski. A24, B-Reel Films, Nordisk Film, Square Peg, released 2019. DVD: A24 Films, LLC, Lions Gate Entertainment (2020, USA). Start time: 00:02:38.
3 *Gravity*. Directed by Alfonso Cuarón, Cinematography by Emmanuel Lubezki. Warner Bros., Esperanto Filmo, released 2013. DVD: Warner Bros Home Entertainment (2017, USA). Start time: 00:12:20.
4 *The Incredibles*. Directed by Brad Bird, Cinematography by Andrew Jimenez, Patrick Lin, Janet Lucroy. Pixar Animation Studios, Walt Disney Pictures, released 2004. DVD: Buena Vista Home Entertainment (2005, USA). Start time: 1:02:58.

Chapter 2
Foundations in the script

The life cycle of the story

In Chapter 1, we looked at examples that illustrate how the pictures help us feel the story. The pictures present story information and the movie conventions help us put that into context. We are now going to build up a functional framework for how that works. We will start at the foundation – the scripted storytelling – and build from there.

It is common to consider the script to be akin to a blueprint, providing instructions but lacking the vivid qualities of performance and imagery. Perhaps that sells the script short. The script is, in almost every way, the full and complete story. A good script conveys all the flesh and blood emotions and feelings that we want and expect from the movie. It will have all the revelations and surprises, the emotional resonances and reverberations. Filmmaking requires the fostering and nurturing of that story. It is useful to understand how a script conveys story information and inferences in order to find out what requires creative interpretation and invention in the filmmaking. We must understand how to transfer and translate storytelling on a page into a cinematic version.

Script to screen is a kind of metamorphosis

Some creatures go through a natural process of metamorphosis. The essence of the creature – its DNA – is faithfully transmitted and optimized in an entirely different form. A caterpillar chews leaves, while the butterfly sips nectar. A dragonfly nymph hunts underwater, while the dragonfly adult hunts in the air. After a stage of metamorphosis, these creatures leave behind one set of attributes to take up an entirely new set, with new capabilities. It is the same creature, totally transformed.

This is quite similar to what happens when a script is transformed into a movie. The story essentials remain the same, while the artistic presentation is fully reorganized to maximize its effectiveness in the next phase of its life.

When this works well, it can be wondrous. When it falls short, we might say "something got lost" or "it didn't live up to its potential." Maybe it feels like the acting was weak, but in actuality the coverage undermined the

DOI: 10.4324/9781003080657-2

performances. We might think it's boring, when really it lacks any shape that nudges us to feel story progress. Perhaps we get no emotional impact from story events that should be meaningful, because the chain of cause and effect wasn't made clear.

Story metamorphosis requires faithful transmission of scripted storytelling, plus the creative invention needed to make it fully alive in its new form as a motion picture. Throughout this book, we will examine how this has been done in a wide range of examples. At the end, we will concretize this as a process, going from a script example to the full plans for cinematic storytelling.

Scripted versus movie storytelling

We need to understand a little bit about scripts in order to make movies. Let's look at salient ways that scripts deliver storytelling, compared to how motion pictures do the same job. These differences define the transformational gaps that we must bridge.

Symbolic versus sensory presentation

A picture is worth a thousand words. Let's look at this concept from the other direction. How many pictures is the word *wilderness* worth? What about *mother*? Or *destitute*? There is no fixed relationship between words and images. Each one can unpack into a thousand of the other. This sobering thought spares us wasting time hunting for a Rosetta Stone that easily and directly translates words into pictures.

Instead, let's look at a few lines of an imaginary script, and consider the imaginary motion pictures that might result. This will provide insight into the differences between word and image storytelling.

```
EXT. THE CLIFF - DAY

Ocean waves CRASH on the rocky base of a sheer cliff.

A solitary figure stands at the edge.
```

Let's consider three options for how to present these words in motion pictures, for us to "watch" in the theater of imagination.

1   We could start with the camera flying along the base of the cliff, swooping up in the nick of time to avoid being smashed by a wave. It rises up the cliff, slowing, until we peer over the edge and find the solitary character.

2   The camera could start by looking down the cliff at the waves, then pull back to reveal the character, and look past them to the blustery sea.

3   A wide shot from a distance could show us all the elements at once – the waves, the cliff, and the small figure near the cliff edge. After absorbing that for a few seconds, we go to a shot of the character.

The first option engages kinesthesia – the sensation of movement – which is something that motion pictures do supremely well. We arrive at the character, loaded with dynamism. Will that energy suffuse our sense of the character, revealing a bit about who they are? Perhaps.

The second option engages the sensation of dizzying heights. That is another bodily sensation that movies do very well. The pull-back of the camera results in looking past the character at the setting, encouraging us to imagine being on that cliff with them. Perhaps they are afraid of heights, perhaps totally immune to that fear. We await their reaction, to reveal some information about what kind of person they are, or what kind of story events might follow.

The third option is objectifying and observant, from our exclusive vantage point. We have time to feel the awesome setting for ourselves before joining the character. Their loneliness, and the isolation of this setting, might be what we bring to the character as its own form of revealing some aspect of the character.

Any of the camera ideas might serve, depending on the story being told. The first two options exploit the camera's ability to transfer sensations through imagery. The third provides a way into the scene that feels like a romantic landscape painting from the 19th century. We meet the same character, but the three options bring quite different feelings to this introduction, perhaps revealing something about them. They provide the same information in different contexts. The choice of cinematic presentation should be based entirely on the story, how it unfolds, and how you, as a filmmaker, interpret the script.

The declarative story information is what can be seen (and heard). The declarative story information bridges the gap between forms. What is explicitly described on the page becomes the subject matter of the images. The images present what is plainly visible.

The inferential story information is what we feel, emotionally or physically. The stimuli for inferences are different in writing and in movies. We "read between the lines" in a different way. The cinematic storytelling doesn't add information; it points to what is implied within the script. It presents story information in a manner that supports the deeper inferences.

Let's try another example, to look for the social and psychological dimensions of this metamorphosis from words to pictures.

```
INT. THE DINING ROOM - DAY

BILLY (9), a skinny kid in school uniform, sits at the
table. STEPFATHER (52), in a grey suit with frayed
cuffs, steps into the room and pulls out a chair at the
opposite end of the table.

Billy flinches at the SCRAPE of the chair.
```

Let's imagine some options for how this could be presented visually.

1   We could start with a shot of Billy at the table, all the way through his
     notice of Stepfather entering, and his reaction to the sound of the chair.
     Then go to a shot over Billy's shoulder, showing Stepfather settling into
     his chair.
2   We could start with a wide shot that shows Billy sitting, Stepfather
     entering, and cut to a close-up of Billy reacting to the chair.
3   We start with a shot through a doorway of Billy at the table, and enter
     the room with Stepfather, stopping at a shot over-the-shoulder of Step-
     father on Billy, awaiting his fate.

There are endless possibilities. The words give us a fairly clear idea
of Billy's response to Stepfather. But even in the imagination, the
images of Billy's reaction are a faster and more penetrating indication
of his emotional state than words can easily convey. Movies are more
like real life, where we can sense emotions and relationships almost
instantaneously.

The declarative story information is that Stepfather comes into the room
and sits at the table with Billy. Part of the inferential story information is that
Billy is scared. Maybe he's scared for good reason. But maybe his Stepfather
is kindly and loving, and gaining Billy's trust is central to the story. The total
arc of the story should guide your choices.

For the audience to feel that they are in good hands, filmmakers need
to know the story completely, in order to make choices that are true
to both the script and their creative interpretation of all the possible
inferences.

Fluid and elastic reading versus fixed-duration viewing

Scripts are a literary form of a very specialized type. Reading allows us to
disconnect from strict clock-time in a way that movies do not. When we
read, we can skim through information but stop to take a breath after strong
emotional moments. We feel the pacing and may rush along or linger, but
this is a time-stream – a temporal stream – that we can dip in and out of at
will. The storytelling happens in sequence, but reading time is fluid, elastic,
and under our control.

Movies are more like recorded music, taking exactly a fixed amount
of time to experience, never stopping from start to finish. We receive

storytelling in sequence, through time, but we have no control over how long anything takes, and there are no breaks except those provided by the filmmakers.

Filmmakers need to account for the transformation from a fluid to a fixed temporal form. This cuts both ways. The audience may need to follow a series of character actions. If they miss some critical moment, the story events won't make sense. But it may only take an instant to register the social and psychological information conveyed by characters' expressions. In movies, we can "read" people without a thought, just like in real life.

```
. . . The attacker swings the butt of his gun. THUD.

George slumps, a puppet whose strings have been cut.

Claire jumps the attacker - grapples for the gun.

The gun SKITTERS across wet pavement.

Claire dives - rolls - SHOOTS.

The attacker drops, disbelief in his eyes. Then
nothing.

Claire crawls to George. He's lifeless. A thing. He's
gone.

Claire is alone, kneeling in a dirty puddle, oblivious
to the gun she still grips.
```

Let's play this out in the theater of imagination.

We are starting in the middle of the action. A close-up of the gun traces its arc down to George's head. A medium shot follows him slumping to the ground, lifeless, bleeding.

From behind Claire, a handheld shot stays with her as she jumps the attacker. A close-up shows the grappling for the gun. It flies. We see Claire trace its path. We see the attacker trace its path. A close-up shows the gun skittering, then coming to rest.

Handheld, we follow Claire's leap and grabbing the gun, turning, and shooting. The reverse shot shows the attacker hit by the bullet, his expression of disbelief, and his death.

Handheld, we follow Claire to her kneeling beside George. A close-up shows the shock and series of realizations flowing through Claire.

A wide and stable shot shows the tableau of Claire kneeling beside George's body. The camera slowly pulls back, leaving her a lonely figure in an alley, her life changed.

There is a general convention among filmmakers that one page of a script equals one minute of screen time. That is, in my experience, fairly accurate if averaged over the total script. It is not uncommon for action to take longer on screen than you'd expect from the script, while dialogue may actually take less time. Or vice versa, depending on the writer and the specifics of the storytelling. The connection between time on the page and on the screen can be quite elastic.

As this excerpt is about one-quarter of a page, you'd expect it to be about one-quarter of a minute, or 15 seconds. I've timed my silent reading of this small script excerpt, and it comes to about 15 seconds. Perfect. I've timed my reading aloud, and it comes to about 25 seconds. I've timed my "watching" the movie in my imagination, and it comes to about 30 seconds, or twice the expected time, due to the temporal differences between reading and watching.

The scripted form accounts for the pacing of the action through short sentences and white space to make it fast and punchy until the end, when it becomes almost languid. Each significant story event in the chain of cause and effect is given its own paragraph. But on screen, the audience needs more time to register the gun flying, and each combatant's reaction to that.

It takes longer on screen to register the gun landing and stopping, because the audience must clearly see it to grasp its significance. But it takes little time on screen for George to fall, because we can instantly "read" his face and body language going lifeless.

It takes only a moment on the page for Claire's final actions and realizations. The reader can take their eyes away from the page to register all the emotions and story significance. But on screen, we need to provide that time as actual experienced time, to permit the audience to register and process all the emotions and significance for Claire. Time is needed to allow the performance to work through all the interior thoughts and feelings, and for the audience to grasp that and give it proper weight.

Pulling back lets us leave Claire to her grief and all the implications of being left alone, irrevocably altered. The pacing slows, to match the weight of the moment. The stable framing is a contrast to the handheld instability of the physical action, reflecting the release of tension we feel at the conclusion of the fight. The slow pace allows the audience to ponder the dramatic change in the story arc. Depending on the genre of the story, we might imagine Claire's future to include crushing guilt, or we might perhaps imagine that she becomes a badass vigilante killer.

What is common in all three examples

What is plainly visible – the declarative information – will transfer from one form to the next, giving us a solid anchor in the scripted storytelling. That is what the images present. Creative use of cinematic means will be required to help the audience grasp story interpretations – the inferential information. That is what filmmakers can point at through cinematic storytelling, aligning the physical and emotional feelings of the movie-watching experience with the story. This is how the visualization of the movie stays organically connected to the written form of the story. It is how the unique qualities of the story, and the unique interpretations of filmmakers, are brought to the screen. The way the images present information can point toward the way it should be felt or influence the way we feel it.

Summary

In Chapter 1, we looked at how pictures help the audience feel the story without having to be conscious of how that happens. For filmmakers to accomplish this, we need to compare and contrast the ways that a script and a movie convey the same storytelling.

To achieve this transformation from words to pictures, we need to identify what is carried forward, basically untouched, and what must be invented.

- Stories go through a metamorphosis or transformation from script to screen. Filmmakers need to faithfully preserve the written storytelling while optimizing its potential in the new form as a movie.
- The differences in written versus movie storytelling show us gaps that must be bridged to account for the major differences: symbolic through words versus sensory through images; and fluid versus fixed temporal experience.
- The non-stop temporal experience of motion pictures demands giving the audience the time to register and process critical emotional events.
- The performance-based nature of motion pictures makes social and psychological understanding closer to real-life experience, and faster on screen than through words.
- The declarative story information is the same in both forms – the plainly visible people, places, things, and events that are described in a script are seen on screen. These are the elements that bridge the transformational gap between the forms.
- Everything that the audience puts together in their imagination or responds to physically – the inferential story information – has to be interpreted from the script. Then, it can be pointed at and felt, physically or emotionally, through the pictures. This demands invention through cinematic means.
- No information is added by the cinematic storytelling. The declarative story information from the script is presented, and the inferential story information is supported, according to how it should be felt.

What you can do . . .

Find the script for any movie or show you know, love, and can watch for the sake of comparison. Pick a scene or short sequence and do the following analysis and comparisons:

- What is the declarative story information? What do you actually see?
- What is the inferential story information in the script? What do you feel and know from the words that isn't stated outright and explicitly? How did you know?
- What part of that inferential story information is emotional? What part is contributing to physical sensations?

Chapter 3
Coverage defines attention

Coverage delivers story information in context

Let's begin with a short review. *Coverage* is the word for all the different shots in a scene. Any given shot will record or "cover" some section of the script. For example, a scene of two characters sitting around talking might have **conventional coverage** that presents:

1   A wide enough shot to let you know where people are in relation to each other, and what they are doing. This would be called a **Master** shot because all of the action can be seen from that one vantage point, start to finish. It could be followed as the "master plan" to sort out and reconcile any differences in the rest of the coverage during the editing process.

2   A shot close enough to the characters so that their social presentation to each other is the focus of attention, ignoring the setting. This would be called a **two-shot**, with the two characters as the focus of attention.

3   One set of mutual, mirror-image, reciprocal shot pairs that present character dialogue would be called a **shot-and-reverse** pattern. In standard, conventional coverage, this would likely be OTS (over-the-shoulder). Most importantly, the two-shot will have character A on frame left and character B on frame right. That same orientation will exist in the OTS shots. Character A will still be frame left, and character B will still be frame right. So we have a Master, two-shot, and close-ups (CUs) in a shot-and-reverse pattern.

4   You might have closer CUs of each character, using matched and reciprocal frames of each, and continuing to have the same orientation on the left and right sides of the frame. That tighter shot-pair will feel more intense or intimate. Going back and forth between these shots provides the editor with the means to shape the scene and what is called rising and falling action, roughly defined as the increase or decrease in the dramatic energies over time. That is the benefit of conventional coverage – it gives the editor the means to shape how the audience will feel about the story, moment to moment.

DOI: 10.4324/9781003080657-3

Conventional coverage – Master, two-shot, and CUs – is a starting point for many filmmakers, and it can work quite well for scenes with dialogue between two characters. The scene of the holiday dinner from *Cast Away*,[1] (Figure 1.1, Figure 1.2) follows that form, more or less – wider to let you know what's happening and progressively tighter until we are seeing a shared interaction between the two main characters.

Simply by switching from a wider shot that includes the setting to the shot-pairs of dialogue, we feel the story moving toward the interaction between them and the emotions conveyed. Going closer or pulling back can feel like the ebb and flow of intimacy or intensity between the characters. Even the most basic of conventional coverage is shaping how we feel about the story.

Storytelling before mechanics

Coverage should go beyond simply recording performances. It should also inform and orient the audience to story perspective, pacing, and subtext. At that point, the coverage is truly carrying story weight and functioning cinematically. The imagery becomes almost like an accompaniment to the performances – seating and shaping, elevating and deepening audience engagement.

The declarative subject matter of the story becomes fully activated when housed and carried by imagery that helps the audience assess and understand story meaning. This is central to the definition of **context** – the circumstances that form the setting by which something can be assessed or fully understood. Context serves up content on a platter and helps us understand what to make of it. Cinematic coverage delivers story information in context, assisting the audience in feeling the inferential story information. That's what supports the specifics of the individual story and what supports performances so that the audience feels the emotional importance of events to the characters, the emotional journey of their story, and the physical sensations intrinsic to their experience.

The problem with starting from a shot list – describing what is seen in terms of camera mechanics – is that it skips all the truly significant issues of cinematic coverage. Jumping to decisions about shots leaves out all the concerns of contextual presentation that are at the heart of cinematic storytelling. For these reasons, the creation of a shot list should be at the end of a process of determining cinematic coverage, not at the start. That may seem odd or frustrating. But if you think about it in terms of storytelling, it might make more sense. Many screenwriters create things like character backstories, plot outlines, storyworld descriptions, and thematic constellations long before any scene is written. This is to ensure that the writing will follow a compelling and coherent plan and not go off the rails. The plan is not blindly executed; it is the scaffold for creative invention.

Working through the context-shaping aspects of coverage – before making a shot list – is like developing the cinematic equivalent of backstory and outline. The creative and emotional rationale for all the subsequent camera work will be firmly rooted in your interpretation of the scripted storytelling. The shots will follow the cinematic plan and not go off the rails.

In the traditional sense, shots are the basic unit of film production, but they are not the basic, underlying units of contextual decision making. A better analogy might be that shots are more like complete sentences, while framing is more like key words and phrases – the containers of the central ideas. These can be expressed in any number of ways while still retaining the intended meaning. If you fall in love with a beautiful sentence that doesn't convey your idea, you might feel an emotional commitment to it that thwarts your real communication purpose. The same can hold true for a beautiful shot that doesn't support the storytelling.

It is framing – specifically the patterns formed from framing through time – that serves the story-tracking and information-contextualizing functions. The fundamental cinematic reasoning for framing decisions is to create a contextual connection to the scripted storytelling. All the rest stems from that. All the interpretive freedom comes from the grounding in story-based decisions.

Framing = story attention

Framing presents subject matter to us with qualities of attention that orient us, moment to moment, about how we are supposed to understand the storytelling. In every well-produced movie, every image is serving the storytelling. This means that the center of story significance at any given moment will act as a sort of attention-magnet for framing.

Looking at part of a sequence from the film *Alien*[2] (Figure 3.1) illustrates the way that framing brings attention to what is central to the storytelling.

The framing is always centered on whatever is important to the story in the moment – cutting off the helmet, then the CU reactions of the characters. Reactions always tell us how information is received in the storyworld, through character response – true in social situations, as well as physical actions such as this.

Consider how, in real life, we may be in an unfamiliar situation and the reactions of those around us tell us what is expected. If we are watching an unfamiliar sports event, we know if something good or bad happened to the home team from reactions. If we are in a brand-new social situation, we will pay exquisite attention to others' reactions so we don't step on toes or do the wrong things. This also works in movies.

Our observation of the scene, showing all three participants, functions as a way to align us with the crew and their reactions. The framing is revealed to be an approximate POV of the crew, waiting anxiously in the hallway outside the medical laboratory. Clarity in the chain of cause and effect in the

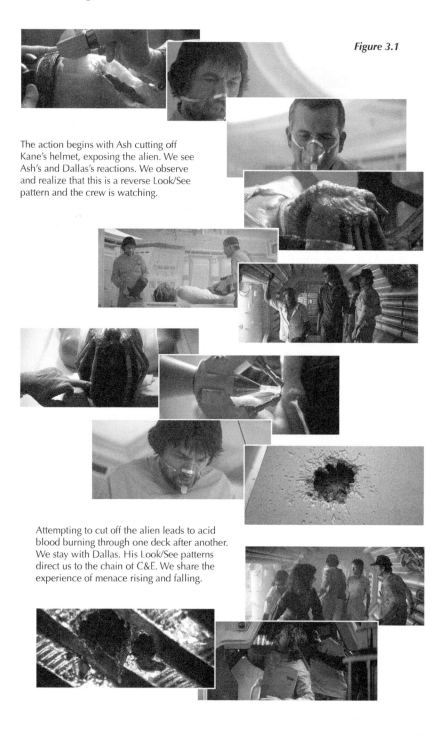

Figure 3.1

The action begins with Ash cutting off
Kane's helmet, exposing the alien. We see
Ash's and Dallas's reactions. We observe
and realize that this is a reverse Look/See
pattern and the crew is watching.

Attempting to cut off the alien leads to acid
blood burning through one deck after another.
We stay with Dallas. His Look/See patterns
direct us to the chain of C&E. We share the
experience of menace rising and falling.

lab gives the scene a feeling of precision and measured pacing, soon to be interrupted. Ash's finger points to where he will attempt to cut off the alien, so that it's completely clear what the next ECU (extreme close-up) means. Taking time creates tension.

We see the acid blood spurt out – we see Dallas track it through his focused gaze – then a CU of a hole being melted through the floor. Suddenly, the fate of the ship takes priority and Dallas rushes from the lab, through the gathered crew, who follow behind. The action is no longer slow and deliberate but instead a headlong rush. Down one ladder after another, we follow in front of Dallas, seeing him track the damage until it peters out. At each stage, his focused look puts the subsequent CU of melted metal into context. We see the acid-burned hole and smoke as it is depleted and stops. At each stage of this example, the framing is bringing some piece of the story puzzle to our attention, for us to put the pieces together.

One final thing to note is that this is called a *sequence*, which is a group of scenes that constitute one continuous piece of action. The main reason this feels like one scene is that the patterns of framing and action are continuous, without reset. When we discuss the many ways to cross scene-to-scene boundaries, we will review how sequences work.

Envisioning framing

Now let's look at an imaginary story to consider how framing choices can bring attention to the storytelling in a way that contextualizes the action, helping us make sense of it and giving each aspect its proper story significance.

When our protagonist inches along a window ledge outside a high-rise building, we may see the vertiginous view down, with certain death if she falls. We share the story perspective and stakes of her predicament. We share a physical sensation of dangerous height, induced through our vicarious attachment to the character. When she peeks into the next window and sees a bad guy, we will share her attention, aligning us with her subjective experience. When she gathers herself, then jumps inside and fights, we will feel the adrenaline through framing that dynamically tracks the action. The camera will track her actions that control the frame, letting us feel her agency in the story's drive and forward movement.

It makes no difference how many shots this takes, or how fancy they are. The important part is how the declarative story information is framed to provide the richest contextual presentation of everything sensed, felt, and inferred from the script. That is what tracks the story. The shots are the final, mechanical containers of framing decisions. The distillation of framing decisions – cinematic context formation – into shots may end up influenced by numerous factors such as practical considerations, budget, or your personal philosophy. As long as the contextual intent of the framing is carried out, the imagery will serve the cinematic purpose of carrying story weight. As with serving up food, more expensive ingredients might make it tastier, but good plain food is always satisfying.

We will discuss the process of shifting from a stage of coverage planning – the contextual application of framing patterns – to the logistical and technical stages of shot listing but only at the very end, after questions of context formation are fully considered. That is what makes it possible to have unique coverage suited to your unique story and creative intent. The final shot list is just the end product of that exploration and decision making.

Framing patterns underlie cinematic coverage

Watching cartoons as kids, we've enjoyed happy hours immersed in cause and effect. From adventure films, we've discovered and eagerly anticipated the physical thrills of kinesthesia. From love stories, we've given our sympathies based on knowing clearly which character's perspective was favored at what point. We've all been trained in how to assimilate motion picture storytelling, to make sense of it, to be willing and able to enjoy the simplest or most elaborate, overt or subtle storytelling.

All of this common experience allows filmmakers to use and build upon a common set of approaches to the presentation of story situations. Identifiable patterns of framing are the building blocks of storytelling in context.

Our next example, from the movie *Altered States*[3] (Figure 3.2), shows how framing can evolve and transport the story attention through a series of contextual moments.

In this example, there is a strange CU that is more evocative than informative. It is its strangeness that orients us to the storyworld and obsessions of the protagonist, Eddie. A continuous shot starts with that frame, then evolves into one that shows a glowing tank in what seems like an industrial setting. The single shot continues to new framing that finally reveals a scientist, Arthur, observing the tank, with extensive instrumentation surrounding him. There are multiple moments where our attention is reconfigured through the inclusion of new story information, until we realize that this is an experiment. What could conceivably be multiple shots are instead strung together like beads on a string, to give a sense of evolving attention and evolving attribution of provisional meaning.

Now oriented to the laboratory setting, we can understand the shot of Arthur working, shown to us from the opposite angle. We understand where Arthur is in the room, so it isn't disorienting to see him looking back at the tank, which returns us to Eddie's experience. This becomes quite subjective, as we see Eddie spasm inside the tank from an angle that reveals his full body motion from a peculiar but possible angle. Then we connect to his face, but his eyes are covered, and his view must be inward. It shuts us off from him. His inner state is unreachable, but we can feel that it is an active and intense state.

This is quite a cinematic way to introduce the main character as someone inexplicable and willing to do strange and extreme things to pursue his

Figure 3.2

The movie opens with a very abstract image of a person in some sort of apparatus. A continuous, dynamic pull-back reveals that this is a cylindrical tank. Framing on the object evolves into the laboratory setting. We observe Arthur making notes. His look is followed by seeing his POV of the isolation tank.

We reattach to Eddie's perspective with more otherworldly images, including a view inside his womb-like experience. He's a spaceman in technical rebirth.

internally motivated quest for self-knowledge. He is a mad scientist in search of existential truths.

In this example, patterns of framing lead us from a detail, to a setting, to the characters within the storyworld. These are plainly visible elements of the script. The framing of those elements will become something I call **keyframes**. Keyframes represent landmark moments in the presentation of scripted elements, shown in a way that delivers contextual cues. The visible elements are the subject matter; the contextual cues are what I call the qualities of the keyframe. The huge pull-back at the start of the *Altered States* example demonstrates many keyframes within a single, evolving shot. All of the screenshot examples in this book are comprised of keyframes and important transitional moments between them.

Those of you who are familiar with computer-based editing or motion graphics will be familiar with the term keyframes, as the important points for actions or operations.

When analyzing cinematic coverage, the only keyframes that need to be identified and selected are those that, in a connect-the-dots manner, outline the highlight moments and indicate when change happens, providing a shape that tracks story progress.

In that way, keyframes are like landmarks when giving directions – turn left at the yellow house. You don't have to pay attention to every corner, just the one with the yellow house. Keyframes are like snapshots that tell the essential story. At a birthday party, blowing out the candles might be a keyframe moment. Grandma nodding off in her comfy chair might be another. Keyframes are highlight moments of the story. The story passes through them.

Plainly visible scripted elements link to framing patterns

Everything within the scripted storytelling hinges on those elements that can be seen. Those scripted visible elements are critical in bridging the gap between script and screen, providing the subject matter for keyframes. Keyframes work as the underlying fundamentals for cinematic storytelling, through variations in their qualities and their connections from one to the next, forming patterns.

There are six broad categories of scripted elements that are plainly visible: Character Actions, Character Looks, Character Dialogue, Settings, Objects, and Evocative Imagery. Everything plainly visible in a script – the declarative story information – will fall into one of these categories. Each category is associated with patterns of framing qualities that present the visible elements in context that help us feel the inferential story information.

An overview of the six visible elements is provided next. Chapter 4 explores how patterns provide context, pointing toward story implications and inferences. After that, individual chapters dig deeply into each category to explore how they work.

1) Character actions

Actions might be physical, like dancing, running, or climbing. They might be activities in the sense that driving, computer operation, bomb assembly, and cooking dinner are all focused activities rather than highly physical actions.

Usually, it's important for the audience to clearly understand what the actions involve. At other times, it may be important to raise questions that won't be answered until later. Both situations demand knowing how to provide or mask information through our *observation* of the action. In addition, there is often a desire to engage a sense of audience *participation* in character actions. Often, *connection* with the character is the most important, in order to grasp their thoughts, feelings, and intentions. These may have story significance in anticipation of, in the middle of, or in reaction to events. Chapter 5 is devoted to the patterns for Character Actions.

2) Character looks

A main indicator of character thoughts, feelings, and intentions is their focus of attention. That is what enables other story elements to be understood as given singular attention by a character – the Look or focused gaze. There is a cause-and-effect relationship between the Look and whatever is seen. Because of this relationship between a character's attention and what we see, we have entered the realm of subjectivity – the audience sharing the subjective attention of a character.

The Look/See framing pair lets us know that we are finding importance in, and vicarious access through, the relationship between the character and subject or object of their attention. It places story perspective in that character and makes the storytelling in that moment dependent on the character. We have seen this in a few of our examples in Chapter 1, and we will explore more examples and options in subsequent chapters.

There are also Looks that circle between characters, letting us understand mutual, unspoken understandings. This is comparable to real-life looks between people – perhaps at a dinner table or when playing a card game – checking on each other for any indications of thoughts, feelings, or intentions that might affect the situation. Chapter 6 is devoted to Character Looks.

3) Character dialogue

The other main part of scripted scenes is the interaction between characters, known as Dialogue. Usually this involves two characters, but it sometimes involves more. Dialogue is based on reciprocal attention of characters, with balance and imbalance, symmetry and asymmetry, stasis and change, configuration and reconfiguration, all in service of context formation. Dialogue patterns are framing pairs. That pairing is precisely what lets us know that what is between these characters is the focus of the storytelling. The primary Dialogue pattern – shot-and-reverse – is a mutual Look/See pair, with each character engaging focused attention upon the other. That makes it not just dependent in perspective but also interdependent.

Because the social, psychological, and story implications of character interaction are so huge, we will spend a lot of time examining some of the many possibilities in their presentation. Two chapters are devoted to Dialogue – Chapter 7 outlines the structures underlying their presentation, and Chapter 8 provides examples of how these structures can be employed.

4) Settings

From ancient Rome, to spaceships, to a big city, Settings will be described in the script to the extent that informs the storytelling. Settings may be limited to background or act as major story elements, such as a ship at sea (or in space). Settings are physical but also social, informing and orienting the audience to the opportunities and constraints that are affecting characters and the overall storytelling. Even knowing that a story location is public or private has big implications on character behavior and reactions to that behavior.

Entrances and exits of main characters are often shaped by the direct connection of Setting to Action patterns. We will explore these in detail in Chapter 9 on Settings, and we will generalize about presenting Settings in static increments akin to a slideshow or the evolving, searching quality of a tour or survey.

5) Objects

From tokens of affection to rings of power, from nuclear submarines (both an Object and a Setting) to a Thunderbird convertible, from books to guns, Objects may be described in the script that have intrinsic significance or pure utility. Some objects are presented to the audience outside of, or prior to, any character awareness of them. The bomb under the table is the classic example of how an Object can create tension. Sometimes a character singles out an Object, lending it story attention, as in detective stories when a clue is found. From these two examples, we can generalize that the framing of Objects will help us understand story perspective, whether it is independent of character mediation or dependent upon their subjective attention.

A character might give singular attention to people, animals, or creatures that do not engage in a reciprocal interaction. This "objectification" has storytelling potential. The phrase "object of desire" comes to mind, as does the targeting of prey, the fearful glimpse of an adversary, or the comforting presence of a loved one in the distance. Chapter 10 on Objects will delve into these concepts through examples.

6) Evocative imagery

A tunnel of light resolves into a paramedic's penlight when a character regains consciousness. The surface of the ocean becomes flickering light. Firelight turns shadows into dancing shapes. Swirling checkerboard vortices replace normal vision, going through a wormhole. Lovers become silhouetted shapes that flow together.

The last category of scripted visible elements is Evocative Imagery. These are purely sensory visuals, and the feelings they evoke are the point of their inclusion in the story. Whenever the perceptual nature of imagery overshadows the conventional presentation of subject matter, the storytelling is shifting toward a place where aesthetic response is central.

Chapter 11 on Evocative Imagery explores these ideas, and how a pure visual aesthetic response can contribute to the storytelling.

All patterns come equipped with contextual cues

We learn how to watch movies from childhood onward. As mentioned in Chapter 1, we can feel the interaction of Dialogue through pairings of shots, even if no words are spoken. We quickly grasp that a character's focused Look is connected to whatever we see next – and even that their look might retroactively be understood to be focused on whatever we just saw.

Framing patterns are what we respond to, through our unconscious training as movie-watchers. These patterns support and confirm our understanding of what is happening in the story. They are so ingrained in us that we don't even think about them; we just respond. Now we have to think about them in order to put them to use.

The established patterns and their variations are how we, in the audience, track the twists and turns of a scene. The variations function cinematically – visually assisting the storytelling – precisely because the framing directs our attention without conscious thought. We feel that character interaction is central in one scene, and physical danger is central in another. We understand how characters are reacting because we are given access to their expressions. A set of generalized contextual cues are built into the patterns. The specific modulations and variations in pattern usage help us feel the specific changes and story progression of the movie.

For example, the pair of shots in a Dialogue pattern is a round-trip electrical circuit of mutual attention and interaction. As with relationships in the real world, the closely observed sense of reciprocity can indicate balance and fairness, while imbalance or asymmetry between the shot-pairs of dialogue can indicate imbalance or asymmetry in the relationship. Let's consider this in the theater of imagination.

The character Mary is interested in the social scene at a dance club, and the character Jean just wants to go home. That might be inferred through customizing the framing patterns so that Jean is facing and trying to connect with Mary, but Mary's attention is shifted toward the dance floor. The asymmetry in the shot pairs carry the contextual cues that allow us to interpret and expand what we read from the performances of the actors playing Mary and Jean.

The pattern sets up our anticipation of conventional story presentation, and the story-centered modifications point toward an inference of failed emotional connection. A very simple pattern, with the potential for modulation, can cinematically engage the audience with recognition of subtextual and story-significant events.

Coverage patterns function through time, like music

We can think about visual presentation as something like music – notes, timbres, and rhythms adding up to patterns through time. In an essential way, the music **is** the patterns repeating, modulating, and changing through time. The music, like a Platonic ideal, exists outside of any single instance of its performance. We know that because different players with different instruments can play the same music. They can even perform it in radically different styles.

Music is temporal pattern formation. In the verses of a song, patterns repeat and modulate. Then we are alerted to a change, and we hear a new section of the music – the chorus. Transitional sections called bridges connect sections in a way that provides surprise and creates anticipation.

Framing also comes in patterns that are repeated, transitioned, and changed. The patterns can interconnect and be recombined in a temporal flow. That is how the contextual function of framing can track the storytelling, and why we will use framing and patterns as the basis for our work. The way they inform and orient us can be consistent, go through slight modulations, and give us wholesale change.

We can feel the shift between framing patterns and are stimulated to follow the contextual implications for the storytelling. For example, our character Jean has left the nightclub and is walking down a city street. Mary exits the club seconds later and sees her friend in the distance. We know this is the story progression because a fundamental pattern is a frame that clearly shows one character's focused gaze, and whatever is seen next will be interpreted to be the object or subject of their attention. That pattern lets us understand this, without thought. We see Mary's gaze, we see Jean walking away in the middle distance, and we instantly understand that the storytelling is now with Mary and we are sharing her subjective attention. Mary enters this frame, and we are pulled along with her, participating with her as she catches up with Jean. When Jean turns, we are now in a CU dialogue frame OTS of Mary. The pattern would anticipate a reciprocal frame of Mary OTS Jean.

We have seamlessly gone from Action, to Look, to Dialogue patterns of framing. This fluidly shifts our sense of what to expect from the storytelling, contextualized by the expectations of the framing patterns. We have shifted story perspective from Jean to Mary. We have fluidly moved from the Action of Jean leaving, to the Look of Mary finding her, letting us understand through the fixation of her attention and our subsequent participation with her that she is intending to catch up with her friend, not just going for a brisk walk on her own. When they face each other, we have organically arrived at the Dialogue pattern contextualizing interaction and social communication.

Recombination of patterns allows flexible context shifting

In music, the same notes, underlying patterns, and changes can be used again and again for entirely new and different songs. In film, the same underlying patterns and changes are employed in continuously new combinations to support entirely new and different motion picture stories.

In fact, if patterns are used in a stale manner that doesn't reflect sensitivity to some unique narrative drive, we can feel it almost immediately. This is why some movies can feel stale, unoriginal, and distinctly un-cinematic. The context-generating cinematic means have become detached from the storytelling source, and it all feels mechanical and emotionally distant.

It is our job, as filmmakers, to make sure those types of problems never happen. It is our job to take advantage of the cinematic tools of framing and framing patterns. With those tools in hand, we can clearly present story information in a way that is contextualized to support the story meaning. We can nourish and foster the story, helping to make it come alive.

Summary

- Coverage that is cinematically functional delivers information in context. It enables the audience to feel much of what is inferred in the scripted storytelling through visual presentation.
- By thinking in terms of framing, not shots, we can remain focused on where story attention is placed, and how it should be housed contextually to register with the audience in the way that we, as filmmakers, want. Then we have creative freedom in final shot selection with "built in" connection to the scripted storytelling.
- Patterns of framing are attached to the visible scripted elements. These patterns immediately and unconsciously orient and inform us about what we see, housing performances, action, and dialogue in an activated, context-rich presentation.
- Because these are time-based patterns, we can use modulations and changes in the basic framings to track twists and turns of the storytelling. This keeps the motion picture coverage closely aligned with the scripted storytelling.
- Because the patterns are modular, configurable, and interlocking, we can create endlessly different combinations that conform to the unique story demands of individual projects.
- It is clear presentation of story information with contextual nuance that makes story-based coverage cinematic. It carries weight in the storytelling. This connects the audience to the story through faithful transmission of scripted storytelling through cinematic means, fully integrated into the overall filmmaking and performances.

What you can do . . .

Pick a scene from any movie or show you know and love, and do the following analysis:

- Is the framing always limited to what is important to the storytelling? Is there ever a shot that presents anything that isn't important to the storytelling?
- If characters are seen in wide shots that include the setting, does the physical or social setting provide informative context?
- If some action is seen in close framing, is it the center of the storytelling in the moment?
- Are you ever observing characters and the actions from some objective vantage point?
- Are you ever participating with characters, moving with them, or seeing the situation they face over their shoulder?
- Are you ever connecting with character expressions and reactions? Does that happen at a moment when their emotional reactions are informative and significant to the storytelling?
- Do you ever see a character's focused gaze and then see who or what they are looking at?
- Could you take a series of screenshots that outline the storytelling and provide a record of storytelling decisions (cinematic keyframes)? Would that collection of keyframes provide the highlights of the story?

Notes

1 *Cast Away*. Directed by Robert Zemeckis, Cinematography by Don Burgess. Twentieth Century Fox, Dreamworks, released 2000. DVD: Twentieth Century Fox Home Entertainment (2001, USA). Start time: 00:14:06.
2 *Alien*. Directed by Ridley Scott, Cinematography by Derek Vanlint. Brandywine Productions, Twentieth Century Fox, released 1979. DVD: Director's Cut, Twentieth Century Fox Home Entertainment (2004, USA). Start time: 00:36:18.
3 *Altered States*. Directed by Ken Russell, Cinematography by Jordan Cronenweth. Warner Bros., released 1980. DVD: Warner Bros. Home Video (1998, USA). Start time: 00:00:16.

Chapter 4
Cinematic thinking

Breaking free from shot-first thinking

For most of us involved in filmmaking, it's an almost unstoppable reflex to think in terms of shot size, from long shot (LS) to extreme close-up (ECU). I've been referring to shot size in examples, precisely because an image quickly comes to mind. It is very hard to be patient and think in story terms of attention to the visible subject matter before leaping to the end result of determining shot size. It's worth the wait. That first leap to shot size can close off valid, exciting, or unusual options that might be supportive to the story and feel fresh.

Arbitrary or mechanical decision making – falling into a rut – is a real danger of shot-first thinking instead of story-first thinking. Of course, the actual doing of filmmaking demands mastery of things such as shot size but being mechanically oriented in your creative thinking can put the cart before the horse. A shot description only tells us the subject matter, shot size, and what part of the action is covered. To root the coverage in the story, we will work toward these factors, starting from the scripted story. Shot descriptions come at the end, not the start, of the process.

We will practice with a condensed and scaled-down version of the full process, focusing on contextual presentation to suit an interpretation of the script. This is groundwork in story-based thinking about coverage. We will work from the visible elements of the script to considering representative keyframes that support a desired interpretation, then to creating patterns, and finally to the actual shots. This is the cinematic storytelling process in miniature.

When we go further and deeper in the next chapters, we will be expanding this thought process of keyframes, patterns, and context creation as the core of cinematic storytelling. Our end goal for the entire book is a full and comprehensive process that will let you tackle complex and complete scripts, bringing them to the screen in a meaningful way. Groundwork comes first.

Presenting the scripted story through keyframes

It's useful to look at examples that haven't been made into actual movies. Although existing movies can provide great examples of cinematic choices,

DOI: 10.4324/9781003080657-4

it is almost impossible to consider alternate choices, because they would no longer be the movie we know and love.

```
EXT. SIDE STREET - DAY

Row houses of red brick. Scraggly trees heave up
through the sidewalk.

Mike cuts across the street on the diagonal, slides
between parked cars and up onto the sidewalk.

Taking the steps - one, two, three. Quick RAPS on the
door.

EXT. MAIN STREET - MOMENTS LATER

Mike and Barbara push down the sidewalk, side by side.
They take a left, leaning into the corner.

EXT. CENTRAL PLAZA - MOMENTS LATER

Mike and Barbara slow the pace. Up ahead - the edges of
the crowd, now in sight. PROTEST CHANTS reverberate.

They stop, catch their breath and turn to each other,
reflecting their resolve.

Barbara turns and enters the crowd, Mike right behind.

They disappear into the mass of bodies.
```

Here we have three scenes that function as a single sequence or block of storytelling. The only plainly visible elements are Settings and Character Action, keeping our discussion simple. Each scene features characters on the move, not stationary. One implication is that conventional coverage for a dialogue-based scene probably won't work. No single shot – no Master shot – could encompass all of the action. A lot of movies have either sequences or scenes so long or complex that no single Master shot is functional. A lot of scenes that are primarily action or physical movement aren't suited to that type of conventional coverage. So what do we do?

We will think of the action as a series of keyframes that represent the landmarks of each scene. Let's dissect the factors that go into conventional shot descriptions and rethink them in terms of providing contextual cues.

Subject matter in terms of singular, compound, and plural

The choice of how subject matter is presented becomes one of the contextual cues that point the audience toward the story interpretation. Thinking of framing as the directing of attention, it is useful to consider what contextual cues the subject matter can provide the audience.

If attention is directed toward a crowd, you have a plural subject. There is no concentration of attention. The overall, undifferentiated, and general subject is the focus of the story in that moment. Scenes often begin or end with a plural subject. Settings are typically plural subjects, such as the residential street. Its contribution to story meaning is taken in aggregate, not considering each house, car, or sidewalk as meaningful in isolation.

If attention is directed toward subjects that are connected but still differentiated, it is a compound subject. Mike and Barbara form a compound subject. Each is individuated. Being seen together gives us context. Mike and the residential street could be considered a compound subject, because Mike is not seen in isolation but in the context of a Setting that influences the way the audience understands the action.

If attention is isolated on just one component, it is a singular subject. This tells the audience that story meaning can be found in that one person or thing. Mike could be a singular subject, if we wanted a sense of what was on his mind before knocking on the door. Close framing on his face would give us indications of his thoughts, feelings, and intentions. The door could be a singular subject, as the endpoint of one stretch of the action.

Subject matter isn't simply a given – Mike, or Mike and Barbara, or the crowd. The degree of concentrated attention points the audience toward an interpretation of the story. This is part of the bundle of contextual cues that form keyframe qualities.

In one interpretation, the story function of the setting is to inform us of Mike's destination, not having truly specific story significance. Therefore, the setting could be background, requiring no dedicated coverage. We will get the residential feeling through observation of his actions.

If we needed a break after the last scene, we might use a keyframe of the street before Mike's entry turns it into the next keyframe, centered on the character as the subject matter. That break in action and in engagement with a character would point toward the interpretation of beginning a new stage or thread of the story.

If we wanted to guide the audience toward an interpretation of Mike's actions being emotionally urgent, we could load him with dynamism by having the camera move toward and converge with him at the parked cars. That would rapidly shift attention to the singular subject, giving it the feeling of energetic shift concentrating on him. Lots of options exist. That's what interpretation is all about – making creative choices.

The next scene has a compound subject – Mike and Barbara. You might ask what purpose this scene even serves. Functionally, it creates compression of time and space to sketch out a longer journey without the boring details. This forms a kind of ellipsis, to indicate leaving out superfluous stuff. It is the cinematic equivalent of a written description: They meet up . . . travel through city streets . . . to the protest in the plaza. The in-between parts are left out. Films do this a lot, allowing us to pick up the action without the boring parts. This middle scene functions to concisely illustrate that the protest is far enough away that it requires a small jump in time and distance.

It implicitly makes sense of their need to hurry – it's a bit of a hike, and they don't want to miss it.

The last scene in the sequence goes from compound subject, Mike and Barbara; to matched, reciprocal, singular subjects, the two of them in silent dialogue; to the plural subject, the crowd, which they merge into. The start of this scene invokes sight – the goal is now apparent. As with many scripts, it isn't explicitly stated that we see this through a character's POV. Therefore, we have choices. We could present it as a Look/See pair – one or both character's Look followed by seeing the crowd. Or we could use the reverse order for an inverted Look/See, if we want a sense of finding the crowd, then sharing that experience with the characters who arrive and see their destination. Or we could arrive as participants with them, seeing it over their shoulders or past them, as we face the situation in the same way that they face it.

Each option feels different to the audience and will point toward a slightly different interpretation of the story. It is critical that you, as a filmmaker, decide on your interpretation of the story first – before selecting the shots – so that your cinematic choices express your creative intent.

The shot-first way of thinking about subject matter is a subconscious selection of attention. To make this story-based, we need to take into account the contextual cues that point toward interpretation of the action. Considering whether to select singular, compound, or plural subject involves actively considering how the audience will absorb the action. It isn't willynilly. It is derived from what is visible in the script, presented in the best way to focus the audience on story meaning and interpretation. **Cinematic thinking demands conscious choice.**

Energy and flow

To me, this entire sequence feels like the characters are bringing energy to the protest. Then we can feel the big energy of the crowd, a gathering of all the individual droplets of energy. Therefore, I'm considering movement, not stasis or fixation, as an important element – but movement that centers on them, not something imposed by the storytelling. The only moments of stasis are before Mike crosses the street, after the knock (editing choices can make that part of continuous flow), and their moments of connection before taking the plunge.

I also feel a story perspective shift from Mike to Barbara in the last scene. Therefore, I'm going to make sure that framing movement is following – almost magnetically controlled by – the character whose perspective we should be sharing. That's Mike at the start, the two of them in tandem in the middle, and Barbara at the end.

Because this sequence builds up to the moment of entering the crowd, it functions more like the shape and flow of a single, longer scene, in a series of events that make the story move forward. Because movement is such a vital part of cinematic storytelling, an in-depth discussion of movement is covered in its own chapter (Chapter 5). Right now, we are practicing, in miniature, the thought process that underlies these kinds of decisions.

How shots can emerge from contextual choices

We have not gone in depth on keyframes and their range of qualities in this condensed process of envisioning coverage. But we do have enough analysis of this simple example to consider coverage and possible shots in a way that supports the storytelling. We start from conscious decisions about how things like presentation of subject matter and use of movement can provide contextual cues. These decisions will become part of a comprehensive coverage plan, before it is reduced to individual shots. Working toward shots from contextual decisions makes it possible to adjust to the realities of production in a way that shot-first thinking cannot do as effectively.

Maybe you can't shoot in the street, or the characters need to take a right instead of a left. Maybe a medium shot, not a close-up, ends up feeling "right." Thinking about what is being presented and how it should be contextualized will make any resultant shot list resilient and functional, even if conditions change or practicalities make one idea impossible.

Here is one set of ideas: We start in the side street. Mike enters frame, looks back over his shoulder to make sure cars aren't coming. A head-and-shoulders framing should work, but that can be adjusted to whatever lets us know that the storytelling is centered on and attached to Mike. As he crosses on the diagonal, we fall in behind, participating in this walk. That's probably a medium-size framing, sticking with the character and facing the way they face. When he slips between parked cars, we stay on the street, observing the character cross the sidewalk and up the steps. As the rest of the action takes very little time on screen, I might decide to sustain that shot from the street all the way through the knock, the wait at the door, Barbara's emergence, and the two heading down the street.

But I'd like an option to stay closer to the action, meaning greater attention on the character's experience. More distant observation could feel sterile and less engaged with his experience. Perhaps a CU of his feet up the stairs that follows the action up to a CU of his knock. These are not time-consuming options, so we can evaluate the final choices in the editing. Mike's full body might be more expressive of impatience than facial expressions, after the knock. Maybe we'll end up using the CU of feet and knock, then go back to the wider shot.

The second scene might be a single shot, backing up as they approach. We can see and identify them, then let their foot speed pass the slower camera as we follow, falling behind, until they exit the frame at the corner. We feel the attachment of story to the two of them in a kind of teamwork, their speed, and feel that this is an in-between moment in a more extended journey.

This is one shot, but identifying the keyframes lets us connect the dots on set in any way that feels right. They enter full shot (full body) framing, evolving into medium shot framing, evolving into full shot framing again as they exit. When a single shot contains different framings, it will have the sense of fluid development through time rather than being discrete, incremental steps that result from the editing between relatively fixed framings. Flow and evolving action feels more like the dynamic I want for this sequence. In one shot that isn't logistically difficult, we connect with the characters, observe them, and participate with them.

The only thing planned to be discrete and incremental is the non-verbal dialogue in the third scene, of Barbara and Mike after they arrive at the protest. The back-and-forth tennis match of social interaction is well supported by reciprocal, alternating frames.

I interpret the last scene as feeling like we should experience arriving at the crowd through the characters' experience, rather than as something independent from their experience and merely observed.

One option is that their entrance will capture and pull the framing, like a magnetic attraction to the centers of story agency. This following of their action will then fall in behind them, seeing the scene over their shoulders. That is similar to the first scene. We participate in their movement and we (the audience) will recognize their destination through their story perspective, not independently of them.

Another option is to stress connection to their reactions, not our participation in their actions. They enter frame and we back up with them, seeing their reactions – perhaps wonder, gratification, and resolve – as they arrive and slow to a stop. The whole time, we are reading their emotions, thoughts, and intentions. When we do see the vast crowd, our reaction will already be informed by their inner state, and we will experience it, knowing that it elicits strong emotions for the characters.

Based on either option, when they stop, we can have them turn to each other, with Barbara framed over Mike's shoulder. The shot evolves through keyframes from participation or connection, into the interconnection of a dialogue pair. A matched framing of Mike OTS Barbara completes the pair. If we start and end with her, and follow her movements after, we can effectively shift the sense of story agency centering on her action and agency. We have shifted to her story perspective and experience. When she enters the crowd, the frame will follow her, and Mike will fall in behind.

We may pull back, track to the side, or (if we have the budget) crane up – any option that evolves from the characters as subjects, to the plural subject of the crowd. If we first saw the crowd only through their reactions, a big crane shot up will feel like a revelation of an event with great energy that, in retrospect, rewards their efforts and reactions. As long as the coverage suits presentation of the crowd through character experience, we can have a wide range of different creative choices, any of which could be valid. Interpretation of the feel of the story and its flow will guide the final selection from usable possibilities. I have diagrammed one set of possibilities as a sample reference (Figure 4.1).

Building up contextual cues leads to final shot selection

Only after considering the storytelling implications of a range of decisions, do we finalize our choice of keyframe qualities, including the presentation of subject matter. After that, we can consider how keyframes will be allocated to specific shots.

Every keyframe choice does not have to result in a separate shot. Instead of a CU as a separate shot, you might have a character walk into a tighter framing, or have the camera push-in, or do both at once for an intense injection of dynamic energy. If Mike wears a zebra-striped jersey, we might be able to clearly identify him without needing to see his face. But we may decide that checking in with his feelings, through some form of CU, is good for the storytelling, even if not needed for purely informational reasons of letting the audience know who is in the scene. Keyframes may be strung together like beads on the string of a continuously evolving shot, as in the second scene from our example.

We never want to get hung up on the precise shot size. Anything that works to provide the desired contextual cues becomes a useful possibility. The contextual cues – including subject choice, story perspective, and flow – have more importance than shot specifics in contributing to cinematic storytelling. Later in the book, these will be fully explored and ordered into a complete process for going from script to screen. This condensed version with a simplified example is intended to orient your thinking, rather than serve as a comprehensive process model.

Moving forward to patterns of keyframes

In previous chapters, we've covered how the audience feels the storytelling without conscious thought, assisted by cinematic framing. We've compared and contrasted scripted and visual story presentation, to determine what firmly connects them and what must be rethought cinematically. We've isolated the role of coverage to the presentation of what is seen and the support of story interpretation.

In this chapter, we oriented thinking away from a shot-based and toward a story-based decision-making approach, through a simplified script example and a condensed version of the cinematic storytelling process.

Figure 4.1

Mike and Barbara go to the protest

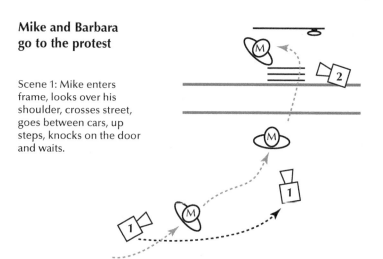

Scene 1: Mike enters frame, looks over his shoulder, crosses street, goes between cars, up steps, knocks on the door and waits.

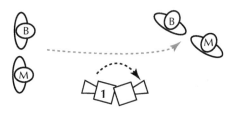

Scene 2: Mike and Barbara walk toward, then past camera. It pans with them. They exit frame.

Scene 3: They enter, then face each other…

…then Barbara enters the crowd. Mike follows.

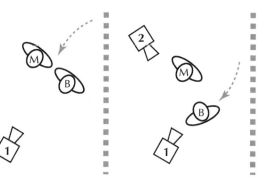

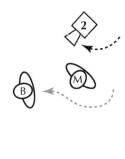

In the next chapters, we'll dive into the patterns we'll use to convey the six plainly visible elements of a script. Employment of these patterns provides the contextual cues that will affect — at the subconscious level — how your audience understands and responds to the storytelling.

Summary

Cinematic choices express the filmmaker's creative intent. Starting with what is seen or plainly visible in the script, we use cinematic options to point toward desired story interpretations and evoke feelings and emotional responses in the audience. Cinematic thinking demands conscious choices based on what is appropriate at each significant story moment.

- Storytelling ideas come before shot definition. The immediate leap to considering shot size might take our eyes off the story flow and interpreted meaning, resulting in rigid, formulaic, or arbitrary choices.
- Consider the presentation of subject matter in terms of singular, compound, and plural. These provide a contextual way of thinking of subject matter, pointing to story interpretations and directing attention to what is most important.
- Consider camera angles in terms of the way they feel, in terms of observational, participatory, or emotive connection with character experiences.
- The desired flow and pace of the action integrates movement with the total bundle of contextual presentation. Evolving story flow will tend to connect keyframes like beads on a string, as one keyframe evolves into the next through movement, within a single shot. Incremental story progress will tend to link keyframes to individual shots, as in conventional Dialogue shot-and-reverse pairs, that will be edited from one to the next.
- One set of framing qualities can exist across multiple shots, as in Dialogue shot-and-reverse pairs that are balanced and symmetrical. Matched pairs share one set of keyframe qualities.

What you can do . . .

Pick one or two scenes from any movies with characters "on the move." Consider the following:

- Are you seeing conventional coverage, with a single Master shot that encompasses all the action? Does it follow conventional coverage and go from a Master to a tighter two-shot, and then immediately into alternating CUs of dialogue pairs?

- Does the coverage instead observe (from the side), participate (from behind), or connect (from in front) with the characters? Does it use only one or two of these perspectives?
- If characters do engage in dialogue, does the coverage go directly and fluidly from following them into either OTS or CU dialogue shot-and-reverse pairs?
- If the characters leave one location and go to another, is there a time gap (ellipsis) to leave out boring parts? Does the action stop and restart? Or does it flow seamlessly, as if the sequence were one continuous scene?

Chapter 5
Patterns for character actions

Character actions

Character-based storytelling is told through actions or activities – the things that characters do. The broad-based nature of character action patterns employ simple components. These can be used flexibly in a myriad of ways.

Let's review some basics of script formatting. This is a slugline:

```
INT. DINING ROOM - NIGHT
```

The slugline tells us whether this is an interior or exterior scene, the location, and whether it is day or night. The following are "action lines," or the descriptive parts of the script:

```
Elizabeth and Melissa listen to the wind HOWL and the
rain POUND against the windows. A shutter BANGS loose
and Elizabeth strides across the room to secure it.

Candles flicker then burn steady.
```

Anytime we see action lines, we are reading those things we can see and hear. (The sounds are in CAPS.) We find out who is in the scene and what they are doing. We find out anything about the setting or objects that is pertinent to the storytelling. The following are dialogue lines, the spoken words:

```
                    MELISSA
        How long till the electricity comes back on?

                    ELIZABETH
          Who knows? Could be days.
```

When we look at script formatting, we will see action lines that offer descriptions of what is happening, and dialogue formatting that provides the words spoken. Generally, we might think that action lines in a script will match up to action patterns. Usually that is true. But it is within the

DOI: 10.4324/9781003080657-5

action lines that Settings are also described, and where Looks and Objects are nested. We are focused on Character Actions and will distinguish those other elements when they arise.

Physical actions like fights, chases, or exuberant games fall under this umbrella of Character Actions. Stationary activities – sewing, reading, defusing a bomb, operating a spaceship, even daydreaming – are also types of story actions. Dialogue can even be seen as a kind of action. When we see characters talking, it is an interaction. When we discuss Dialogue patterns in detail, we will see that those patterns stem directly from action patterns, and we will discuss how this works with the conventional shot-and-reverse patterns of Dialogue.

Action patterns tie camera angles to storytelling functions

The Action pattern includes three perspectives – Observation, Participation, and Connection. These roughly correspond to camera angles relative to the characters. These broad strokes of shot angle will be refined as part of the process to suit an individual story. In addition to the angle in relation to character, there is the question of how much of a character is seen in frame, which feels like how close we are to them in proximity. We are thinking in broad strokes about where the center of storytelling is at a given moment. Facial expressions might be most important, giving the audience access to thoughts, feelings, and intentions. Or their social presentation and gestures, or the expressive physicality of their full body, might best suit the moment.

With these broad strokes of perspective (translating into angle) and of proximity (translating into shot size), you can analyze action scenes in any movie in a productive way (Figure 5.1). You can borrow the cinematic strategies that have worked in terms of perspective and proximity. You don't need to copy shots. These broad-stroke decisions will funnel down into a specific shot list through this story-centered process, avoiding arbitrary or mechanical decisions.

Sometimes the situation clearly calls for a particular perspective – Observation, Participation, Connection – but often we need to figure out what will do the best job in pointing the audience toward the interpretation we think is best. The goal is to align the presentation of the visible story information with all the emotional or physical feelings that are important to a story's meaning.

Sometimes, framing that splits the difference can serve two functions at once. The three-quarter view from in front of a character can be very useful. We can read expressions but still be sufficiently removed from the character line of sight (the way they face) to have some emotional distance, letting us observe and often judge their actions. In like manner, a three-quarter framing from behind the character can be both observational and encourage

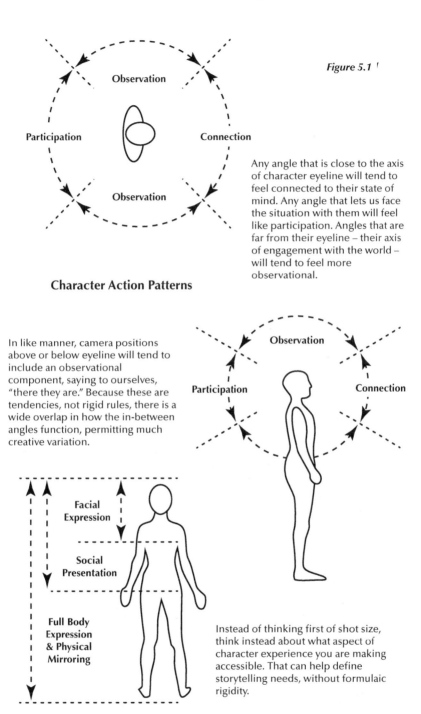

Figure 5.1 [1]

Observation

Participation

Connection

Observation

Any angle that is close to the axis of character eyeline will tend to feel connected to their state of mind. Any angle that lets us face the situation with them will feel like participation. Angles that are far from their eyeline – their axis of engagement with the world – will tend to feel more observational.

Character Action Patterns

In like manner, camera positions above or below eyeline will tend to include an observational component, saying to ourselves, "there they are." Because these are tendencies, not rigid rules, there is a wide overlap in how the in-between angles function, permitting much creative variation.

Observation

Participation

Connection

Facial
Expression

Social
Presentation

Full Body
Expression
& Physical
Mirroring

Instead of thinking first of shot size, think instead about what aspect of character experience you are making accessible. That can help define storytelling needs, without formulaic rigidity.

the sense of participation. All of this fine-tuning of choices depends on the interpretations of the story by the filmmakers.

Think first of what shot size will mean in the conveyance of story information, before getting caught up in the mechanical definitions. The majority of all shot sizes from medium close-ups (MCUs) to extreme close-ups (ECUs) are providing connection to the character's inner state, so you can think of the storytelling need for access to character expression in one general category. This prevents getting pinned down to mechanics before clarifying the general contextual cues desired. The waist-up framing of a medium shot can serve to deliver information on social presentation. Consider the person with arms crossed, or the person leaning forward or back. Thinking in terms of social presentation keeps the discussion of framing qualities centered on storytelling. The full body has expressiveness, too. Consider the powerful feeling of a person triumphant after a win or slumped after a loss.

As with all creative means that have a dynamic range of choice, the power of connection with characters can benefit from selective use. Filmmakers may want to save the tightest close-up of the protagonist for a big moment. In the movie *Midsommar*,[1] there are many CUs but only one ECU of the main character, Dani. It happens at the midway point (1:04:12) of the movie, after she witnesses the first gruesome death. It marks a "point of no return" for the character and the movie. No other frame is like this one peak moment.

A creative choice may also be made to sustain a character's relationship to their setting because it informs everything they do. What's an astronaut without space? What's a cowboy without the West? You might not want to take the character out of that setting by close proximity that loses contact with the setting. Creatively, you may want that effect if the character is emotionally removed or alienated from the setting and isolated within their separate thoughts and emotions.

Observation

The first perspective on character Action is **observation**, which is typically the relatively objective viewing of character actions. Observational framing is giving us (the audience) a vantage point that allows us to see and judge for ourselves. It is independent of the character's internal, emotional state.

The other side of this coin is that observation of the character's body gives us the "mirror" experience of their physical state. This is why sports and dance, which depend on the feeling of movement, typically show us a wide enough framing to feel expressive movement of full bodies.

In the movie *Midsommar*[2] (Figure 5.2), we connect with Dani as the May Queen dance forces her round and round the May Pole. Everything connects to her subjective state, following in front of her to catch her alternately giddy and alarmed emotions. Multiple times, she must spontaneously go

Figure 5.2

Dani's May Queen dance is filled with subjective sensations of motion. For the complex moves as they weave in synchrony, we observe full body actions, to feel the difficulty and precision. For her giddy and alarmed states, we move with her through space. The frame is never firmly oriented to anything but her experience.

into a complex weaving with the other dancers. We feel the near misses and need for precise control of movements in our own bodies. In a very real sense, this scene challenges and exhausts us, very much in line with Dani's subjective experience.

The way framing works is also closely aligned with our own real-life experiences. If you can think of a character having a social-psychological "zone" that is along the axis of their attention – the way they face – you can imagine observational framing to be outside of that zone. In real life, if we get into someone's line of sight, we will interrupt them because we intrude into that social zone of their attention. If we read over someone's shoulder, we get that same effect. But if we are off to the side or above, we can observe without intruding.

All three perspectives are interactive with proximity. The farther away we are, the more observational the perspective. It is the ability to observe the whole body that permits us to feel the physical, bodily sensations of the athlete or dancer. The closer we are, the more we stray from an observational perspective to become increasingly occupied by and engaged with the character's mental and emotional experience of the situation.

Participation

The second perspective relates to the audience sense of **participation** in the action or activity portrayed. Facing the way that the characters face will facilitate that sense of vicarious participation in the action and align us with the characters' experience. If they are walking, we participate, a few steps behind them. If they are hacking a computer, we are over their shoulder. Framing that encourages a sense of participation with the character is central to our subjective understanding of their experience.

The perspective of participation is always character-dependent, but it also allows us, in the audience, a degree of independence in our experience. It is their "outer experience" – an objective experience – that is the focus of Participation framing.

In the movie *Saving Private Ryan*[3] (Figure 5.3, Figure 5.4), we get a tutorial in selective use of perspective. This aligns our experience with the soldiers – sometimes with time for conversation, sometimes facing deadly threat. Choosing when to connect, when to observe, and when to participate with the characters gives these two scenes a solid shape and clear story progression from one phase to another.

Connection

The third component of the action/activity pattern is **connection** with character thoughts, feelings, and intentions. This is to give the audience access to a character's interior state. Now we are fully inside the character's social zone. Most often, this means seeing the character's face and especially their eyes (the windows of the soul). This lets us employ our own innate abilities to "read" people's inner state through expression.

Our example from *Midsommar*[4] in Chapter 1 (Figure 1.3) provides almost continual connection with the character's emotional state, seen through CUs of Dani's face. Gifted actors clearly convey the thoughts, emotions, and intentions of the characters they portray. Supporting performances, through carefully calibrated CUs and the presentation of new angles to shape the scene, allow us to connect with the character's inner state and are central to engaging with their subjective experience.

Connection to a character's inner state is not exclusively a substitute for saying "close-up." Consider a character slumping to the ground after a loved one has died. Would we get more information about their inner state from a CU? There may be times when a hand gesture is most evocative, as when clenching a fist or dropping an object that was held tightly a moment before.

The main function of framing for connection is to allow us to engage our social-emotional intelligence in understanding character thoughts, feelings, and intentions. This places story perspective in a dependent state – entirely focused on and mediated by character experience.

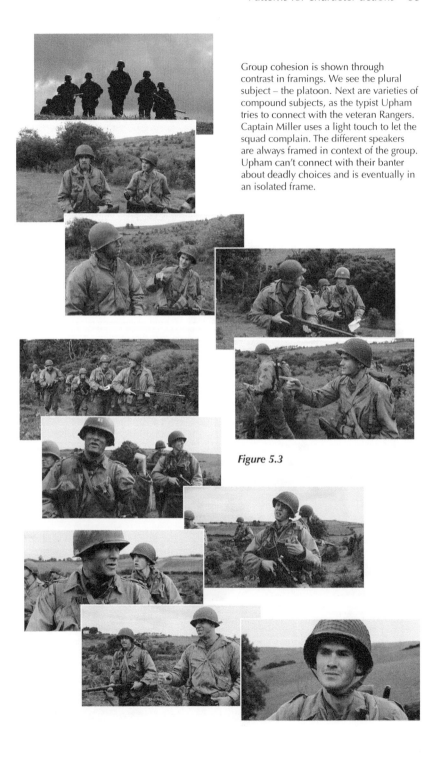

Group cohesion is shown through contrast in framings. We see the plural subject – the platoon. Next are varieties of compound subjects, as the typist Upham tries to connect with the veteran Rangers. Captain Miller uses a light touch to let the squad complain. The different speakers are always framed in context of the group. Upham can't connect with their banter about deadly choices and is eventually in an isolated frame.

Figure 5.3

Figure 5.4

A slideshow presentation of rain building is used to compress time between the calm patrol and the next fight. As they advance, we follow, facing the situation with them. We look past Miller, seeing the civilians as he does.

With a plan for attack, the perspective shifts to moving in front, connecting to their alert state and creating suspense. Wide shots let us observe and grasp strategy.

Perspectives are used selectively, giving each phase a distinct feeling and aligning us with character experience. Prioritizing one at a time shapes the scene, with modulations through movement.

In the movie *Harry Potter and the Goblet of Fire*[5] (Figure 5.5), we observe, participate with, and connect with Harry in his challenge with the dragon. But we also have a third party – the spectators. Their reactions shape our understanding of the significance of events and how they are judged in the storyworld. We root for Harry along with his friends, and we hiss at his enemies.

We observe most of the dragon attacks from whatever angle gives us the best vantage, while maintaining a perspective from Harry's side of the action. As his chances diminish, the flames start coming at us, too. When he lifts his wand, we see it from a new angle, breaking the axis between Harry and the dragon for a moment of hope and turning the tide in his favor.

How actions function in the storytelling

Writers use story events to reveal character, plot, and theme. The broad strokes of Action patterns provide the necessary qualities of presentation that enable audiences to clearly understand the visible, declarative aspects of story information, while feeling a strong nudge toward the inferences revealing character, plot, and theme. The variations of framing, through time, can also contribute to mood and tone, story perspective, and pacing.

Actions and events are providing links in the chain of C&E (cause and effect), revealing aspects of the story and fueling anticipation of the effects that will result from some observable or emotionally implied cause.

In the movie *Fury*[6] (Figure 5.6), we see a clear chain of C&E from explicit, declarative story information. As with many war movies, the emotional content of the scene is bundled with the battle, in the reactions to life-and-death moments. How these are felt through framing qualities point toward these interpretations. Each frame in the example is a link in the chain. The total scene is a solid example of clarity in presenting physical action and connection to each crew member's actions and reactions under tremendous psychological stresses.

In true physical action, such as fight scenes, chase scenes, or overcoming physical obstacles, the C&E happens like a set of dominoes, one hitting the next in a chain reaction. Physical C&E is external to the character and observable. With emotional C&E, the reactions and shifts in trajectory are happening within characters. These are comprehensible through their expressive reactions that let us feel what they feel, or through inferences from our sense of participation in facing the story situation.

Action is also the gateway to audience physical sensation, shared or vicariously experienced through characters. Motion pictures of a roller coaster can elicit the sense of kinesthesia. Every blockbuster "ride" movie uses this principle. A character standing on the edge of a tall building can evoke the bodily sense of fear of heights. Many suspense and horror movies root audience fears in these sensations.

Harry Potter faces a dragon. The crowd follows each step of the action. It starts with Look/See patterns – Harry thrown off by the setting, then seeing the golden prize. The dragon attacks – a blast of fire, sweep of the tail, swipe of claws – and Harry defends. Each is followed by crowd reactions. This three-part pattern gives us the full scope of physical and emotional C&E.

Figure 5.5

The next phase is started by Hermione's reminder of his wand. The close framing helps us believe she can be heard. Harry starts using magic.

The center of the story is Harry's experience, but we also share the crowd's. Like us, they are the audience.

Figure 5.6

The commander calls the shot. The loader grabs a shell, loads the gun. The gunner takes aim – his foot hits the trigger. We see the explosion through his POV. We feel the deadly efficiency of crack teamwork.

The enemy crew runs. The commander shoots. They fall. Norman takes aim, fires, kills, and roars in triumph. Clear presentation lets us follow rapidly changing physical and emotional C&E.

In the movie *Out of Time*[7] (Figure 5.7, Figure 5.8), we see how connecting and participating angles can carry a fight scene, along with the occasional observational perspective to clarify the situation. The action is dynamic, the camera moves are dynamic, but the basics give it clarity and solidity. We can follow the fight, know what trouble Matt is in, and feel his desperation reaching for the gun. In the second section of this example, when his attacker drives Matt through glass and over a balcony edge, we feel the physical sensations as if we were participating. Matt's fight to climb the railing to safety, while battling his attacker, makes for nail-biting excitement through physical sensation.

Quite often, it serves the storytelling to mask or obscure story information in order to raise questions that will be answered later, fuel anticipation to know what's next, or to provide misdirection and intentionally lead the audience to erroneous conclusions. Framing choices allow for creative control over both the clear presentation – and withholding – of information.

Because the three components of the action pattern – Observation, Participation, and Connection – have different potentials for providing information, filmmakers may exclude some component in order to keep that information from the audience for dramatic purposes. For example, if the audience really needs to know a character's reaction to some situation, we may not see the character's face for a while, to keep us guessing. The inverse may be true. When a character is approaching some terrifying unknown, we may only see their expressions of fear, and not be given any view of what they are actually facing until the moment of a big scare.

In the movie *The Ring*[8] (Figure 5.9), we see how horror movies withhold information and use deliberate pacing to raise tension. We mostly see the body language and expressions of fear by Katie. We are never following behind or seeing what's in front of her. We can only anticipate something bad – we don't know what it is until the trap is sprung on her and us.

Action patterns don't always fit conventions of coverage

The three components of the patterns for character actions and activities are directly related to the storytelling needs for presenting observation of the action, or participation and connection with character experiences. Many movies contain scenes that do not neatly fit into what is generally taught as conventional or Master-scene coverage. For review, that is a Master shot that encompasses all the action in a scene, then typically a two-shot or tighter group that focuses on the social relationships, and then sets of CUs of any kind in pairs that suit dialogue.

Many examples in this book have nothing that would function as a Master shot. Consider any scene of Character Action in terms of what is observation, participation, and connection, and you will likely unlock a way to understand the choices. The choices may, in fact, seem ultra-simplistic in "pointing the camera at the characters," but more careful

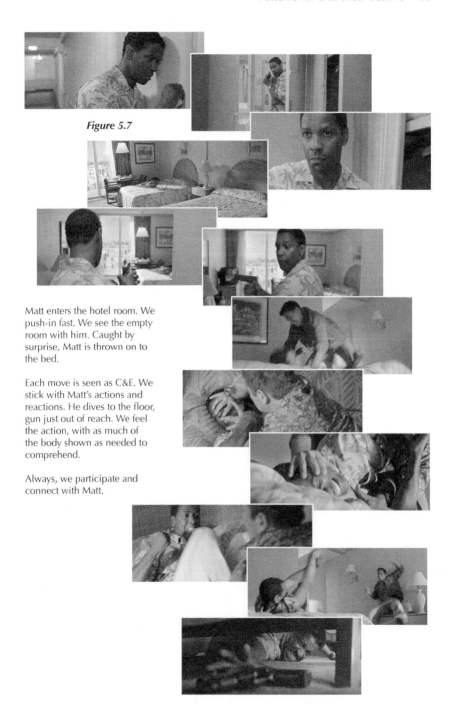

Figure 5.7

Matt enters the hotel room. We push-in fast. We see the empty room with him. Caught by surprise, Matt is thrown on to the bed.

Each move is seen as C&E. We stick with Matt's actions and reactions. He dives to the floor, gun just out of reach. We feel the action, with as much of the body shown as needed to comprehend.

Always, we participate and connect with Matt.

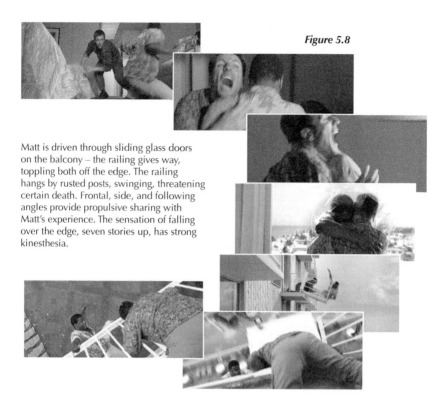

Figure 5.8

Matt is driven through sliding glass doors on the balcony – the railing gives way, toppling both off the edge. The railing hangs by rusted posts, swinging, threatening certain death. Frontal, side, and following angles provide propulsive sharing with Matt's experience. The sensation of falling over the edge, seven stories up, has strong kinesthesia.

analysis will show how the perspective shifts in keeping with story flow, varying the nature of our understanding of the action and our feeling of its interpretation.

Action patterns are particularly flexible

These three storytelling perspectives of observation, participation, and connection give filmmakers a path for following story perspective shifts with great flexibility. Through Action patterns, we can move from relatively independent observation of character action, to dependence on character perspective in facing the situation along with them as participants, to full story dependence on their inner state – thoughts, feelings, and intentions – when reacting to the situation they face.

In practical use, Action patterns are the "universal connectors" that permit fluid storytelling movement from one pattern to the next.

In the movie *No Country for Old Men*[9] (Figure 5.10, Figure 5.11), we see how the Action pattern embraces and encompasses Look/See patterns and Dialogue patterns without missing a beat. The first part of Llewelyn's hunting trip features his focused gaze, the subject of his attention, and a clear

Figure 5.9

Until the "jump scare" of the evil video, we only observe and connect with Katie's fearful approach to the room. We never follow behind.

The Look/See is the scare. A rapid pull-out from the TV cuts to a rapid push-in on her, as if the evil leaps across the room to possess her.

Figure 5.10

We see a true POV through Llewelyn's rifle scope. A chain of C&E is clear. Picking up the shell is characterization – he doesn't leave a mess behind. This action is repeated in the wide shot for fluid editing. We follow his footsteps, participating in his experience.

chain of C&E. The second part illustrates how following with a character lets us participate, facing the situation with them. Observation orients us and gives us the scope of the action.

When we see inside the first vehicle, we are shocked by the bloody remains of a dead body. Llewelyn's movements and attention – his focused gaze – lead us through the scene. When we arrive at the surprise of the dying man, we are just as shocked as Llewelyn. His POV of the man is reciprocated and we have a Dialogue shot-and-reverse pattern consisting of mutual Look/See pairs. The Action perspectives facilitate fluid interconnection of patterns, shifting context instantly and organically.

One thing is almost universally true: the main characters are known by the degree to which we are encouraged to participate and connect with them, through coverage choices. If there is a singular protagonist, the audience will be with them more than anyone else, encouraging us to vicariously share their experiences. Simply put, we see more of them, and in closer proximity.

Figure 5.11

Llewelyn's hunting trip leads to bigger game. Action patterns flow into Look/ See without interruption.

Characterization plays a role in framing and sequence. First, we see a horrifying bloody body. The next shot is his Look, revealing that he is unaffected. His reaction is not like ours.

From his methodical action and controlled emotions, we can believe he's a war veteran.

His look leads to the next truck and we follow, revealing a dying man, begging for water. This becomes Dialogue – a mutual Look/See pattern of reciprocal framing.

Action patterns lead seamlessly into interaction. The mutual Look/ See pair of dialogue creates mutual intersubjectivity.

Vicarious engagement and audience judgment

Storytelling often relies upon both comprehending and judging why characters do the things they do, or why the storyworld's social or physical laws work the way they do. Consider likable characters doing questionable things. Or characters we may dislike but can sympathize with, when they are faced with a corrupt society or no-win situation that is inherently unfair. Over the course of the story, we may decide that justice demands a bad ending for one character, or that another character had a good ending they didn't deserve.

Consider the example in this chapter from the movie *Fury*.[10] The character Norman is the innocent thrust into a brutal world. Before that scene, he couldn't stomach the act of killing. By the end of this scene, we see his shouts of triumph after the battle, capped by his shooting of the enemy commander. He has been irrevocably changed in ways that suit survival but damage his psyche. The slight angle away from his face gives us the space we need to respond to his (deserved) emotional release, while still questioning and judging the transformation of an innocent young man into a killer.

The multilevel nature of audience judgment – of characters and the story – is tied to the multilevel vicarious experience. As the audience, we visit this storyworld and its inhabitants, living through character experience, and we can feel it as they feel it, empathetically. But as the audience, we also view the story in relation to our own values and experiences. We imagine how we might react if we were in the character's shoes. The implications, in terms of coverage, are that the broad-stroke perspectives of Action can and will tip the scales in favor of one or the other – either the dominance of feeling subjective character experience through participation and connection, or the feeling of more "objective" judgment by the audience through observation. Careful balancing can bring both to bear.

When to invoke character subjective experience, when to participate with them, and when to observe from a cooler distance give filmmakers sophisticated choices with fairly simple means.

Physical action is fast and easy to understand

Action patterns can be employed very freely during editing. It is possible to jump between any of the three perspectives, at almost any time, and the audience won't get lost. My conjecture is that, particularly with physical action, there is a low cognitive demand on us in terms of comprehension. Physical actions may have heart-pounding impact, but they can be comprehended in an instant.

In the movie *Jurassic Park*[11] (Figure 5.12, Figure 5.13), we see how chase scenes use Action patterns. In a chase scene, there is an axis of action between the two parties – the chaser and the chased. Along that axis, we see the back of the Jeep getting closer when the T-Rex is catching up, and getting farther away at the end when the characters drive away. We clearly

Figure 5.12

The chase starts with a Look/See pair of Ian seeing the vibrations in a puddle. Everything is part of the chain of C&E or character reactions to ground us in their experience. They hit the gas just as the T-Rex bursts through the trees. Details like the stick shift are introduced early, so they won't need explaining when they figure into events.

Chases employ perspective and proximity. When the T-Rex gets closer over Ian's shoulder, it's gaining on us. When the car gets closer, it's gaining on them.

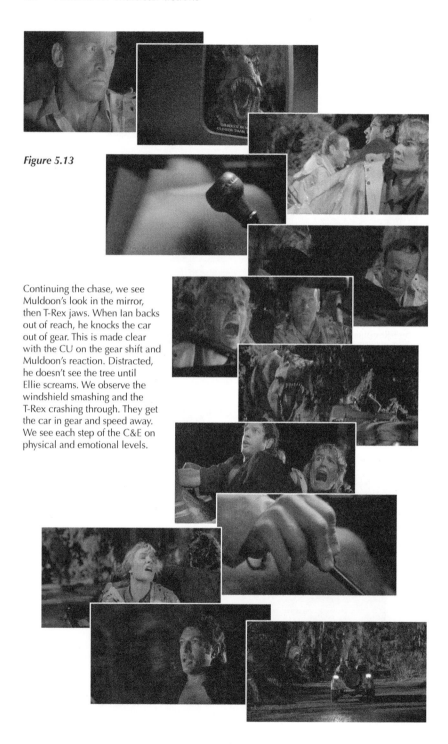

Figure 5.13

Continuing the chase, we see
Muldoon's look in the mirror,
then T-Rex jaws. When Ian backs
out of reach, he knocks the car
out of gear. This is made clear
with the CU on the gear shift and
Muldoon's reaction. Distracted,
he doesn't see the tree until
Ellie screams. We observe the
windshield smashing and the
T-Rex crashing through. They get
the car in gear and speed away.
We see each step of the C&E on
physical and emotional levels.

see each element in the chain of physical C&E. Character reactions give us the emotional component in response to each step of the chase. When we need to see wider action to understand events and stay oriented, we observe from a greater distance.

Setting up or establishing anything that will be part of a chain of C&E is absolutely required prior to encountering it in the heat of the action. There is no time in the midst of action to introduce new elements without messing up the flow.

The gear shift lever is a good example of an Object that has functional story significance. As with all Objects, its coverage is nested within a bigger pattern like Action. It is needed to drive the vehicle. When we first see it in CU and the car is put in gear, we may wonder why we see it. But in the heat of action, it gets knocked by Ian, taking the car out of gear and making them sitting ducks. The gear shift must be established ahead of time in order to take its place in the chain of C&E.

Social interactions are complicated

In contrast to physical actions, a deep and conflictual conversation between characters can have very high demand on our ability to comprehend at multiple levels. We are thinking of each character's inner state, their reactions, their assessment of the reactions of the other character, plus our own reactions and judgments as the audience. The social-psychological complexity and density of emotional interactions is probably the most demanding thing to grasp in movies. And it's all happening in real time.

This is what leads me to the conviction that fast and flashy coverage can comfortably embrace Action, but complex or busy camera work can be competitive and not supportive to scenes of complex emotional interaction in Dialogue.

Summary

Character Actions are central to cinematic storytelling. Patterns for presenting Action are embracing much that is central to the audience experience. Subsequent patterns for Character Looks and Dialogue will build upon these Action patterns.

- Actions in scripts reveal character traits, plot information, and thematic content, as well as affect mood and tone. Big and small actions count because they build the story in the minds of the audience.
- Actions and events provide links in the chain of C&E (cause and effect) on both the physical and emotional-psychological levels.
- Actions can provide a physical sense of kinesthesia.
- Selective choices in perspective and presentation can mask clear information, for the purposes of raising questions that need answering and for surprise.

- The three perspectives of action – Observation, Participation, and Connection – roughly correspond to camera angles relative to the characters.
- Considering proximity in terms of access to expressive performance helps in selecting shot size for story meaning.
- Action patterns have the freedom and flexibility to present events and situations that wouldn't necessarily fit the conventional boxes of standard coverage.
- Action patterns put camera angles in the service of audience perspective on the storytelling and point toward interpretations of how the action should be interpreted.
- The storytelling need for access to a character's full body, social presentation, or expression will lead to decisions that are story-based.
- Shifting perspectives and proximity in Action patterns are critical tools for filmmakers to affect and guide the audience experience, pointing toward interpretations of character subjective experiences for empathetic engagement or emotionally distancing for critical judgment of their experiences and responses.

What you can do . . .

Watch a scene of vigorous physical action from any movie you know well. Turn the sound off to help you concentrate on story information and context through the images.

- Can you find observation, participation, and connection?
- Do you see single, compound, and plural subjects, and do they inform your understanding of the action? What about frames that use the full body's physicality, social presentation and significance of gestures, or access to character expression?
- Do you see chains of physical C&E through direct and clear presentation?
- Are there any conventional Master shots that encompass the entire action?
- Are there any moments of kinesthesia (movement through space) or proprioception (body awareness of position in space)? How do they contribute? What shots were used to create these strong physical sensations?
- Did you see a range of angles and shot sizes in a short period, and were they clear or confusing?

Notes

1 *Midsommar*. Directed by Ari Aster, Cinematography by Pawel Pogorzelski. A24, B-Reel Films, Nordisk Film, Square Peg, released 2019. DVD: A24 Films, LLC, Lions Gate Entertainment (2020, USA). Start time: 01:04:12.
2 *Midsommar*. ibid. Start time: 01:41:52.

3 *Saving Private Ryan*. Directed by Steven Spielberg, Cinematography by Janusz Kaminski. DreamWorks, Paramount Pictures, Amblin Entertainment, released 1998. DVD: DreamWorks (1999, USA). Start time: 00:42:40.
4 *Midsommar*. Ibid. Start time: 00:02:38.
5 *Harry Potter and the Goblet of Fire*. Directed by Mike Newell, Cinematography by Roger Pratt. Warner Bros., Heyday Films, Patalex IV Productions Ltd., released 2005. DVD: Warner Bros Home Video (2005, USA). Start time: 00:57:50.
6 *Fury*. Directed by David Ayer, Cinematography by Roman Vasyanov. Columbia Pictures, QED International, released 2014. DVD: Sony Pictures Home Entertainment (2015, USA). Start time: 1:18:31.
7 *Out of Time*. Directed by Carl Franklin, Cinematography by Theo van de Sande. MGM, Original Film, Monarch Pictures, released 2003. DVD: MGM Home Entertainment (2006, USA). DVD. Start time: 01:10:06.
8 *The Ring*. Directed by Gore Verbinski, Cinematography by Bojan Bazelli. DreamWorks, MacDonald/Parkes Productions, released 2002. DVD: Dreamworks Home Entertainment (2003, USA). Start time: 00:06:40.
9 *No Country for Old Men*. Directed by Ethan Coen & Joel Coen, Cinematography by Roger Deakins. Paramount Vantage, Miramax, Scott Rudin Productions, released 2007. DVD: Buena Vista Home Entertainment (2008, USA). Start time: 00:05:12.
10 *Fury*. Ibid.
11 *Jurassic Park*. Directed by Steven Spielberg, Cinematography by Dean Cundey. Universal Pictures, Amblin Entertainment, released 1993. DVD: Universal Studios (2000, USA). Start time: 01:20:04.

Chapter 6
Patterns for character looks

Character looks

Why take something as fleeting as a look and turn it into a big deal? Don't actors look wherever it makes sense in their portrayal of a character? The specific and focused line of sight of a character is a hugely important storytelling tool in motion pictures. Their Look guides us. From their Look, we understand their mind and emotions through their placement of attention on something or someone with story significance.

Watch a dialogue scene with any actors you respect. Chances are, they will spend some time looking at the other character, giving them their full and complete attention, but they will sometimes look away, giving us the sense that they have disengaged their attention to be inside their own thoughts and feelings, before reengaging. The look is hugely important for our social and psychological understanding of where a character's attention is focused. We understand it in our own lives, in assessing when someone is paying attention, losing focus, or going inward to assess thoughts or feelings. What do parents say when they want their child's full and complete attention? "Look at me."

The gateway to subjectivity in motion picture storytelling is through the presentation of character attention and our (audience) understanding of their engagement with the storyworld and other characters. The basis for this is framing that includes a character's focused attention through their eyes and attentive gaze.

The Action pattern perspective of ***connection*** gives us access to a character's inner state through facial expression, providing the platform for grasping their subjective attention. Their attention is usually engaged with what is in their surroundings, but it might also be inwardly looking and engaged with what they think, feel, or intend. The Action pattern perspective of ***participation*** gives us a shared view of the subject or object of their attention. When the participation framing does not include any OTS framing, we are no longer simply with them, facing whatever they see; we are actually sharing their subjective attention. This often comes in the form of a POV (point-of-view) shot along their eyeline. It is sometimes called a direct POV, and I would label it as dependent. It could

DOI: 10.4324/9781003080657-6

also be a different angle that gives us, in the audience, a better or clearer view – sometimes called an indirect POV, which I would label as independent.

When the storytelling points toward a character's attention as a contributor to events, it will usually have two components forming a simple pattern. Those two components form the ***Look/See*** framing pairs. Occasionally, a Look will be part of the declarative, visible part of the scripted story, as in "Joey sees the keys fall through the sewer grate." If the script doesn't tell you that Joey sees this, you will need to interpret whether or not Joey's Look and subjective experience is important, in either a forward Look/See that anticipates the event or a reverse Look/See pattern showing the event first, then Joey's reaction through the Look.

Let's look at some examples that show a variety of Look/See patterns. The variations show how different combinations and permutations are used to suit the specific story being told. The nuanced application of a basic pattern is providing contextual support, pointing toward the inferential story information and our understanding of it.

Figure 6.1

Look/See patterns can connect a character's focus of attention to their inner selves. Here, Arthur announces the arrival of his oddball genius friend. Emily sees Eddie standing against a field of light, like a supernatural being. A push-in on her shows the situation hitting her. Her CU is matched with Eddie's framing. This is love at first sight, shown through Emily's subjective experience.

In the movie *Altered States*[1] (Figure 6.1), we see examples of both a straightforward Look/See pair corresponding to the character's POV and the leap to a vantage point that supports the subjective importance of the subject being seen. Emily is at Arthur's party, the two talking in a frame that shows their social presentation – basically waist up – enabling gestures to carry meaning. Emily has been told that she might be interested in the equally smart but strange scientist, Eddie. Her POV shows him at the end of a hall, in dramatic fashion, framed by white light. A push-in on Emily feels like the injected impact of her immediate attraction. When we next see a comparable frame of Eddie, we get a matched pair of frames. The characters are put on the footing of interaction – dialogue – that is still all in her mind. That isn't and couldn't be a POV shot; it's her subjective and focused attention that we share.

As a point of clarification, this is different from the Dialogue shot-and-reverse pattern in one important way. Her Look is not reciprocated, making this a Look/See pattern that feels like imagined interaction. The lack of Dialogue reciprocity has the effect of objectifying. This helps us feel the sense of Eddie being the object of her desire.

The Look pattern is often in pairs, even if it is a chain reaction that goes beyond one character. Consider a movie moment with two parents, lovingly watching their toddler sleep. One looks at the child – we see the child – and then we see the other parent, who breaks their gaze from the little one and looks to their partner. Their partner looks back, and they share the love.

In the movie *Out of Time*[2] (Figure 6.2), we see Looks used for non-verbal interactions, like silent ping-pong between characters. At the same time, a straightforward Look/See pattern of Detective Alex examining phone records lets us know how close she is getting to incriminating evidence on her ex-husband, Chief of Police Matt. As in real life, silent exchanged looks add another level to a social situation, only shared by those making eye contact.

Note that even though the phone records are shown in alignment with Alex's eyeline, they are magnified to let us read the page. If this were truly what she sees, the type would be too small on screen for us to read. What we see is the focus of subjective story attention. This scene features a breakneck series of constant non-verbal cues between Matt and Chae and Look/See patterns on the mounting evidence.

Subjective attention is not always true POV

The degree to which this second part of the pair – the See part – aligns with the character's line of sight is the degree to which it is fully dependent on character's attention, regardless of whether it is mimicking looking "through their eyes" in terms of purely optical criteria. We are usually sharing subjective attention first and foremost, with true POV a rare subset.

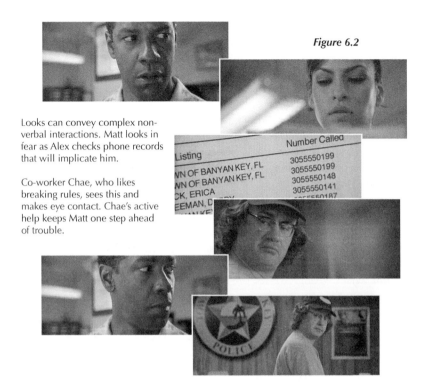

Figure 6.2

Looks can convey complex non-verbal interactions. Matt looks in fear as Alex checks phone records that will implicate him.

Co-worker Chae, who likes breaking rules, sees this and makes eye contact. Chae's active help keeps Matt one step ahead of trouble.

The See part of the pattern will often present some angle or proximity that would be impossible in a true POV. We assume that we are seeing what they are concentrating on, not really their field of vision. That is usually to provide a better, more informative view – such as a CU of a clock tower some distance away, so we can tell that it's almost high noon, or an angle on some object that is most comprehensible from a different angle, such as seeing the complete shape of a rifle and not just a piece of it that might be hard to figure out.

A shift from character eyeline axis can also indicate that they do not or cannot grasp the full nature of what they see, giving us more story information than they possess.

Why Look/See and not simply POV

Sometimes the second part of this pattern is called a POV-look. This certainly indicates story perspective, but it sounds like it can exist without the definitive character Look and still be understood. This is fine for film analysis but could be a dangerous coverage omission for the practicing filmmaker. The term POV (or point-of-view) also has multiple meanings, so it can be a little confusing. As long as filmmaking collaborators share a definition, all is well.

The storytelling may demand framing for the See part of the pair that has little or nothing to do with what might be considered a POV frame from the character's position or distance from the story-significant subject.

In the movie *Cape Fear*[3] (Figure 6.3), we get three examples of Looks from different scenes. The first example shows Sam's look, which connects to a view that is beyond what either character can actually see – a bird's-eye view of the beatdown and fight. The storytelling is independent of character experience, and we know more than him. Then we get a Look/See with Cady looking and his true POV. Then we look past Sam, hiding, to see Cady, in a participation angle rather than Look/See pair. In another scene, we see Leigh looking through blinds at fireworks and seeing the criminal Cady sitting on their wall. Here, the See part is her focused attention, not truly looking through her eyes in a literal, optical POV. The last scene shows how this pattern works with hearing, as well as sight, to show us the focus of Sam's attention on a surprising missing note on the piano. His turned head indicates his focus on hearing, just as it would in real life, but he can't figure out what's wrong. We see the absence of the piano strings, once again knowing more than the character does, helping us connect the piano strings to the murderous chain of C&E.

Look/See forward and reverse

Because we are trained by years of movie watching, we understand the Look/See pattern without explanation. We understand secondary attention – noticing what someone is seeing – as it happens in real life. We even understand chains of secondary or tertiary attention: George looks at Fred, who is looking at Sheila, who is looking at her phone. Secondary attention guides us to follow story significance like a bouncing ball.

The Look/See pattern works in either forward or reverse direction. Done forward, with the character's look followed by what they see, the audience has clarity in presentation and sequence. We see the subject, loaded with story significance through character attention. Interestingly, done in reverse, we see something, then we see the character's focused Look. The subjectivity of presentation is retroactively applied. If we have been introduced to a setting, maybe a waterfall, and then we see a character who is looking at it, we will get the sense of having had our own vicarious experience first, modified by the realization that we are sharing a character's experience. It can feel like a shared experience. That can be powerful and can bond us to the character, just like a shared experience in real life.

In the movie *Midsommar*[4] (Figure 6.4), we have both forward and reverse Look/See patterns plus the relatively rare true POV, as if looking through a character's eyes, sharing their perspective in a first-person, vicarious placement in the character's body. We experience the drug being blown in our faces, then see Christian's stunned reaction. We actually fall with him, connected to his subjective experience. From his sideways view of the world, we have a forward Look/See of Christian looking and then his POV of the

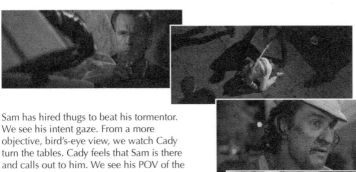

Sam has hired thugs to beat his tormentor. We see his intent gaze. From a more objective, bird's-eye view, we watch Cady turn the tables. Cady feels that Sam is there and calls out to him. We see his POV of the dumpster – then frightened Sam hiding behind it. The suspense comes from knowing more than either character does.

We see Leigh's Look, then Cady sitting on their wall. There are no blinds in the frame of Cady – we see the focus of her attention, not through her eyes.

Figure 6.3

We have an "aural" Look/See. Sam hears a missing note – we see the missing piano string. This increases his attention – through hearing – and we get an ECU confirmation. The strings will be a murder weapon.

Figure 6.4

We observe Christian being drugged, entering a relatively rare true POV, as if through his eyes. We connect with his reaction and fall, the world tilting around us. We return to his true POV when a villager closes his eyes. This bridges to the next scene, where another villager opens his eyes, as he is paralyzed.

villager shutting his paralyzed eyelids. This bridges to the next scene, where a reverse Look/See gives us his POV of eyelids being lifted open, after which we will see Christian, having shared this experience of being help-lessly trapped and unable to communicate.

In general, every reverse Look/See pattern will give us a sense of expe-riencing something before we connect to the character's reaction. That can align us with character experience and give us the space to simultaneously judge character reaction against our own. We see an example of that in Chapter 5 (Figure 5.11), when Llewelyn finds the drug deal gone bad and isn't shocked by the bloody mayhem. Because we saw it first, we can com-pare our shock with Llewelyn's complacency. We now know that he has experience with deadly violence.

The framings for Look/See pairs are usually housed in separate shots, although sometimes swift camera moves might connect the frames into a single shot. We saw this in Chapter 1 (Figure 1.4), with the look of astronaut Stone and the continuous move to her view of earth.

Because these Look/See pairs will usually be recorded in separate shots, there are both practical implications and creative options. If in doubt, the choice of forward or reverse Look/See can be left to editing, responding to the total story flow. The practical implication is that a critical Look/See, as seen in the example with Christian in *Midsommar*, must be carefully noted in your coverage plan so it isn't considered a low-priority shot on set.

Look/See and inner vision

In real life, we instantaneously understand if someone is looking at us or at something else. We can read eyelines. We can tell when someone is day-dreaming, lost in thought, or having strong internal emotions simply by the way their gaze is unfocused. We register this inward attention. Cinematic storytelling can make use of that in interesting ways.

As with standard Look/See patterns, the inward gaze works in either for-ward or reverse. This is also true with dreams. We may see strange or unreal visions, out of context, and then the character waking up, letting us real-ize that this is internal vision and we have just seen their dream. Someone might even need to snap a character out of reverie and bring them back to the present.

The inner gaze can also be used to cross scene boundaries. A scene may end with a character's inward gaze (where we don't see any physical, exter-nal subject), giving us a sense that whatever we see next was on their minds, was in their hearts, or is part of their fate. A character sees the news that the country has gone to war, and we end on their inward gaze. The next thing we see is a troop carrier crossing the seas or a battle scene. Or a teen-age character is adamant about not wanting to have children, and we end on their inward gaze. The next thing we see is the character reaching for a pot that's boiling over, with a toddler on one hip and a baby screaming in a highchair.

In the movie *Saving Private Ryan*[5] (Figure 6.5), we see inward Look/ See patterns masked by real things that are seen. The start is Captain Miller being asked to comment on the view, but the push-in emphasizes his inner gaze – not toward the world around him. We have the strong sense that he is still in the grip of the bloody battle for Normandy Beach, with his inner gaze connected to the scenes of mass casualties. The emotional connection of his inner look makes the next scene a continuous story thread of battle and near-death trauma.

Then camera takes on a life of its own. This is called an "unmotivated move," because the camera is not following a moving character or object but is moving on its own. I think it's worthwhile to consider all unmotivated moves to be driven by the story situation – whatever is outside of charac-ter agency and motivations. They are independent of character experience. Here, it is the trauma of battle which motivated the first push-in to Miller, now motivating the search for something of story significance – the death of one of the Ryan brothers.

Figure 6.5

After the trauma of battle, Captain Miller's inward gaze connects us to his inward vision. We see a series of images of the dead on the beach. His inner Look crosses the scene boundary, connecting the story thread.

Then our view swoops over the beach toward one casualty with the name "Ryan" on his gear. This kinetic move is storytelling independent of character and brings us to a key link in the chain of C&E.

A reverse Look/See bridges us to the next scene, where staff in a war office look down on something of significance, as if they shared our view of the beach. They are typing death notices. When a supervisor notices one family getting multiple notices, the story goal is set in motion.

The next thing we see are Looks of two women. At first it feels like they are looking down on the aftermath of the battle, but they are actually looking down at typed death notifications of the Ryan brothers. This emotional connection through the attention and inner state of characters – the Look – gives filmmakers an effective connection of story threads across scene boundaries, a "soft" continuity of story meaning. We will refer to that when we explore scene-to-scene interconnections in greater depth.

An interesting filmmaking subtlety is that this series gets to have it both ways. There actually is something concrete for the characters to focus their Looks upon, but we get all the emotional benefits of the inner Look on both ends of the series. My conjecture is that this prevents the literal-minded in the audience from getting lost or confused, while taking advantage of the poetic quality of the inner Look for those who feel the cinematic storytelling more strongly. This is a great example of using sophisticated cinematic storytelling without losing broad audience appeal.

Look/See patterns are the gateway to subjectivity

The Look/See pattern tells the audience that whatever is seen has story significance, clearly defined by the character's attention to it (or redefined, in a reverse pattern). By sharing their attention, we have entered into their subjective experience in a way that ratchets up our vicarious involvement. It is beyond participation, where we face the same way but are following behind the character, for a feeling that is slightly independent from their direct experience. With the Look/See pattern, we are fully engaged in their subjective experience.

In the movie *The Shawshank Redemption*[6] (Figure 6.6), we see how character attention pulls us to sharing the subjective experience of Red, newly released from prison and ill equipped to cope. We know, from earlier scenes, that another older inmate committed suicide in the very same room that Red now occupies. From his depressed voiceover narration, we know that he is struggling and has a dreadful longing to be back in prison, where life made sense and he was respected. With the pawn shop sign in the background, we see something catch his attention, and we find out it's a gun. We worry about his committing a crime just to get back into prison.

The interesting cinematic twist is that, after his Look, we are not aligned with his eyeline. Instead we are observing him, separated from him, encouraging us to evaluate and judge his intentions. This is a subtle but effective storytelling choice. When the framing that signifies his interest shifts to the compass, we can't tell if it's his intention or wishful thinking of our own.

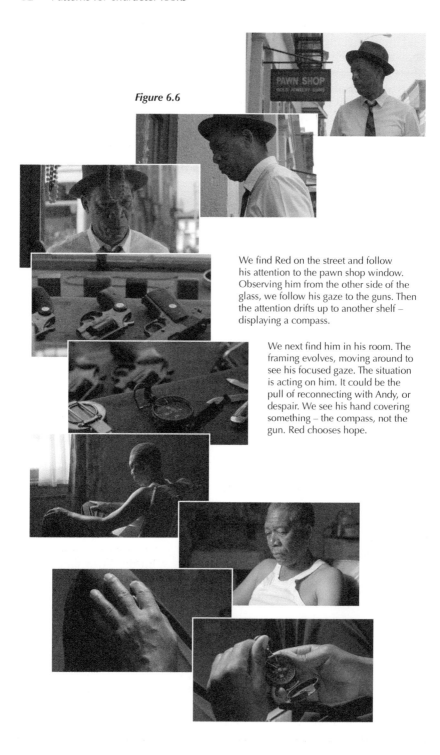

Figure 6.6

We find Red on the street and follow his attention to the pawn shop window. Observing him from the other side of the glass, we follow his gaze to the guns. Then the attention drifts up to another shelf – displaying a compass.

We next find him in his room. The framing evolves, moving around to see his focused gaze. The situation is acting on him. It could be the pull of reconnecting with Andy, or despair. We see his hand covering something – the compass, not the gun. Red chooses hope.

The somber scene that follows prolongs this tension until the reveal of the compass and the triumph of hope over despair. As with much dramatic tension and suspense, it comes from knowing things in the story that seem to inevitably lead to a bad end.

The extent of subjectivity possible through the Look/See pattern is suggested by movies that have a character experience some intensely subjective state, such as being drugged or feverish. Within the realm of realism, but equally subjective in regard to character experience, would be a sweeping survey of a setting after we see the character's sweeping gaze.

Avoiding looks for creative reasons

There are some stories where it makes sense to hold at the level of vicariously witnessing character events, rather than using Looks to enter the characters' subjective experience. The filmmakers may want to encourage the sense of being an honest witness and not presume to enter the character's thoughts, thus keeping the experience more objective and perhaps respectful of limits to what we can truly know about another. Stories about a character who is enigmatic may fall into this category. A story based on a biographical character may demand that we not invent things that we can't be assured are part of their real-life experience.

Look/See becomes dialogue

The effect of the Look/See pattern is to place us within the character's subjective experience. We see what they are intent upon, and their interest drives the storytelling. Just as the Action perspective of connection leads into the Look/See pair, the Look/See pattern is the building block of dialogue patterns. Dialogue pairs are mutual, reciprocal Look/See patterns. We share the feeling of mutual subjective attention or intersubjectivity.

In the movie *Michael Clayton*[7] (Figure 6.7), we get the character's Look, but the subject of his attention is withheld for a moment, lending surprise when we see the graceful horses on a misty hill at dawn. In simple Action patterns, we stay with Michael. The participation angle melds into what can only be called a Dialogue pair – mutual Look/See frames – of him and the lead horse. It is an otherworldly communication.

We already know this character's sense of self-disgust, corrupted by his job as a "fixer" for a high-priced law firm, and his loss of money from both a failed business venture and a gambling habit. He is hitting bottom. His need for redemption and a moment of spiritual cleansing make sense of his need to connect with this innocent and noble animal. When his car explodes, the magic is shattered and forced with the ugly reality that he was the target of a murder attempt. It feels like a divine intervention, where his attention to the beautiful and ungrasping nature of the horses has saved him from the consequences of greed.

Something catches Michael Clayton's attention – we know this through his focused gaze. We connect with his wonder, replacing his dour mood. We participate with his walk up the hill to the horses . . .

Figure 6.7

. . . where he is entranced by an encounter that feels like unspoken dialogue, using reciprocal shots of him and one of the horses. An explosion scares the horses. He turns to see his car blowing up, realizing he was saved from certain death.

Summary

Character Looks provide the essential means to put the audience in the character's shoes – seeing what they see, feeling what they feel. We immediately know that what we see has story significance through the fixation of character attention. This is the storytelling importance of character Looks and the basis of the Look/See pattern. Here are the main points:

- Connection with the character lets us read their concentrated attention.
- A series of shared looks presents non-verbal communication, providing a private layer of communication, just as in real life.
- The Look/See pattern pushes us beyond the connection to character emotions and into their head and the source of their reactions. We share their subjective attention.
- True POV (as if through the character's eyes) is not necessary or common. Mostly, we observe whatever they are focused on, in the clearest, most understandable way.
- In the forward Look/See pattern, what we See is the subject of their attention.
- In the reverse Look/See pattern, we See something, and then the character's Look provides a sense of shared experience and allows us to judge the character's reaction against our own.
- The "inner" Look/See pattern is an excellent way to cross scene boundaries with story momentum intact and redirected.
- Because the character's Look is the gateway to subjectivity, it can be used extensively to achieve storytelling that remains close to one character's or a group's subjective experiences.
- Conversely, avoiding the Look/See pattern can provide objectivity, resisting presumptions of subjective "mind reading" and serving for "honest witness" storytelling.

What you can do . . .

Watch any section of your favorite movie and stop it whenever you see a character's focused gaze, with the subject of their attention in the shot just after or just prior.

- Did the Look take you inside of character interests and provide a sense of their subjective experience?
- Was it a forward or reverse Look/See? How did the order of that pattern pair affect your understanding?
- Did the Look/See pattern cross a scene boundary? In which direction? How did it carry across story thread, character feelings, or mood from one scene to the next?

- Did you see any Looks exchanged between characters? Did this happen in a social setting, with others present who weren't privy to that other level of shared communication?

Notes

1 *Altered States*. Directed by Ken Russell, Cinematography by Jordan Cronenweth. Warner Bros., released 1980. DVD: Warner Bros. Home Video (1998, USA). Start time: 00:06:36.
2 *Out of Time*. Directed by Carl Franklin, Cinematography by Theo van de Sande. MGM, Original Film, Monarch Pictures, released 2003. DVD: MGM Home Entertainment (2006, USA). Start time: 00:56:48.
3 *Cape Fear*. Directed by Martin Scorsese, Cinematography by Freddie Francis. Amblin Entertainment, Cappa Films, Tribeca Productions, released 1991. DVD: Universal Studios (2005, USA).
4 *Midsommar*. Directed by Ari Aster, Cinematography by Pawel Pogorzelski. A24, B-Reel Films, Nordisk Film, Square Peg, released 2019. DVD: A24 Films, LLC, Lions Gate Entertainment (2020, USA). Start time: 02:09:13.
5 *Saving Private Ryan*. Directed by Steven Spielberg, Cinematography by Janusz Kaminski. DreamWorks, Paramount Pictures, Amblin Entertainment, released 1998. DVD: DreamWorks (1999, USA). Start time: 00:27:08.
6 *The Shawshank Redemption*. Directed by Frank Darabont, Cinematography by Roger Deakins. Castle Rock Entertainment, released 1994. DVD: Warner Bros. Entertainment (2007, USA). Start time: 02:10:02.
7 *Michael Clayton*. Directed by Tony Gilroy, Cinematography by Robert Elswit. Samuels Media, Castle Rock Entertainment, Mirage Enterprises, released 2007. DVD: Warner Bros. Home Video (2008, USA). Start time: 00:13:25.

Chapter 7
Patterns for dialogue – structure

Character dialogue multiplies complexity

Physical action is straightforward and easy to comprehend rapidly. In Action, story perspective is fairly straightforward. Compared to Action, the human interaction of Dialogue can be fiendishly complex and thus very rich in meaning.

In Dialogue, the story perspective could conceivably flip back and forth. The audience is connecting with each character through facial expression. The audience may be simultaneously participating with each character's experience, looking over their shoulder facing the other character. Dialogue is complicated on almost every level.

Not only are we, in the audience, taking in the plainly visible story information of character interaction, but we are also paying close attention to words spoken, the subtext underneath the words, and the non-verbal information from body language and expression. Social and psychological questions loom large, with questions inside questions, like a nested set of dolls. What does each character think of the other? What does each think of themselves? What does each think about what the other thinks of them? Now add the questions of how we, the audience, think about each of these questions, and how we judge each character's words, actions, and reactions.

One of the most engaging aspect of films is how they can challenge our social intelligence and force us to grapple with all these interesting, complicated questions. Let's try to build up from what we know and see if we can make sense of it.

Interaction and reciprocal pairs

In contrast to the complexity of dramatic meanings, the basics of Dialogue patterns are simple. The bottom line of dialogue coverage is the observation of interaction between characters. Commonly known as the **two-shot**, we see two characters talking to each other, which is simply an extension of Action patterns for this social activity. Some scenes of dialogue never go further than that. It's worth considering the observation of interaction as a valid and useful choice in coverage. We will see examples where the fact of interaction and how the characters interact is at the center of the storytelling.

DOI: 10.4324/9781003080657-7

We've seen an example in the chapter on Action patterns (Chapter 5), from *Saving Private Ryan*[1] (Figure 5.3), where the conversations between various groups happen while on the move through the landscape. The Action perspective of connecting with the characters allows us to see expression and body language between them, as the character Upham is socially isolated and cannot instantly be "one of the guys." He doesn't want to be there, and they don't particularly want him there, either. This is Dialogue through Action, using the frontal angle that lets us connect with expressiveness and varying proximities. It's all fairly impersonal, and we never get the reciprocal shot pairs emblematic of dialogue and the sharing of subjective social experience. We witness and listen, but we never get fully inside the mutual and shared subjective experience between characters.

The Look/See pattern is the gateway to subjective character experience. The reciprocal Dialogue pattern mirrors the Look/See pattern to become the gateway to **intersubjectivity** – characters in a shared subjective experience. The core dialogue pattern is reciprocal Look/See pairs – the conventional **shot-and-reverse** or A-B-A-B coverage. The shot-and-reverse pattern lets us enter this vicarious mutual engagement. Each character's focused attention is on the other. Each character is, in turn, the subject of the other's focused attention. The center of the storytelling is between them, each granting story significance to the other, each one's words and reactions the focus of attention. Through mutual, reciprocal attention, we share their experience.

The alignment (or misalignment) and balance (or imbalance) of these reciprocal framings is at the heart of cinematic storytelling for dialogue scenes. It is the way characters are physically aligned relative to each other – **staging** – that determines shot pair specifics. Therefore, one of the structural elements of dialogue patterns is the staging of characters. We will look at five different staging patterns that are commonly used. Each has its own typical shot pairs with different associated feelings.

Let me briefly note that some filmmakers are adamant that staging decisions should only happen in rehearsals or on set, working with the performers. They may feel that any predetermination of staging is hobbling creativity and the valid discovery of what feels right and true to the characters and the moment. For many – not all – stories, that is also my preference, but with some groundwork in place. Broad strokes on staging options and intentions can help develop the cinematic storytelling, leaving freedom in the specifics to a discovery process in rehearsals.

If you know the common options for staging and their implications for molding context, you can analyze movies and make sense of the decisions. With that in the back of your mind, you can work with actors to discover the best staging without painting yourself into a corner.

You need to know how to set up and support performances through cinematic means, so that the audience receives the best and clearest emotional impact. You do not want great performances undermined by cinematic choices that are dissonant or contradictory to the inferential meaning of the scene. That would be a shame.

Staging and the 180° Line of Continuity

In Action, we stay oriented simply by being with the characters. A range of angles can be completely comprehensible and not disorienting. The major need for careful, technical consideration of orientation and continuity is in situations like battles or chases, where two individuals or groups are interacting. That makes those situations a lot like dialogue.

The **180° Line of Continuity** is probably familiar to most of you. If not, here is an overview. In the first illustration (Figure 7.1), we see the common staging with characters directly across from each other. We have seen this staging in one of our examples from the movie *Cast Away*[2] (Figure 1.1, Figure 1.2), where Chuck and Kelly are across from each other and engage in spoken and unspoken dialogue. It is that reciprocal framing pattern of shot-and-reverse – something we've seen all our lives in movies – that notifies us of their dialogue. We've seen it in the movie *Michael Clayton*[3] (Figure 6.7), where that pattern tells us that the person and the horse are engaged in what feels like dialogue.

In our first diagram of camera positions and staging patterns (Figure 7.1), we have the basics of how shot-and-reverse pairs relate to character staging. The camera positions shown are basic choices. Use these as a starting point for understanding how reciprocal pairs can be set up and how they might feel. You can expand from there.

First, let's look at the 180° Line of Continuity. **The Line** (as it is called on most sets) is an imaginary line or axis connecting the mutual eyelines of the characters. The simplified framing, shown below the plan view (overhead) camera diagram, illustrates how a wider shot of the interaction – the two-shot – from one side of the line will show the characters oriented frame right and frame left.

Following the Line of Continuity, camera positions 1, 2, 3, 4, and 5 have the character in the dark outfit always frame left. The character in the lighter outfit is always frame right. Any camera position on that side of the Line would typically show that same orientation. That is what keeps the audience from getting confused. Later on, we will see an example that "crosses the line" or uses shot pairs from different sides of the 180° Line for creative storytelling. In the vast majority of cases, maintaining the orientation of the Line is a good thing because it prevents confusion. There is already a lot for the audience to think about. The Line lets us know where characters are "coming from" because they sustain orientation in framing and all shot pairs.

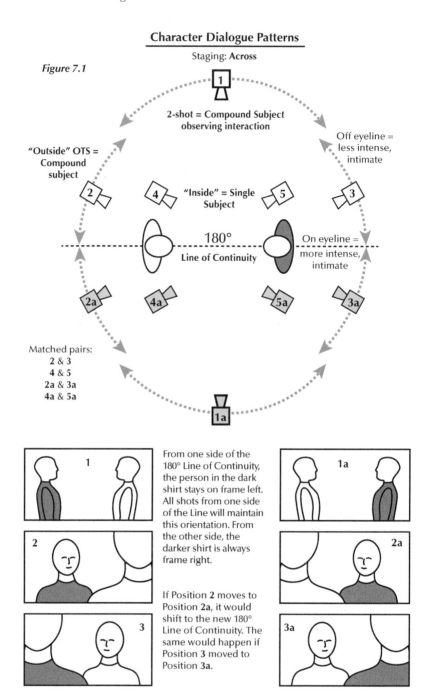

Character Dialogue Patterns

Figure 7.1

Staging: **Across**

2-shot = Compound Subject
observing interaction

"Outside" OTS =
Compound
subject

Off eyeline =
less intense,
intimate

"Inside" = Single
Subject

180°
Line of Continuity

On eyeline =
more intense,
intimate

Matched pairs:
2 & 3
4 & 5
2a & 3a
4a & 5a

From one side of the 180° Line of Continuity, the person in the dark shirt stays on frame left. All shots from one side of the Line will maintain this orientation. From the other side, the darker shirt is always frame right.

If Position **2** moves to Position **2a**, it would shift to the new 180° Line of Continuity. The same would happen if Position **3** moved to Position **3a**.

Resetting the Line of Continuity

One of the major ways to shape scenes is to reset the 180° Line of Continuity, which is done in three common ways. One is simply to jump to a new camera position on the other side of the Line and then maintain that new Line. That method is abrupt and momentarily throws us a bit off balance, which can be a good thing for some story situations. The second way to reset the Line is to move the camera across or behind the characters – for example, with the use of a dolly or other mobile camera mount. This resets the line without confusion because we see it happen. It still feels like a new phase of the scene but without the "bump" of a sudden reset. The third way is to have the performers move or shift into a new staging that automatically resets the line because their mutual eyeline has changed.

Resetting the Line generates the feeling of a new context and a new phase of the scene. Once we go over the structural basics of Dialogue scenes, we will focus on that idea – using cinematic means to shape scenes and support performances, through changes in the context provided by coverage. We will see examples in our chapters on Patterns and Movement, and references in our chapter on Scene Shaping.

Staging across offers a big range in intensity and intimacy

As seen in Figure 7.1, characters face each other directly when staged across from each other, whether standing or sitting. Let's consider framing variables within that staging. We know from Action patterns that the most objective and observational angles are off the characters' eyeline, more to the side or above or below. The perspective and angle alter our sense of dependence on, or independence from, character subjective experience. The closer we are aligned to the character's eyeline, the stronger the sense of connection to their subjective emotional responses. The mutual and shared attention of dialogue magnifies this effect. The further off the axis of their mutual eyeline, the more observational and objective the shot pairs will tend to feel. The closer on the axis of their mutual eyeline, the more subjective and emotionally intense the shots will tend to feel.

We know from Action patterns that being closer to a character in visual proximity will give more importance to their facial expressions and thus their thoughts, feelings, and intentions. That gets magnified in dialogue, where mutual attention pings the attention back and forth in a closed loop. The end result of story-based proximity decisions is shot size. The most common and widely understood way to ramp up intensity or intimacy is by getting closer to the characters in tighter CU pairs. The reverse holds true for ramping down intensity or intimacy by creating more distance. This shifts attention from the inner state of the characters to their social presentation in frames that show more of their body. When characters are staged across, there is a wide range of usable angles and variations in shot size, providing a great amount of control.

From the camera positions 2 and 3 shown in Figure 7.1, we have OTS (over-the-shoulder) framings that put each into the other's context. From camera positions 4 and 5 (and their corresponding positions on the other side of the Line), we have singular subject framing that can support either the sense of more autonomous story agency for each or the sense of isolation. As with everything related to cinematic storytelling, the story and performances provide the meaning, and the framing points toward it.

I will refer to these structural diagrams of staging and the 180° Line of Continuity when we get into examples from movies in Chapter 8. We will not only see each staging but also how one staging may flow into another to shape the dialogue scene. For now, let's plow through the mechanics in order to have background knowledge needed to understand the movie examples.

Staging on a diagonal offers front or back angles

Characters on a diagonal, or "catty-corner," are commonly used in both standing and sitting dialogue (Figure 7.2). Socially, this is less intense than directly across. Even though we expect the characters to turn their heads toward each other, their body positions are not so directly confrontational. Envisioned in the imagination, you can see how camera positions 2 and 3 are quite different than what we would see in the "across" staging. In a diagonal staging, we would be looking past the foreground character, not truly over their shoulders. That feels quite different. It puts both characters into more of a shared context. It splits the difference between "across" staging and what we will look at next, which is "side-by-side" staging.

The major feature of diagonal staging is that we have completely different feelings if we are on one side of the 180° Line or the other. From a frontal angle, the sense of connection predominates. These camera positions would be very much like connection angles in Action patterns. From the back or over the back shoulders, we are in a position that is like the participation angle from Action patterns. That can feel more like eavesdropping on their conversation, getting to peek inside their shared subjective attention.

Camera positions 4 and 5, which might be angled or straight-on, will feel more isolated, with each character in their singular frame. The more common camera positions at 2 and 3 (and the reverse side) will likely be compound subject framings that put each into the other's context.

Staging side-by-side offers a shared view

Moving even farther from the potentially confrontational "across" staging, "side-by-side" staging lets the characters be shoulder-to-shoulder, facing the same way (Figure 7.3). Sometimes this is forced on the scene by a setting such as inside a car. When the setting permits greater freedom, this will tend to feel the way it does in real life. Facing the situation side-by-side just feels different from facing each other. Most parents understand that sitting next

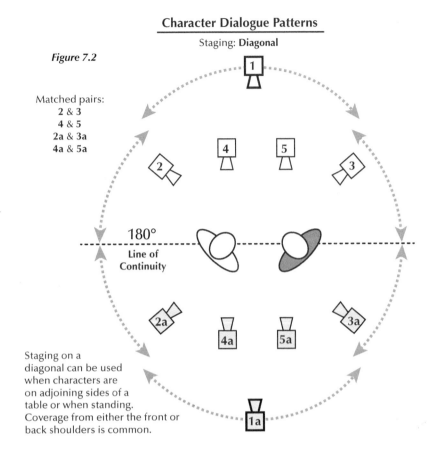

Character Dialogue Patterns

Staging: **Diagonal**

Figure 7.2

Matched pairs:
   2 & 3
   4 & 5
   2a & 3a
   4a & 5a

180°
Line of
Continuity

Staging on a diagonal can be used when characters are on adjoining sides of a table or when standing. Coverage from either the front or back shoulders is common.

to a child who is wrestling with a problem creates a feeling of working on it together, whereas sitting across from the child can feel confrontational.

As with the "diagonal" staging, the camera positions 2 and 3 will not be true OTS but instead will be looking past one character at the other. It is putting them on the same side. And as with the "diagonal" staging, side-by-side offers both frontal and back-shoulder options, which will feel different from each other.

In contrast to "diagonal" staging, it is relatively easy to select either compound subject framing or single subject framing from positions 2 and 3 (or 2a and 3a), because the characters aren't in each other's way. That provides a slightly different set of options to explore. I have left out the straight-on camera positions from the back shoulder because there is less utility in seeing the backs of heads. You can easily achieve a profile shot in the "diagonal" framing, but it isn't as practical in this side-by-side framing.

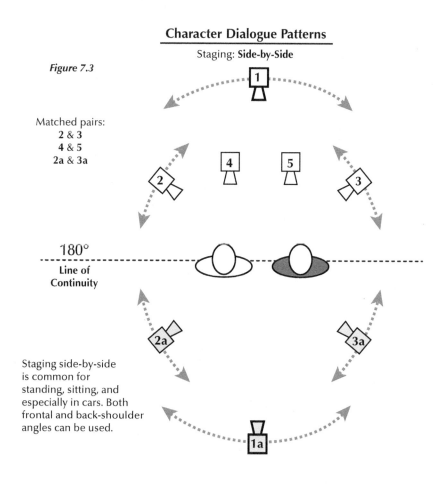

Character Dialogue Patterns

Staging: **Side-by-Side**

Figure 7.3

Matched pairs:
  2 & 3
  4 & 5
  2a & 3a

180°
**Line of
Continuity**

Staging side-by-side
is common for
standing, sitting, and
especially in cars. Both
frontal and back-shoulder
angles can be used.

When characters are in the front seats of a car or a similar setting, the side-by-side staging is inevitable. That is where the camera positions 2 and 3 might be much more to the sides to see through a side window, past the foreground character at the other. Movies have the chance to "cheat" into a more confrontational staging "across" by having the characters fully turn toward each other. Although this would be dangerous for a driver to do in real life, we can do this safely in movies, as long as it doesn't seem too unrealistic.

Staging in depth offers the masking of emotions

When characters are staged in depth, the foreground character's face and expressions cannot be seen by the background character (Figure 7.4). This is often used for moments within scenes, rather than being the predominant pattern throughout the scene. Consider a story situation where

Character Dialogue Patterns

Staging: **In Depth**

Figure 7.4

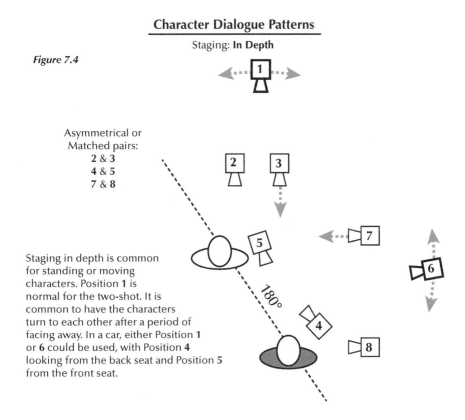

Asymmetrical or
Matched pairs:
2 & 3
4 & 5
7 & 8

Staging in depth is common
for standing or moving
characters. Position **1** is
normal for the two-shot. It is
common to have the characters
turn to each other after a period of
facing away. In a car, either Position **1**
or **6** could be used, with Position **4**
looking from the back seat and Position **5**
from the front seat.

the foreground character doesn't want the background character to notice a deception or wants to hide their feelings. Sometimes courtroom dramas will use this to show the clever lawyer turned to us, setting up a guilty defendant who can't see their plans. But we can, because we see both expressions when the characters are staged in depth. Staging in depth might also be used for a moment when the foreground character is regaining their composure while turned away. Then, the dialogue will return to a more conventional staging.

This staging might be sustained if the characters are in a car, or in any setting with seats or benches one behind the other. In those cases, the camera positions 4 and 5 could be used to look from the front seat character to the back seat character and vice versa. Also, the two-shot from position 6 might be used if the desire is to have more observational and less emotionally connected coverage. This might be used for a spy movie where characters don't want to be observed meeting, so they sit in different seats on a bus, not facing each other.

Staging offset provides a diagonal that isn't shared

The less common offset staging is useful to exploit the expressive possibilities of a setting that might have benches or rows of chairs that face each other (Figure 7.5). This allows for characters to only share a mutual eyeline and not mirrored positions. This mismatch makes asymmetrical shot pairs feel natural and unforced. The characters are in an awkward or intentionally disconnected relationship already, and the use of asymmetrical shot pairs can feel appropriate.

Staging and "the situation" to help feel the options

One way to consider the differences between the common staging options is in the realm of a thought experiment. Strictly for the sake of cinematic decision making, you can bundle all of the story agency that is outside of the characters and label it "the situation" (Figure 7.6).

Let's imagine we have a scene with two kids talking about skipping school for an adventure. The factors outside their agency – "the situation" – might

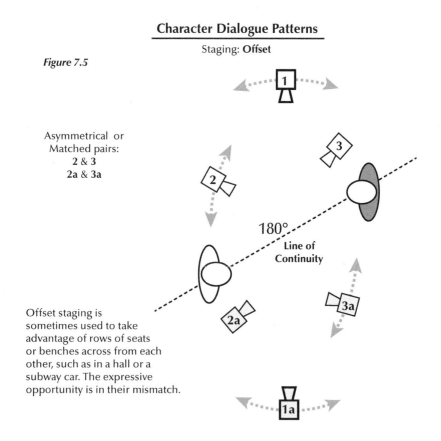

Character Dialogue Patterns

Staging: **Offset**

Figure 7.5

Asymmetrical or
Matched pairs:
2 & 3
2a & 3a

180°
Line of
Continuity

Offset staging is
sometimes used to take
advantage of rows of seats
or benches across from each
other, such as in a hall or a
subway car. The expressive
opportunity is in their mismatch.

Staging & "The Situation"

Figure 7.6

Across

180°

When characters are staged directly across from each other, we can see "the situation" as being between them.

Consider all story agency outside of the characters present as one big story bundle of "the situation." Character orientation relative to "the situation" can be a tie-breaker when thinking about staging and for changes in staging.

Diagonal

180°

When characters are staged on a diagonal, we can think of "the situation" as being halfway between in front and between them.

Side-by-Side

180°

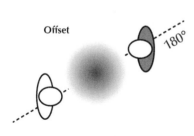

When characters are side-by-side, we can think of "the situation" as being something they face together.

In Depth

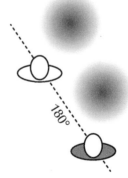

When characters are staged in depth, we can think of each having their own separate view of "the situation."

Offset

180°

When characters are offset in staging, neither one faces "the situation" directly.

include their parents, their parents' differing approaches to discipline, the school, the judgment or endorsement of their peers, the weather, the kind of adventure they pick and its risks, etc. They might argue, but "the situation" and all of the influencing factors outside of their own individual agency loom as something outside of them.

I am not suggesting that you dump your existing methods of dramatic analysis and replace them with this simplistic and binary concept. I'm only suggesting that dialogue coverage can be very complicated and that simplifying some issues, through broad strokes, can help clarify your decision making.

Setting up context and changing the context

Figuring out coverage for dialogue requires setting up and establishing a context with consistency. The basic staging patterns are a good starting point because they offer some natural options. For each, a two-shot and matched, reciprocal shot pairs are available as a consistent "bundle" of coverage. The two-shot plus shot-and-reverse pairs provide a total pattern.

Shaping the dialogue scene happens through changes in that context. Like songs going from verse to chorus, it is the change that signals the audience. Where will we find these mechanisms of change? They will be in the variations of angle and perspective, proximity and shot size – just like in Action patterns. They will also be in the staging of characters and the effects of setting and resetting the 180° Line of Continuity. Any and all of these, in various combinations, will provide the means to conform coverage to the storytelling, be supportive of performances, and give shape to dialogue scenes.

Reciprocal framing pairs – the core of dialogue context – provide a big opportunity to shape the context for the audience. The use of matched and symmetrical, or unmatching and asymmetrical, shot pairs can effectively alert the audience to the nature of the characters' relationship. Proximity to characters can also be either balanced or unbalanced. Whether we see each character within the context of the other in OTS (over-the-shoulder) shots or see each in a "clean" single subject shot will also influence the feeling of the interaction.

Movement and restaging is used to shape the phases of a scene, creating a new 180° Line of Continuity and resulting in new reciprocal shot pairs. **A new angle in the coverage signals a new angle in the storytelling**. This is perhaps the most essential tool for creating cinematic Dialogue coverage that supports the storytelling. And it is a major factor in how we, in the audience, feel story shape and progress, as the coverage has one set of qualities, then breaks free to move to the next set of qualities. This is how the coverage provides context that informs and elevates performances without competing for audience attention.

Summary

- Character Dialogue patterns start with the observational Action pattern of seeing characters engaged in an interaction. With two characters involved, that results in two-shot framing.
- The basic pattern of Dialogue is a mutual Look/See pattern that has each character's subjective attention focused on the other. This results in shot-and-reverse framing or matched, reciprocal framing pairs. Mutual subjective attention is the focus of the storytelling. Reciprocal dialogue pairs signal shared intersubjectivity.
- Dialogue is socially complex, requiring more options for contextual support of the story specifics.
- Staging, or the placement of characters relative to each other, is an important structuring mechanism of dialogue coverage. Staging does not need to be rigidly fixed in order to make productive cinematic decisions, leaving options open for different filmmaking styles.
- Staging creates a mutually shared eyeline that is the basis for the 180° Line of Continuity. Changes in staging can be used to reset this Line in order to convey story progress.
- Each of the five basic staging options – across, diagonal, side-by-side, in depth, and offset – have their own storytelling strengths, and each will result in their own reciprocal shot pairs to convey the intersubjective sections of a scene.
- The factors that go into dialogue interaction and reciprocal shot pairs include the perspective (or angle) on characters, the proximity (or shot size), and the staging. Changes in one or more of these factors will be the way we shape scenes in order to signal story progress through changes in contextual presentation.
- Working through these options helps filmmakers turn the complexity of Dialogue into something that can be clarified through coverage choice. All options let us see the visible action, and all the options have their own particular feeling that can be used to point toward desired interpretations of the interaction.

What you can do . . .

Take a look at the diagrams for staging and basic camera positions. Now fast-forward through some of your favorite movies and see if you can identify any of these within Dialogue scenes.

- Does the coverage of the dialogue follow the 180° Line of Continuity? Do the characters stay on "their side" of the frame as the coverage progresses?
- Do you see the full interaction in some form of a two-shot or group shot, plus shot pairs?

- Do the shot pairs show symmetrical and mirror-image framing? If so, what were the qualities of the shots in terms of single or compound (OTS) frames? What about perspective or angle on the characters? Proximity or shot size?
- If the shot pairs are unmatched or asymmetrical in any way, what are the differences? Are they different angles, shot sizes, or single versus compound subject framing?
- Can you find examples of more than one staging? If so, did they feel different? Have you seen any restaging in a long dialogue scene, and how was it achieved? Through movement?

Notes

1 *Saving Private Ryan*. Directed by Steven Spielberg, Cinematography by Janusz Kaminski. DreamWorks, Paramount Pictures, Amblin Entertainment, released 1998. DVD: DreamWorks (1999, USA). Start time: 00:42:40.
2 *Cast Away*. Directed by Robert Zemeckis, Cinematography by Don Burgess. Twentieth Century Fox, Dreamworks, released 2000. DVD: Twentieth Century Fox Home Entertainment (2001, USA). Start time: 00:14:06.
3 *Michael Clayton*. Directed by Tony Gilroy, Cinematography by Robert Elswit. Samuels Media, Castle Rock Entertainment, Mirage Enterprises, released 2007. DVD: Warner Bros. Home Video (2008, USA).

Chapter 8
Patterns for dialogue – examples

Examples of the variety in dialogue pattern usage

In Chapter 7, we laid out the structures that support dialogue patterns. Let's briefly review.

1   The observational witnessing of interaction, in a two-shot of both characters, can convey a tremendous amount of information about how they interact.

2   In the alternating shot-and-reverse pairs of Dialogue, the perspective or angle relative to mutual eyeline modulates subjectivity. When the angle is off the axis of mutual eyeline, the perspective can be relatively objective and independent of character experience. When closer to their mutual eyeline, the perspective tends toward dependence on subjective character experience.

3   In Dialogue shot-and-reverse pairs, proximity to characters helps to shape the audience's expectations. Seeing the characters' upper bodies and gestures places the focus on social presentation. Access to facial expressions places the focus on the character's thoughts, feelings, and intentions. Closer is more intense or intimate.

4   OTS (over-the-shoulder) framing keeps each character in a compound subject, within the context of the other character in frame. Singular framing, or "clean" singles, can give each character a sense of greater individual autonomy of story agency and individual goals but can also feel more isolated. Framing choices should, of course, be made based on the interpersonal dynamics at play.

5   Five common staging configurations – across, diagonal, side-by-side, in depth, and offset – provide a range of opportunities to influence how we see the characters relative to each other and to the forces arrayed outside of them in the story. Staging can provide consistent mutual orientation. Changes in orientation can signal story progress to another phase of the scene. Changes in staging allow for new angles and new combinations of shot pairs.

DOI: 10.4324/9781003080657-8

In this chapter, we will see how all these factors can be brought into play in order to suit a specific scene in a specific story. In your own work, creative freedom will be found in the fluid application of these patterns and in the adjustment or modulation of the variables that give them a range of contextual options. Let's see how that works out for these examples.

Observing interaction may be all that's needed

In the movie *Se7en*[1] (Figure 8.1), we see what is known as a "walk & talk." Sometimes a walk & talk is used to hide exposition – story information essentials – camouflaged as a social interaction. In this case, Somerset does not want a partner and Mills won't give up. How they interact is central to the story.

This is a single shot that relies upon coordinated character and camera blocking that moves through a variety of keyframes. The observation of their interaction is active, staying with them through starts and stops and

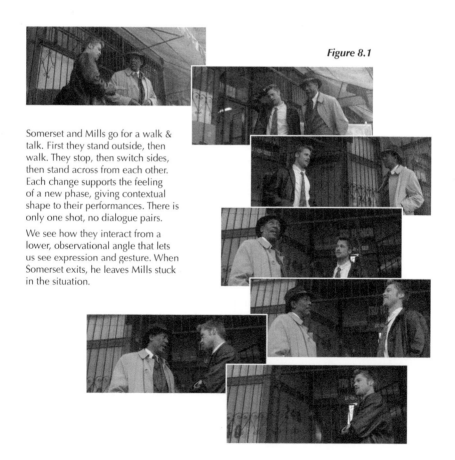

Figure 8.1

Somerset and Mills go for a walk & talk. First they stand outside, then walk. They stop, then switch sides, then stand across from each other. Each change supports the feeling of a new phase, giving contextual shape to their performances. There is only one shot, no dialogue pairs.

We see how they interact from a lower, observational angle that lets us see expression and gesture. When Somerset exits, he leaves Mills stuck in the situation.

realignments. Each phase houses a particular nugget of their interaction. Movement and staging work hand in hand.

Moving, they are side-by-side. When stopped, they might be on a diagonal, or offset, or across from each other, in keeping with the nature of their interaction. This is an example of what might be considered a theatrical presentation of character relationship, where physical staging for the audience is all that counts. Coverage from a single perspective, relative to the characters, is almost like a "moving stage," with the entire audience sharing a common vantage point. There are no reciprocal dialogue shots. There is no need to call attention to reciprocal subjective attention because the scene is about rejecting a shared situation as partners. Somerset leaves Mills behind to stew. Movement and staging do everything necessary to support the performances, letting the actors' work be naturalistic and understated. The audience feels the changes from one phase to the next.

Connection and disconnection through proximity

In a scene from *The Right Stuff* (Figure 8.2), we see a single exterior shot of a cheap hotel. This is establishing and orienting us to the setting, acting as a chapter marker that separates this from the previous scene. The cheap hotel is the only reward for Gus and Betty after his space capsule sank and he nearly drowned – hardly the heroic moment they both anticipated. Gus was blamed for the failure and he is deeply ashamed. Betty is distraught after other astronaut families got parades, fancy hotels, and celebrity meetings. We observe this couple, framed at the level of social presentation in medium and wide shots, where gestures and body language communicate. We stay with them as Gus tries to mask his feelings, evading Betty in the confined space.

Betty finally breaks through. Her single-subject keyframe starts the second phase of the scene. We follow her back to Gus. Because she is the sustained focus of attention and the driver of the framing, we feel her story agency and the shift to her story perspective. Finally, Gus admits his feelings and they embrace, becoming a plural subject – the couple. Abruptly, they are forced back into masks of happiness to satisfy the media's intrusive attention.

This is like a caged walk & talk. We stay with them, witnessing. From this observational perspective and distance, without reciprocal pairs of CUs, we go through various staging options – across, offset, diagonal, and especially in depth, as Gus tries to keep his true feelings from Betty by turning away from her.

The *way they interact* is the focus. This is unlike dialogue through reciprocal shot-and-reverse pairs, where mutual subjective attention is central. The distance in proximity gives them space to move and space for our judgment of them, while connection to their expressions assists in empathetic connection with their pain and conflict. The objective witnessing of emotions so private and raw feels like exposure of their humiliation. This is exactly what they fear. The coverage contextually supports the arc of a deep

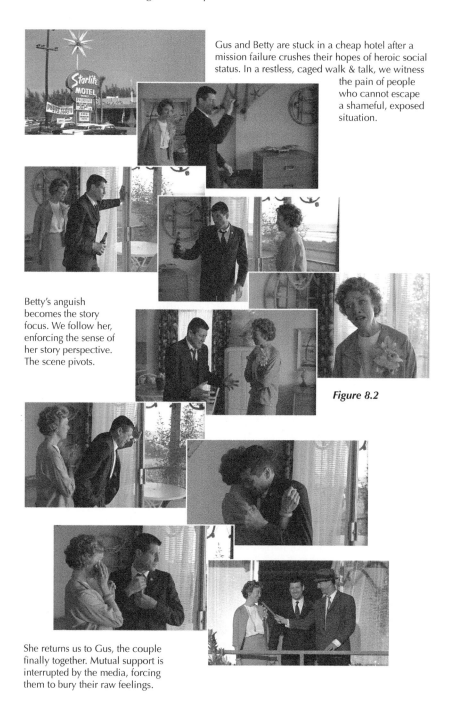

Gus and Betty are stuck in a cheap hotel after a mission failure crushes their hopes of heroic social status. In a restless, caged walk & talk, we witness the pain of people who cannot escape a shameful, exposed situation.

Betty's anguish becomes the story focus. We follow her, enforcing the sense of her story perspective. The scene pivots.

Figure 8.2

She returns us to Gus, the couple finally together. Mutual support is interrupted by the media, forcing them to bury their raw feelings.

emotional disconnection, moving toward understanding – they only have each other in facing the circumstances.

The next example illustrates contextual support for intimate connection, despite great distance.

In another scene from *The Right Stuff*[3] (Figure 8.3), we see an almost opposite dynamic between characters, contextually supported by the coverage. This begins with asymmetrical pairs covering a phone call. On one end is John, with his boss pressuring him (staged in depth). On the other end is his distraught wife, Annie, at home. In a make-or-break moment, we go to tighter framing on John, emphasizing internal decision making. He is also turned away, which raises the tension, casting doubt on his commitment to Annie. He turns back, and their strong bond is reinforced in the mirror-image CUs that exclude everyone else from the picture, happening in tight diagonal staging. It's just them, in reciprocal subjective attention, sharing their private world.

The close, mutually matched frames, facing diagonally toward each other, collapse the physical distance and create subjective closeness. Any time when phone conversations truly connect characters, this type of approach can be supportive. If the characters are in a conflicting or emotionally disconnected phone conversation, the use of asymmetrical or unbalanced pairs and the lack of a mutual eyeline may give us the contextual support the drama needs.

Simple choices support rising and falling action

When the main shape of the scene is rising and falling tension, the simple methods of change in proximity or shot size can be enough. This enables filmmakers to provide shape without creating unnecessary demands on attention that could compete with performances.

In the movie *No Country for Old Men*[4] (Figure 8.4), we see a very simple dialogue pattern, with the characters staged across from each other. In this scene, a gas station owner, in the middle of nowhere, has the misfortune of running into a sociopathic killer. This scene demonstrates the twisted mind of Chigurh, the killer, and his method of using a coin toss to let random fate play a hand in his murderous intentions. The suspense comes from us, in the audience, knowing what he's capable of, while the owner only knows that he's angered by imperceptible slights.

The major variable is proximity, which is increased and decreased to ramp the intensity up and down. Compound subject OTS pairs are used when we feel a shared context, and single CUs are used when we feel their disparate responses to the situation. The angle provided on the deadly coin toss is aligned with the owner's POV but is tighter than actual vision would provide, for a clear view of the result – heads or tails. This helps us share his subjective experience and feel threat from the sociopathic killer. The performances are supported with the simple means, culminating in the physical C&E of the coin toss and the emotional C&E of the innocent owner's relief from building terror.

Figure 8.3

John is called to the phone to convince his wife, Annie, to bow to political pressure. The first pairs are asymmetrical: John and his boss, then Annie. The CU focus on John's inner state lets us see his decision.

He enthusiastically puts Annie's feelings first. Matched intimacy creates a strong subjective connection, despite being physically apart.

Dialogue patterns provide the potential for mutual, intersubjective conflict or connection.

A single shot of the setting brings us into dialogue. Matched, reciprocal framing gets closer and more intense as it progresses. The tightest CUs give each character their own frame, emphasizing separate inner states. The coin toss has great import and is big enough to "read" on screen. This lets us share the owner's stunned reaction. Ending on the wider frame leaves him in the situation – surviving an unknown mortal threat.

Figure 8.4

Dialogue scenes usually give us access to expressions. Emotions are forefront, but thoughts are also readable, as the owner puzzles out safe choices. We can also read the evil intentions of the sociopathic killer.

Action leads to Dialogue, with intimate subtext

In the movie *Out of Time*[5] (Figure 8.5), we see action patterns of observing, connecting, and then participating with Chief of Police Matt as he walks up to the door. Following behind seamlessly becomes an OTS shot. This is mirrored to become the reciprocal shot-and-reverse of Dialogue, with Matt and Ann staged across from each other. Once initiated, the Dialogue pattern is sustained. The CUs become more intimate and more subjective. We get closer in proximity and closer to their mutual eyeline. This encourages and supports the sense that they have a connection that goes beyond a routine police call. The pattern progression, leading to rapid intimacy, supports the inferred storytelling. They are lovers, playing a game. It is a game that becomes convoluted and deadly, all based on misinterpretations of, and within, their relationship.

Offset staging provides meaningful imbalances

The classic, symmetrical framings of the Dialogue paradigm indicate story equivalence between the characters and a degree of balance in the situation. To introduce a level of greater complexity, you can use asymmetry to indicate imbalance between characters or in the story situation.

In the movie *Altered States*[6] (Figure 8.6), we see very simple coverage in a reconciliation scene. There is a Look/See from Eddie to Emily, then a simple two-shot that shows them in offset staging, where they don't share alignment. The resulting shot-and-reverse pairs that follow are asymmetrical, from slightly different angles, which give contextual support to the performances. Their connection increases in intimacy and we feel the shape of the scene moving from distance to closeness. Then a change in staging brings us to a new two-shot with them side-by-side and together. Movement and restaging, from asymmetry and imbalance toward alignment, is contextually supportive and suits this story moment nicely.

Conventional coverage, staging across, relying on proximity

In the movie *Wonder Woman*[7] (Figure 8.7), we have an example of extensive conventional coverage, with characters staged across from each other. A progressive series of shots go from wider two-shots to tighter CUs, providing multiple framings of the characters in mirror-image, reciprocal pairs. There is a pair of wide OTS shots that orients us to their relative positions in the setting. There is a pair of medium, social-presentation–sized shots that allows the audience to see gestures and their negotiated interaction. There is a pair of head-and-shoulder shots that emphasizes each character's thoughts, feelings, and intentions. We are close to the characters and their emotional states for the more personal and flirty dialogue, and also later in the scene when the implications of the dialogue have emotional impact – particularly on Diana, the main character. The wider shots support the more literal and plot-oriented parts of the conversation.

We are led to believe that Matt is on police business. His focused look lets us know where the story is heading. We stay with him to the door. This frames Ann over his shoulder, evolving into Dialogue pairs that get more intimate. Is this real or a game? Questioning the truth of their interactions is central to the story.

Figure 8.5

The great benefit of such extensive coverage is the ability to shape the scene in editing. The nuances of the characters' interaction – getting closer or having distance, being separate or in each other's frame – can be adjusted to suit the feeling and flow of performances. Sometimes the intercut shot pairs are not exactly matched, as Diana's inner state and her reactions have greater story importance.

In one sense, extensive conventional coverage is kicking the can down the road and postponing decisions on cinematic choice to the editing stage. It allows the editor to react to performances and make choices on the right proximity, moment to moment. In another sense, it generates reliable coverage that allows for shaping of the audience's understanding of phases of the scene.

Figure 8.6

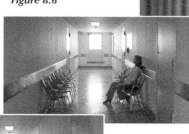

Eddie sees Emily in the hall. He sits across from her in an unshared diagonal. Their dialogue pairs are asymmetrical. They aren't aligned.

His proposal brings them closer. In reciprocal CUs, we share their subjective interconnection.

When he joins her, they become aligned in an emotionally satisfying way. Side-by-side suits this story moment. This variation on basic coverage provides a more nuanced context than a symmetrical approach for this story.

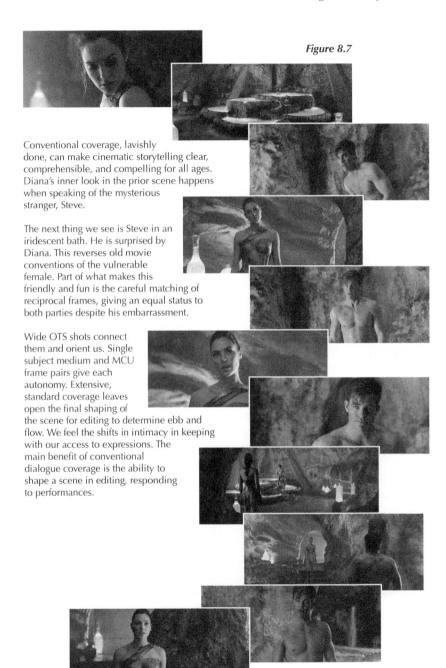

Figure 8.7

Conventional coverage, lavishly done, can make cinematic storytelling clear, comprehensible, and compelling for all ages. Diana's inner look in the prior scene happens when speaking of the mysterious stranger, Steve.

The next thing we see is Steve in an iridescent bath. He is surprised by Diana. This reverses old movie conventions of the vulnerable female. Part of what makes this friendly and fun is the careful matching of reciprocal frames, giving an equal status to both parties despite his embarrassment.

Wide OTS shots connect them and orient us. Single subject medium and MCU frame pairs give each autonomy. Extensive, standard coverage leaves open the final shaping of the scene for editing to determine ebb and flow. We feel the shifts in intimacy in keeping with our access to expressions. The main benefit of conventional dialogue coverage is the ability to shape a scene in editing, responding to performances.

Conventional coverage can serve superhero movies well, especially considering the younger audience members for whom the movie "language" is still fairly new and who might be thrown off by unpredictable or unusual coverage. Steady, gentle, contextual guidance can be very helpful in making the storytelling clear, maintaining immersion in the storyworld for audiences of all ages. For this movie, it is both enchanting and supportive.

Staging in depth and withholding of mutual connection

A scene in the movie *The Wrestler*[8] (Figure 8.8) illustrates coverage that is raw and unconventional. The movie feels like a documentary in many ways, with the handheld camera staying with Randy throughout. That sense of witnessing, participating, and connecting with a gritty reality is fully supported by the coverage. Throughout the movie, the Action pattern perspectives of connecting from in front, and participating by following behind, seamlessly land Randy in a variety of conversations.

Randy waits on the landing. Stephanie comes out the door, pushes past him (and the camera), and walks away. Randy follows, and the framing follows. We pick up from in front of Stephanie, whose rapid walk forces the framing to keep up.

In earlier chapters, we've mentioned that the person who has agency in the moment – who is driving the story – is usually driving the framing. This is motivated movement, where we follow action on a moving character, connecting to their perspective. We see this with Stephanie's movement controlling the frame, while Randy tries to keep up.

We also see the dialogue component of staging in depth, where we can see both characters, but the foreground character's expressions are hidden from the person behind. This gives us more information than either character has and has the feeling of putting the foreground character in a controlling position socially and psychologically. They are closer, and their inner state is increased in story priority.

When Randy catches up and steps in front, we land in an OTS dialogue shot. But Stephanie doesn't want the reciprocal relationship that he wants. This is contextually supported when she steps back into her own frame, creating an asymmetrical dialogue pair. When she walks away, we stay with Randy, who has given up. She returns to face him and tell him how she feels, and they are staged across from each other. This becomes separate, isolated frames of each trapped in their own corrosive feelings.

An interesting aspect of singular framing, not OTS, is that it can support either the more positive reading of autonomy and story agency or the negative reading of isolation. Framing and staging don't carry fixed and prepackaged meaning. The coverage points toward and supports interpretations within the story; it doesn't create meaning. Story specifics will infuse the choice with specific meaning. Filmmakers can reach for a decision that feels right for the scene, trusting that being alone in a frame, just like in real

Figure 8.8

Randy visits Stephanie, the daughter he abandoned years ago. She pushes past him, the camera following her trajectory. Switching to a frontal view, we have staging in depth – enabling us to read the emotions of the foreground person, while the background character cannot.

Randy pushes ahead and she stops, landing us in an OTS dialogue pair . . .

. . . except she doesn't reciprocate, pulling away into her own frame. We stay with Randy. She walks away, then returns. Reciprocal dialogue has each in their own singular frame – one filled with anger, the other with remorse.

life, can have positive or negative meaning, totally dependent on the specific character and circumstances.

Side-by-side with a burst of misleading context

In the movie *American Beauty*[9] (Figure 8.9), we see story perspective attached to Ricky in a psychologically complicated scene. In the scene just before this, we saw the family dynamic of a domineering and hair-trigger father. In this scene, all the coverage favors Ricky's side in this side-by-side staging – with one dramatically important exception.

From the car exterior, we go to Ricky's reverse Look/See pattern. We see notes and figures on paper and a calculator. This encourages us to share the cool and calculated mindset of Ricky figuring out his illicit business profits. We see his dad, the Colonel, past Ricky. But when the Colonel begins to berate him, the coverage switches to mutual tight CUs that suggest an intense and mutual engagement.

This is misdirection. The feigning of mutual engagement is Ricky's deflection of his dad's anger. We share Ricky's subjective experience of

Figure 8.9

We track a car, then we are within that car. A reverse Look/See pattern shows a calculator and notes, which we connect to Ricky's downward gaze. Questioned by his abusive dad, Ricky delivers an intense simulation of obedience in closely matched, reciprocal frames. Mollified, dad leaves him alone. Ricky goes back to work tallying drug dealing profits.

managing his dad through this coping strategy. He's a drug-dealing liar, but we can sympathize with the desire to head off his father's violence and have grudging admiration for his cleverness and risk taking.

Across, diagonal, symmetrical, and asymmetrical

In the very next scene of the movie *American Beauty*[10] (Figure 8.10), we start with two plural subjects – sets of friends – in simple, matched pairs, across from each other. The dominant friend in each pair weights the opposite side of the pairs, for social mirror-imaging. A Look/See pattern leads us to Jane's POV of Ricky arriving. Then we have Angela and Jane in a shared diagonal staging, turned toward each other, for a bit of sharing by Jane and teasing by the jealous Angela. This puts them on equal footing, as Angela usually receives disproportionate attention.

When Ricky arrives, we get the asymmetry of his singular frame versus the two-shot of Jane and Angela. Then we get an intense CU of Ricky that is in asymmetrical pairing with Jane. We feel the uncomfortable effect of her being squeezed into the corner past his shoulder but also feel the effect of Angela being left out of the picture – a welcome relief. This strong asymmetry carries these conflicting positive and negative feelings while enforcing the sense of Ricky's autonomy in the story – he acts on his own interests in ways that suggest self-agency beyond his years.

This is a socially and emotionally complex scene, with good and bad implications in the emotional chain of C&E. But we feel it clearly, supported by the simple shifts in the sets of dialogue pairs – not flashy, just supportive through changing context that signals story progression while enhancing our understanding of characterization.

Dramatic perspectives, only possible with staging across

In the movie *The Silence of the Lambs*[11] (Figure 8.11), we get the first of many scenes with memorable dialogue coverage. The abrupt changes support the characterization of Crawford as someone whose mind quickly jumps around, challenging the trainee Starling to keep up. After an initial informal intimacy, her framing is a more formal head-and-shoulders, letting us see her attentiveness to her boss. The reciprocal pairs are almost directly on their mutual eyeline but never quite matched in proximity and frame size. The contextual work is handled by changes in frame size and the leap from "normal" coverage, off the mutual eyeline, to this special brand of intensity with the angle almost exactly between them.

In the next example, the dialogue pairs will be more closely matched and exactly on the mutual eyeline between Starling and Lecter.

In later scenes from the same movie (Figure 8.12), we see this choice to use an angle directly on the characters' mutual eyeline. This is uncomfortably intimate and supportive of the story and performances. In contrast with Crawford, Lecter can sustain this focused intensity and perfect it. The shots

Figure 8.10

Angela and Jane face off against schoolmates in reciprocal frames with plural subjects – pals versus pals. Jane's look leads us to Ricky, the kid next door who spies on her.

This incites dialogue pairs with Angela, making them co-equals and escaping Angela's social dominance.

Ricky arrives to talk to Jane only, beginning a series of asymmetrical dialogue pairs.

Ricky maintains his own, autonomous frame, while Jane is with her friend.

Ricky's intense subjective attention pushes Jane into a corner, in his context. This is both threatening and welcome. The shifting frames shape the scene and support subtext.

Figure 8.11

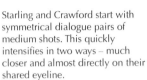

Starling and Crawford start with symmetrical dialogue pairs of medium shots. This quickly intensifies in two ways – much closer and almost directly on their shared eyeline.

Crawford gets down to business. The framing pairs no longer match up. He can be distant or intense at his own discretion. Her frame settles into a formal portrait.

are directly on their eyeline and it feels like he looks through us or inside us, as we imagine being in Starling's position, facing him.

Perhaps this is just my response, but when I see Lecter, I vicariously put myself in Starling's shoes. When I see Starling from his POV, I am vicariously in touch with her thoughts, feelings, and intentions. Being so attached to her story perspective throughout the movie encourages this character-centric affiliation with her subjective experience.

At times, the Dialogue pairs are fully aligned in matched, reciprocal frames of equal intensity. By the end of their last scene together, his subjective attention feels like a controlling demonic presence, with the closest possible framing of his eyes to mouth. Starling stands up to it. The way she is psychologically probed and survives demonstrates enormous courage and strength. The storytelling is supported by these dramatic perspectives that put us deeply inside her subjective experience, which is dangerously intermingled with Lecter's subjective experience. This is only possible with them staged across from each other, directly on the laser-beam of their mutual eyeline.

Crossing the 180° Line for dramatic intent

We have an interesting example of rule breaking for creative purposes in a scene from *Ex Machina*[12] (Figure 8.13). Side-by-side staging in cars or on benches can give filmmakers a degree of freedom in coverage, as we can stay oriented if the overall angle shifts. But that depends on the use of consistently reciprocal shot pairs from whatever angle is used. This example blows up that rule, for subtle contextual support of inferential storytelling.

Here, we participate with Caleb at the door and see his Look, which leads us to Nathan. The light and dark sweatshirts help us keep the geometry of their placement in mind. It is fairly normal to see side-by-side framing both from in front and from behind. What is totally surprising is the asymmetrical pairing of frames from in front on Nathan, keeping him frame left, and frames on Caleb from over the back shoulder, also making him frame left. It creates an uneasy feeling that something is not quite right. We are also closer to Caleb in his shot and he is more prominent in the foreground in Nathan's shot, contextually supporting the sense of his agency driving story progress.

This dialogue pair "crosses the line" and is "wrong" according to rules on continuity. What makes it very appropriate to the storytelling is the way this surprising choice supports the inferential storytelling, giving us the feeling that Caleb is turning the tables on Nathan, who has manipulated him mercilessly up to this moment. It is unsettled and disorienting. They are coming from completely different directions. They do not have a shared subjective interaction. The questions of who is manipulating whom, and where characters are coming from in motivations, is central to the story and leaves us unsure of what to expect.

Figure 8.12

Starling and Lecter go to psychological depths of frightening intimacy. The reciprocal frames are often directly on their mutual eyeline, which is unconventional and socially uncomfortable. Each character's subjective perspective is fully locked in. The intersubjective state between them is central to the storytelling.

In a later scene, prison bars are part of the reciprocal shots. Getting closer, the bars disappear, and nothing separates the characters. Starling earns critical knowledge for the courage to feed the beast her own trauma.

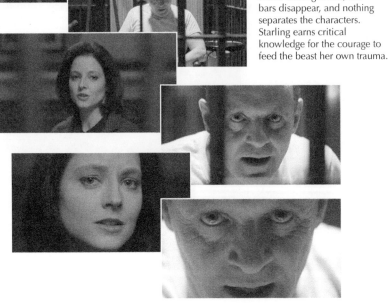

Figure 8.13

Following Caleb's story perspective leads us to Nathan, getting drunk on the hill. We see them from behind, orienting us to the high-tech lab, with Nathan in the dark sweatshirt. Following the view from in front, we see Nathan past Caleb in the foreground.

The reciprocal framing pair would be a mirror-image on Caleb frame right, past Nathan frame left, sustaining orientation.

Instead, we see Caleb over the back shoulder of Nathan. Caleb is also frame left. We've "crossed the line."

The 180° Line keeps us oriented and the characters on their respective sides. The disorienting shot of Caleb has him coming from an unexpected direction. Knowing their positions, we can keep them straight, but it feels like they are at cross-purposes – each with a private agenda. The asymmetry in the shot pairs favors Caleb, assisting in the feeling of his agency, turning the tables on Nathan.

Every rule of filmmaking is there to help you achieve a conventional and normally desired result. Preserving the 180° Line of Continuity maintains orientation and clarity. When the story demands disorientation or confusion, breaking the rule can give you that unconventional result.

Moving beyond two-character dialogue

In the previously discussed examples, we've seen a variety of ways to employ variations in the basic dialogue patterns for two-character scenes. Now let's look at a few scenes with three or more characters to get an overview of how modulations and variations can be used to shape more complex social interactions. The basic staging approaches may no longer apply, or they might be multiplied. The increasing variables can be intimidating, but basic approaches can make scenes with more characters approachable and just as malleable to contextual shaping and support.

Multiple-character dialogue scenes

Variables multiply along with the number of characters. The basic philosophy of coverage for larger groups is to "divide and conquer." This happens through identifying storytelling groups, as well as the main characters, and using the means and methods of scene shaping to move from one set of shot pairs to the next.

We've seen an example of one large dinner scene in Chapter 1 from the movie *Cast Away*[13] (Figure 1.1, Figure 1.2). A wide shot orients us to the total setting. The main characters are initially seen as anchors in the group context, staged across from each other, making it both easier and clearer to connect them in closer framing. Initially, Dialogue happens between them and groups, not individuals, in shot pairs. One wing of the table has the older folks, who are seen as a group or plural subject. Eventually the scene narrows down to Chuck and Kelly, who end up in reciprocal OTS framing, with the rest of the people out of the picture.

Sticking to a very simple approach, such as progressively narrowing down the framing, can bring clarity to what might otherwise be shapeless or confusing to the audience. That dinner scene is very easy to follow, which is a tribute to the clarity of coverage decisions.

Three-person dialogue = 2 + 1

Supporting dialogue between three characters can be tricky. The social cliché that "two's company, three's a crowd" will help clarify a main strategy for coverage. After all, the dialogue pattern is in shot pairs, not triplets. Therefore, finding out which character is the odd person out can help structure the scene and provide story-supportive context. Let's see how that works in two examples – one in which the storytelling hinges on the character who is the arbiter of the scene, and the other in which one character is isolated and excluded.

A scene from the movie *If Beale Street Could Talk*[14] (Figure 8.14) illustrates the two-plus-one principle. It opens with Fonny and building owner Levy awaiting Tish's judgment on the choice of an industrial loft as a potential home (not common or chic at the time). We get two-shots of the guys and singular shots of Tish. An asymmetrical dialogue pair between Fonny and Tish emphasizes that her inner state is central to the storytelling, seen through her tighter CU.

The next phase shifts from the negative feeling of Tish and Fonny at odds to the positive feeling of social connection, as Fonny and Levy play-act at moving invisible furniture around the place. Now we see all three together in a shot from an angle behind Tish, with her as the central figure. The coverage and their interactions become looser as she is won over. She joins in the game. We end up with Tish and Fonny together, at a frame size for social presentation and gestures, holding hands in the streaming light. The total progress of the scene goes from the division of characters into opposing groups – two plus one – to the reinforcement of the couple's bond. This is very supportive visual context for the storytelling.

A three-character scene from the movie *Se7en*[15] (Figure 8.15) shows us the split of three characters into groups of two-plus-one, with a completely different flavor. Unlike the last example, the odd person out is not central. They are excluded. It begins with a basic dialogue pair of Mills and Tracy at the door, with the reverse taking us inside the apartment as they kiss. They part, revealing Somerset, who is as uncomfortable as his unwanted junior partner, Mills.

Instead of a Master-type wide shot that places all three together, we go directly to reciprocal shot pairs, with the main feature being that Mills is left out. Tracy's warmth and easy intimacy encourages a connection with Somerset. They share subjective attention and reciprocal frames. The critical aspect is that both Tracy and Somerset look toward Mills but we do not shift attention to him; it stays with Tracy and Somerset's interaction. This cinematic choice supports the story – Tracy is creating a welcoming bridge that eases her husband's work life and is forming a separate and special bond with Somerset.

This example shows that denying a character their spot in reciprocating dialogue will support the feeling that they are socially marginalized. It also shows that our normal expectation of how Looks function can be upended for storytelling purposes. When both Tracy and Somerset look to Mills, we expect to see him. But we don't. We stick with the more absorbing dialogue between Tracy and her new friend, Somerset. Because Looks typically go to whatever character is deemed significant, the inference is a judgment of Mills's insignificance. That is how he seems to feel – and how we might feel – from being left out of a conversation.

Figure 8.14

Tish is not sold on the idea of living in a loft. We are connected to her perspective. She looks, and we see her POV on Fonny and the building owner. Fonny wins her over through imagination and fun. The barriers between Tish and Fonny dissolve. All three laugh and comfortably inhabit the same frames. It feels like a shared moment of friendship, with the promise of a bright future.

Figure 8.15

In the first frames, married couple Mills and Tracy are together. Then we see Somerset, past Tracy, then Mills's reaction to having the boss over. Tracy looks back over her shoulder at her husband but immediately shifts attention to her guest. Tracy and Somerset have the dialogue pair that shows shared subjective attention. Somerset looks to the side at Mills. Tracy looks at him, too, but both return to their reciprocal interaction. We understand that Tracy and Somerset have formed a bond that leaves Mills out. He's frustrated.

A character Look is usually followed by something of significance. Showing the Looks to Mills but not seeing him in return leads us to the sense of insignificance that he feels.

Grand tour from a central pivot

The final example is shown in two illustrations from a scene in the movie *Jurassic Park*[16] (Figure 8.16, Figure 8.17). This is a luncheon for five, with the host, John, at the head of the table. He will function as the central pivot point for a series of dialogue pairs that move from the characters on one side of the table, all the way around to the characters on the other side. There is a "divide and conquer" element, starting on one side of the table and ending on the other.

This is quite an ambitious scene that could easily be shapeless and flat, or chaotic and confusing. Instead, it is crisp and clear and has the feel of solid story progression. With many larger scenes, there are two usual opening options – either start wide and get closer or start on a detail and pull out to the wider situation. This scene takes the latter approach to preserve an emotional connection with the last scene, where a gruesome feeding of raptors made the guests uneasy. The idea of lunch feels nauseating, which we confirm with Ellie's reaction to her plate.

The first reciprocal pairs, signaling the shared subjective attention of Dialogue, are between the lawyer, Donald, and his boss and host, John. Both shots are past Ian, placing him in the "line of fire" and also presaging his leap into the conversation. A wider reaction shot, past Ellie and John and onto Donald and Ian's side of the table, ends the first phase.

Ian jumps in, initially with Donald in frame but evolving into his singular CU. He has autonomy in this asymmetrical pair, while John is still seen past him. That side of the table has theoretical pragmatists – the lawyer is pragmatic about capitalist theories of making money, and the chaos-theory mathematician is pragmatic about nature's laws that will overwhelm the prideful plans of humans. They are side-by-side, just as Ellie and Alan are side-by-side. John is in diagonal relationship with both sides.

The next phase starts with a rejoinder by Ellie. We are still with the same general orientation from a prior wide shot but adjusted to include Alan. This side of the table is the romantic realists, as we may imagine dinosaur bone hunters to be, not lost in theory or grubby practicality. We are then given a new angle, clinching that the story has moved on. Ellie and John debate, but Alan is always in the picture. Like Ian's presence, we see the character who will play a bigger role, biding their time, ready to speak up. The push-in on Alan ramps up the significance of his thoughts, feelings, and intentions to the storytelling. Like all unmotivated moves (not following a moving subject), it feels as if the pressure of the situation is loaded into his statements, amplifying their central role in the storytelling.

Figure 8.16

We've just left a gruesome feeding of
raptors. Lunch opens with a reverse
Look/See of food and Ellie's reaction.
An evolving wide shot gives us the
layout. We immediately go to the lawyer,
Donald, in dialogue with his boss, John.
Both are seen past Ian. The conversation
opens up, with Ellie now in the shot.
Ian takes over, seen from a new angle
that leaves Donald out of frame. We
carry on reciprocal dialogue pairs with
John. The singular subject in Ian's frames
lend greater sway to his agency in story
progress. Reaction shots of Donald are
interspersed as he becomes the brunt of
comments from all sides.

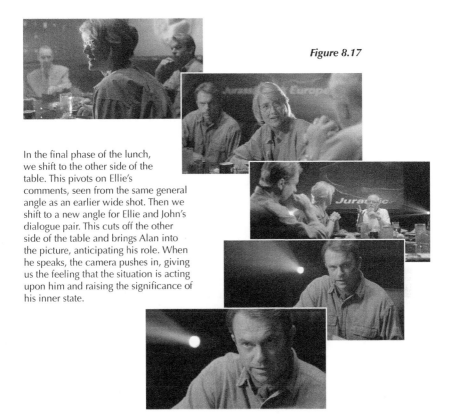

Figure 8.17

In the final phase of the lunch, we shift to the other side of the table. This pivots on Ellie's comments, seen from the same general angle as an earlier wide shot. Then we shift to a new angle for Ellie and John's dialogue pair. This cuts off the other side of the table and brings Alan into the picture, anticipating his role. When he speaks, the camera pushes in, giving us the feeling that the situation is acting upon him and raising the significance of his inner state.

Summary

Dialogue is interaction between characters. Their subjective attention is on each other. The reactions are to each other. We share their attention on each other for a mutual intersubjectivity. Dialogue pairs are simple – reciprocal attention – but the social and psychological complexity can be immense.

- The simple witnessing of interaction, through the observational two-shot of the characters, can carry a lot of storytelling weight in supporting our understanding of how they interact.
- The center of Dialogue coverage is the reciprocal Look/See pair, where each character is the subject of mutual, undivided, and subjective attention. This creates a special zone of intersubjectivity, where the focus of the storytelling is between them and within their interaction.
- Dialogue coverage is adjusted or modulated through perspective or angle on the character; through proximity or shot size; and through changes in staging or physical relationship between the characters.

- A new angle in coverage signals a new angle in the storytelling by breaking the spell of prior consistency in framing. (This is true for all coverage but particularly pertinent to shaping Dialogue.)
- The major goal is to support performances by providing much-needed context that supports, not competes with or undermines, the acting.
- Even though the mechanisms of adjustment are fairly simple, the possible combinations make dialogue pairs endlessly variable.
- Pairs can be matched, symmetrical, mirror-image framings or unmatched asymmetrical framings, in keeping with whatever context suits the interaction.
- Simple coverage can still have nuanced support for inferential and subtextual story information so that the audience feels story progress clearly and effortlessly.
- The five basic staging options have intrinsic qualities and feelings but have more contextual significance in their alteration, change, or adjustment to signal phases of a scene that track the major dramatic beats.
- Conventional, increasingly tight coverage pairs offer the ability to shape the scene and performances in editing, as multiple options exist to ramp intensity or intimacy up or down from moment to moment.
- The 180° Line of Continuity is always important to sustain orientation and flow, but it also can be violated to disorient the audience, in keeping with the storytelling.
- With three characters in dialogue, it is usual to break them up into two-plus-one, either to make one character central or to marginalize them.
- With larger groups, the general approach is to "divide and conquer," with plural subjects matched to main characters in dialogue pairs, usually leading to standard dialogue pairs between the main subjects.

What you can do . . .

Fast-forward through some of your favorite movies and look for the following:

- Do you see any walk & talks? If so, was the content of the conversation exposition, giving you basic story information? Was the way the characters interact of primary importance, or was it something between them as an interpersonal issue? Did the walk & talk feel right to you, for the storytelling?
- If you see a wide shot that feels like a Master shot to encompass all of the scene, how long or how much of that Master shot was used in the scene?
- If you see a seen with no shot that represents a Master shot, how did the filmmakers get into, and then out of, the dialogue? Did you miss the wide, all-encompassing Master shot?

- Find any scene with asymmetrical dialogue shot pairs. What do they represent or inform you about? Is the character relationship shown in their asymmetry?
- Find any scene using OTS shot pairs, then any scene with "clean" single framings for the shot pairs. Do they feel different? What is it about the relationship that feels appropriate to their usage? Are the clean single shot pairs saying something about that character or the relationship? Are they creating a sense of autonomy or of isolation? Or something else entirely?
- Find any scene with a dialogue that lasts more than two minutes. Was it broken into phases to help shape it? If so, how? Did you feel the shaping of these changes?

Notes

1 *Se7en*. Directed by David Fincher, Cinematography by Darius Khondji. Cecchi Gori Pictures, Juno Pix, New Line Cinema, released 1995. DVD: New Line Home Video (2000, USA). Start time: 00:01:58.
2 *The Right Stuff*. Directed by Phillip Kaufman, Cinematography by Caleb Deschanel. The Ladd Company, released 1983. DVD: Warner Home Video (1997, USA). Start time: 02:09:04.
3 *The Right Stuff*. Ibid. Start time: 02:22:04.
4 *No Country for Old Men*. Directed by Ethan Coen & Joel Coen, Cinematography by Roger Deakins. Paramount Vantage, Miramax, Scott Rudin Productions, released 2007. DVD: Buena Vista Home Entertainment (2008, USA). Start time: 00:20:52.
5 *Out of Time*. Directed by Carl Franklin, Cinematography by Theo van de Sande. MGM, Original Film, Monarch Pictures, released 2003. DVD: MGM Home Entertainment (2006, USA). Start time: 00:02:04.
6 *Altered States*. Directed by Ken Russell, Cinematography by Jordan Cronenweth. Warner Bros., released 1980. DVD: Warner Bros. Home Video (1998, USA). Start time: 00:17:36.
7 *Wonder Woman*. Directed by Patty Jenkins, Cinematography by Matthew Jensen. Warner Bros., Atlas Entertainment, released 2017. DVD: Warner Bros. Home Entertainment (2017, USA). Start time: 00:29:37.
8 *The Wrestler*. Directed by Darren Aronofsky, Cinematography by Maryse Alberti. Wild Bunch, Protozoa Pictures, Saturn Films, Top Rope, released 2008. DVD: Fox Home Entertainment (2009, USA). Start time: 00:48:21.
9 *American Beauty*. Directed by Sam Mendes, Cinematography by Conrad Hall. DreamWorks Pictures, released 1999. DVD: Dreamworks Home Entertainment (2000, USA). Start time: 00:25:29.
10 *American Beauty*. ibid. Start time: 00:26:27.
11 *The Silence of the Lambs*. Directed by Jonathan Demme, Cinematography by Tak Fujimoto. Orion Pictures, Strong Heart Demme Production, released 1991. DVD: Criterion Collection (2018, USA). Start time: 00:05:56.
12 *Ex Machina*. Directed by Alex Garland, Cinematography by Rob Hardy. Universal Pictures, Film4, DNA, released 2014. DVD: Lionsgate (2015, USA). Start time: 01:04:21.

13 *Cast Away*. Directed by Robert Zemeckis, Cinematography by Don Burgess. Twentieth Century Fox, Dreamworks, released 2000. DVD: Twentieth Century Fox Home Entertainment (2001, USA). Start time: 00:14:06.

14 *If Beale Street Could Talk*. Directed by Barry Jenkins, Cinematography by James Laxton. Annapurna Pictures, Plan B Entertainment, PASTEL, released 2018. DVD: Twentieth Century Studios (2019, USA). Start time: 01:03:54.

15 *Se7en*. Ibid. Start time: 00:33:15.

16 *Jurassic Park*. Directed by Steven Spielberg, Cinematography by Dean Cundey. Universal Pictures, Amblin Entertainment, released 1993. DVD: Universal Studios (2000, USA). Start time: 00:34:15.

Chapter 9
Patterns for settings

Taking us into the storyworld

In the scripted storytelling, a slugline tells us if the scene is inside or outside, where it takes place, and when it takes place. The Setting is a primary piece of information that can play out in a number of ways to suit the storytelling.

Settings take us into the storyworld, where the action takes place. The storyworld is everything about the physical and social setting where the characters live out the story. The storyworld presents opportunities and constraints that will shape the options for character action and color our judgment of their actions, in light of what we understand about the storyworld. Settings are declarative story information – a spaceship, a high school playground, a big city, peaceful woodlands, or the Normandy coastline in 1944. These are places we can clearly see and where events take place.

But the broader concept of the storyworld includes conveying the passage of time, both in its compression and in orientation to issues such as the relation of flashbacks (and flash-forwards) to the present time within the movie. A change in setting is often a signal that time has elapsed, not just that the location has changed. When absolute clarity on a timeline is needed, information can be provided through some form of titling, such as "Four Days Later."

The social norms of a setting are inferred information, relying on associations to common experience or some clear analog. A family in prehistoric times is still a family.

Character travel through the physical storyworld plays a role in linking story progress to the changes in location and any efforts needed for characters to make the journey. Using a journey is common in storytelling, to make progress physical as well as emotional.

Settings as background with functional significance

Consider how a public or a private setting could influence character actions, providing both opportunities and constraints. Without even realizing it, we in the audience will judge actions based on these factors, as we all have value judgments about what is appropriate to do in a restaurant

DOI: 10.4324/9781003080657-9

versus the privacy of home. It is very common to have Settings function as informative backgrounds with no separate, dedicated coverage needed. Sometimes this is because we've already been in that setting and are already oriented, but just as often it's because the setting is something we understand from daily life and it needs no further introduction.

In Chapter 8, we saw the schoolyard example from *American Beauty*[1] (Figure 8.10). That is just such a situation. There is no broad, overhead view of the setting, no tilt down from a sign over the front entrance. We are just there with the characters. We understand this social setting. Jane and Angela's smoking is clearly against the rules.

Immediately before this scene, we saw Ricky and his dad in a tense car ride. Now we see his arrival at school, connecting his difficult family life to his aloof standing and buttoned-down style of dress, which is unusual in this social setting. Just as the social setting reveals information about Jane and Angela, the juxtaposition of Ricky's family life and this social setting reveals information about his character and coping mechanisms. We find Ricky through Jane's look and assumption of perspective. We now see him through her eyes, reflecting judgment of his general status in the social setting of school, as well as in regard to his behavior toward her.

If a setting only has functional story significance – readily informing us of opportunities and constraints – then the only question for the filmmakers regarding coverage is whether this information is self-explanatory for the audience. Even a setting that might be completely unfamiliar could be comprehensible, such as a police station on Mars in 2159. We'd probably still recognize the setting and wouldn't need heavy-handed, explanatory coverage.

Settings are never arbitrary. If the information on opportunities and constraints can be done in the background of character Actions and Dialogue, there is no need for specific coverage. The exception is when we need an indicator of leaving one scene behind and entering a new scene in a new location, as a cinematic form of a chapter marker.

Establishing a setting as a chapter marker

Establishing means providing story information that will be needed by the audience to understand the upcoming action. Establishing the location is the standard thing to do in conventional coverage, for many good reasons. This orients the audience to a new setting. In many cases, the establishing of a location serves to inform the audience of the simple fact that the story has moved on. The establishing of a Setting brings the sense of a chapter marker or designation that we've left one scene and are beginning the next. Because a single shot is sufficient to perform this chapter marker function – moving on to the next scene – it is common to have an "establishing shot" on the shot list. On bigger-budget productions, that could be done at any time, or by a second unit or auxiliary crew that can record these types of shots that don't require the presence of the actors and the whole movie-making apparatus.

An establishing shot of the lonely gas station starts out a scene in *No Country for Old Men*[2] (Figure 8.4). The Setting is contributing to mood and tone, not just providing orienting information. That gas station, seen from a high angle, gives us the big sign, the shabby building, and the empty landscape in one shot. Looking down on this setting provides a feeling that people in this setting are small and insignificant in a vast and lonely landscape.

In other examples, we might see an apartment building, tilt up to see upper floors, then immediately go into the interior action. From seeing the outside, we immediately assume that whatever we see next is inside. **Whenever we see an exterior setting and then cut to characters inside, we assume they are within that setting.**

This works for any exterior–interior progression, as we saw during Ricky's ride to school (Figure 8.9). We briefly follow a sport utility vehicle (SUV), a marker of bland suburbia in America, then cut to the inside of the vehicle to find Ricky and his dad. The car exterior is a chapter marker in addition to orienting us to the action that follows.

This presumption can be used to intentionally misdirect the audience. I have not illustrated it here, but in the movie *The Silence of the Lambs*,[3] there is an extended sequence that builds great tension. The exterior of a house in the state of Illinois is intercut with the killer's house in Ohio. When the FBI assault team rings a doorbell in Illinois, we see and hear a doorbell ring in the Ohio house. When the killer opens the door, we expect the full FBI team, but instead it is Agent Starling, dangerously on her own. This use of unmatched exterior/interior connection breaks the rules to surprise us and shatter our assumptions.

Settings with intrinsic story significance

Settings that are unfamiliar to us may demand dedicated coverage, especially if that location has major implications for the storytelling. The movie *Alien*[4] (Figure 9.1) opens with an extended tour of the outside of the mining ship *Nostromo*, showing us outer space and inferentially telling us that we are in the distant future. The scale of the ship is indicated by how long it takes for it to pass over our heads. This is an indication of the first level of vicarious engagement – we, in the audience, can be at a vantage point in outer space to witness this. We begin a tour through empty and darkened corridors of the ship, which we (of course) assume is inside the vast ship.

The ship seems to come alive after we enter a control room. A notification through the ship and its central computer, ironically called "Mother," sets off all the action to follow. The ship will be the location of most conflict and action in the movie. Its labyrinthine complexity and its presumed safety both figure prominently in the storytelling.

Figure 9.1

The movie opens with a survey of the setting – the spaceship *Nostromo*. It slowly cruises past us in space, indicating its huge size. If we see the outside of a ship or building, we assume the interior views that follow are inside. We take a tour through corridors and decks – completely independent of character perspective. This is the vicarious experience of entering a storyworld.

It is common to use setting to lead to characters. The first thing that arrests our attention is an automated alarm, making the computer control like a character with story agency. In a chain of C&E, this wakes up the ship. We then find the crew, who serve the ship.

Not only does the spaceship provide a story-specific constraint – you'll die in outer space without a ship or spacesuit – but it's also acting in a manner that feels like story agency, which makes it a bit like a character.

The ship has both functional significance and intrinsic significance, as the conduit of faceless corporate decisions that put the crew's life at risk. We expect people (characters) to have story agency and the ability to drive progress, not just serve as background. But inanimate things like Settings and Objects can have intrinsic story significance and can act as drivers of the storytelling. Many ships, of many eras, figure into the storytelling in this way.

The time taken to explore the ship is a clear indication of its significance. The exploration has a stately pace, contributing to the mood and tone. In any movie using horror or suspense, the feeling of unrushed pacing provides anticipation of what we assume will be the action ahead. It also gives us a before-and-after state of affairs – the ship and crew asleep at one moment, awake and tasked with a mission in the next. It presents links in the chain of C&E.

Settings coverage in slideshows and tours

Consider the meanings of "slideshow" and "tour" in real life. A slideshow is a set of fixed frames that, in sequence, give us a sense of the whole. A tour is a survey that doesn't fixate on any one thing but instead gives us an experience that feels like an overview. Almost all coverage of Settings with story significance uses either the slideshow or tour method of presentation. Most extensive Setting coverage uses a combination of both. Those are the only two components of the Settings pattern.

In the example in Figure 9.1, a tour carries the sense of moving over and through the ship, not settling on any single thing. Once the alarms go off in the control room, we go into a slideshow which presents us with a series of fixated frames on things with significance – alarm messages and lights – adding up to comprehension of the situation. The tour resumes, bringing us to the crew being brought out of sleep-stasis at Mother's command. This shows us the function of most Settings coverage – finding characters.

The example from *Alien* gives us both parts of the Settings pattern. Slideshows feel like a string of moments. The tour feels like an active search.

Characters as features of the setting

Whenever a significant Setting is part of storytelling, it can be used to color and inform our introduction to the characters who inevitably arrive next. In the movie *Leave No Trace*[5] (Figure 9.2), we start with a combination slideshow–tour, discovering our main characters as features or natural inhabitants of the setting.

In this example, the slideshow images are like living paintings or photographs – the frames are still but there is movement within them of leaves and spiderwebs blowing in the breeze. An aesthetic response to the way they feel

Figure 9.2

Evocative images of nature in the forest lead us to "sightings" of Tom and her dad, Will. We observe from above, as if they were wildlife. We feel the ease of their movements. We feel the peaceful beauty of foliage and wind-blown spiderwebs. We see foraging and picking of green leaves. This leads to our first clear connection to Tom and Will as they graze. Finally, we see them going deeper into the forest. At first, we see them as part of the setting – natural creatures of this world. We see the setting through their daily experience. We feel the unrushed connection with nature.

is a major part of their reason for being in this scene. We will refer to this Evocative Imagery in Chapter 11. This example illustrates both elements.

Active frames pick up Tom and then her dad, Will. A tour of the forest leads us to finding them, following them for a bit, then letting them go on. This works like a reverse Look/See pattern, starting with direct audience experience and followed by a character's shared perspective. We start with Settings coverage that we directly experience, with its mood of serenity and natural beauty. We can feel that as a shared experience when we finally meet the characters.

When we move on to their experiences, we are already inoculated with a sense of escapist experience through benevolent nature. They are a natural part of the setting. Like viewing wildlife, we see them as innocent creatures who are meant to be here. The setting becomes characterization, and it becomes our first vantage point for getting inside their subjective experiences without judgment. Without that, the rest of the storytelling would not feel so disruptive or have such ache for their loss of these moments of natural perfection.

We find characters or they emerge from settings

The prison in the movie *The Shawshank Redemption*[6] (Figure 9.3) is certainly a Setting with story significance. This physical and social Setting creates extreme constraints and opportunities. This example is a very shortened version of an extensive tour that makes Andy's arrival a dreadful journey, fraught with the increasing distance from everyday freedoms, to be replaced by the violent and vicious world of the prison. This journey reintroduces us to Andy, now an out-of-place and unjustly convicted murderer, and to Red, who is a leading mover and shaker in the prison. His friendship with Andy is central to the story.

When we find characters through a searching tour, it is as if they are chosen by the story. This is what happens to Andy in this scene. He is transported, against his will, to serve what we will eventually understand as a completely unjust life sentence. The passivity of the character is reflected in the search for him in the back of the bus of "fish" – new convicts ready for victimization.

In contrast, Red makes himself known, standing out from the crowd, holding the camera's attention as we follow action with him. Red is an active – not passive – character at this moment. With his actions holding attention, we grant him a sense of story agency. Anytime a character emerges from a setting, we might feel that they are self-selecting for the story with drive and agency they possess, not granted to them.

This is just one example of the way that Setting can not only bring us to characters but also shape the way we feel about them.

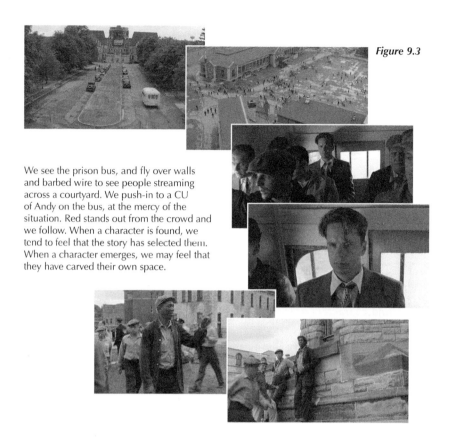

Figure 9.3

We see the prison bus, and fly over walls and barbed wire to see people streaming across a courtyard. We push-in to a CU of Andy on the bus, at the mercy of the situation. Red stands out from the crowd and we follow. When a character is found, we tend to feel that the story has selected them. When a character emerges, we may feel that they have carved their own space.

Settings through character perspective

Our last two examples introduced us to a Setting independently from character experience or mediation. We went aboard a spaceship and over prison walls before we met characters in those Settings. The next example demonstrates Settings presented through character subjective experience. This makes the experience of the characters more significant than the Setting itself, for storytelling that uses a Setting to explore character reactions and even thematic elements.

We see this in an example from the movie *Parasite*[7] (Figure 9.4). Here, we have a tour seen through the subjective experience of the young Ki-woo, arriving at his scam job as a tutor. Most of this is accomplished through the Action perspective of participating. Only at key moments do we connect with his reactions through frontal shots. We also observe, as he walks past the perfect portraits and press clippings framed on the wall.

Central to the story, this Setting is the character's first experience at the top of society. We understand that he wants to step up to the life of the rich.

Figure 9.4

Ki-woo gets his first sense of how the rich live. He steps up to natural beauty, perfect presentation, and symbols of status. He looks through flawless glass at a yard and gardens. We see his reactions and participate with him in his tour of the grounds and house.

This creates a clear contrast with our next two examples from the same movie, *Parasite*[8] (Figure 9.5, Figure 9.6).

Here we have an epic tour of Settings. This gives us our first experience of the vast physical and social distance between our main characters' shabby apartment and the opulent house where the entire family works. Needing to go home from work, they go down steps, through tunnels, and down more steps as the water accumulates. They are at the bottom. The deluge of rain runs downhill. A rainstorm at the top of the hill is a wet inconvenience. At the bottom, it's a desperate fight to stay afloat.

We spend much time observing from a distance, which makes them feel like scurrying ants while also lending an objectivity that confirms the reality of their experience. By observing, we feel the legitimacy of their responses and gain a respect for them that wasn't always at the forefront of the inferred storytelling. Before this, we only had an abstract idea of the distance between rich and poor. This makes it manifested and real. This observation is punctuated by moments of connection with their emotional reactions to the arduous journey.

Figure 9.5

Ki-taek and family leave the rich house on the hill during a storm. We follow their journey down, down, down, to the level where they live.

We observe them, dwarfed by the setting. We connect with Ki-jung's exhaustion – traveling miles, soaked to the skin. Ki-woo is overwhelmed as water rushes past his shoes. The frame becomes unstable as they reach the flooded level of their home, thigh-high in filthy water. We follow the father, Ki-taek, as he nears their home at the bottom of this collection of water and waste.

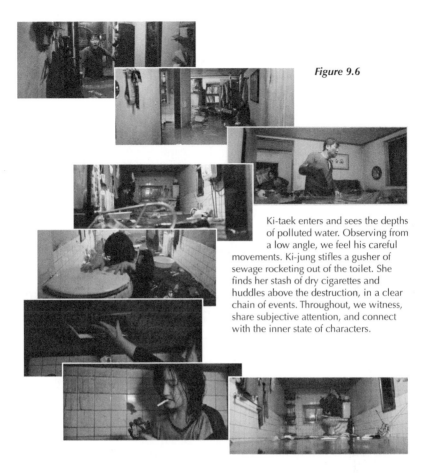

Figure 9.6

Ki-taek enters and sees the depths of polluted water. Observing from a low angle, we feel his careful movements. Ki-jung stifles a gusher of sewage rocketing out of the toilet. She finds her stash of dry cigarettes and huddles above the destruction, in a clear chain of events. Throughout, we witness, share subjective attention, and connect with the inner state of characters.

The final phase of the deluge sequence is the family's arrival at their basement apartment. The Setting and conditions are still central to the storytelling, and now this sequence is in its last phase. Look/See patterns show us reactions to destroyed, pitiful treasures. The action to jam a lid on the erupting toilet leads Ki-jung to finding her last dry cigarettes and, after connecting with her search for respite, we observe her perch over the devastation. As with all Settings, their living situation offers opportunities and constraints. Here, the constraints are terrible, and the family's dogged insistence on living despite the conditions helps us understand their need to cling to the smallest shreds of hope with fierce energy.

Settings for pacing the audience experience

There are two main reasons for using Settings to control the audience experience. Because movies have a fixed temporal nature – movie time is unstoppable – the need for time compression in the storytelling has to be served in a way that is concise and comprehensible. Scripted storytelling can just move to the next scene, but in order for a story thread and feeling to continue, we need bridge elements that serve as a time ellipsis – the dot-dot-dot indicating that time has skipped over.

Settings to visually compress time

A simple slideshow can show conditions that indicate the passage of time without taking up much screen time. In Chapter 5, we saw this illustrated in an example from the movie *Saving Private Ryan*[9] (Figure 5.4). A scene of patrolling is connected to the next scene of a battle by a brief slide-show of images – leaves and trees, as day turns to night and rain begins to pour down. We understand that we have seen hours elapse and the weather change for the worse. When we pick up the action, we understand that the squad has been on the move all night, no matter what the conditions. All of this is done economically.

The images of the Setting function as a chapter marker but don't feel like the start of a new story thread. They feel more like the aftermath of the interpersonal conflicts we just witnessed and a continuation of their mission, unstopped.

Settings can provide time for emotional reverberation

Settings can be used to give us, in the audience, time to absorb the shock of emotional moments and scenes. They provide time for story emotions to reverberate and settle, before we move on to the next part of the story. Without this time, disconnected from the pressures of story progress, deeply emotional and impactful events may not fully register with the audience. We need this time to take in the true significance of critical moments and events so that we move forward, changed by the experience.

In the movie *Children of Men*[10] (Figure 9.7), Theo has just witnessed the murder of Jasper, the last person he really knew, loved, and trusted. Jasper sacrificed himself to enable Theo and Kee to escape. We spend time with Theo, as the reactions of loss and grief settle in. Then we spend just a few neutral moments in a despoiled setting, which evolves into following action on the car they used to escape. We observe from a distance, without emotional demands. We just follow the car through this bleak setting, evocative of Theo's mood. This is followed by an evocative image of sun on the car – a new dawn signaling a new phase of the story – outside an abandoned school, where we pick up the action.

These moments take us out of relentless story progress and let us settle with what's just happened, to feel its emotional reverberations before we go on to the next story events. The emotionally absorbing, evocative images provide the audience with the time needed to process Theo's grief and the irrevocable change in him.

Figure 9.7

Theo has just seen his closest friend, Jasper, murdered. We connect with his private grief, with others present. We see a destroyed landscape, then follow his car. Morning light wakes Theo. The story moves on to a new setting. We've had time to absorb the magnitude of events through evocative settings.

This is another instance of using Settings not to inform or orient but to provide an aesthetic response that suits mood and tone, as Evocative Imagery. In Chapter 11, which discusses this Evocative Imagery, Settings will figure prominently.

In the movie *Gladiator*[11] (Figure 9.8), we see the way that thoughts and feelings from a dialogue scene can imbue the following Settings patterns with feeling. Actors will use a disconnection of eyeline from their partner in the scene to indicate being inside their own thoughts and feelings. Here, Maximus's Look away is connected to the view of a distant lightning storm, for an evocative externalization of his stormy emotions. This progresses through Evocative Imagery – time-lapse images of the sun rising and setting – to create the feeling of time passing using Settings as a temporal ellipsis. We pick up from the Settings slideshow to a tour or survey over the countryside and excited children running to see the sights on the road – the train of caged gladiators on their way to Rome. A frame of the Colosseum signals their arrival.

Figure 9.8

Maximus broods over going
to Rome. His friend Juba
understands his need for
revenge and fear of failure.

Asymmetrical pairs lend
weight to Juba's words.

A Look/See pair shows Maximus
looking away in thought, to a lightning
storm in the distance. This progresses to
Evocative Imagery showing the
passage of time, which becomes a
sweeping survey over the route to
Rome. We join the caged gladiators
on their way to fight in the
Colosseum.

We see Dialogue linked to Settings through the Look/See pattern. We see Settings as Evocative Imagery to externalize emotional reverberations and permit the compression of time and distance, bringing us to the place where Maximus can seek to avenge his murdered family.

Settings, particularly views that are evocative of the feelings of characters or the themes of the movie, are the place where we rest our heads when we need time to cope with the magnitude of some story event. This is what enables us to go forward with the story, having had enough time to process the experience. We are changed by it in our understanding of the depth of the story, and now we face whatever is next with this understanding on board. Without this time, these events could feel rushed and lacking in the significance they deserve.

The use of Settings to assist the audience in processing life-changing emotions can make the difference between the audience feeling like their souls were rocked and feeling like nothing in the story was very meaningful or moving. Anytime a character's life is irrevocably changed, we need time to register the major significance of the event. Creating time – a few moments away from the pressure of story progress – lets us feel these events deeply and allows us to align our emotions with the character's experience.

Summary

- Settings are primary declarative story information, always conveyed in a script slugline even if no further attention is given to specifics in the writing.
- Settings, whether physical or social, are in the service of the storytelling and provide opportunities and constraints that shape character actions. When they are merely background, that is their primary role.
- Establishing a setting through a single shot at the start of the scene serves to orient us to the new location and to act as a chapter marker, signaling that a new scene has begun and the previous scene is left behind.
- Whenever we see the outside of a setting – such as a building, vehicle, or ship – whatever interior we see next is presumed to be inside. This rule can be violated for misdirection.
- Settings with intrinsic story significance are often given extensive coverage to permit us to feel the nature, mood, and tone, so that character actions are understood to be contingent on the special nature of the setting.
- A series of fixated images of a setting, like a slideshow, suggests parts standing for the whole. A tour or survey through roving camera suggests that no single detail is more important than the overall nature of the setting.
- When characters are seen as part of the Setting, they can feel like the natural or normal inhabitants, aligned with the opportunities and constraints that the Setting presents.

- Setting patterns are a primary way to introduce characters in context, and we feel the prolonged setting coverage as a kind of search and discovery of characters with story importance.
- If characters are found through a search in the setting, it tends to feel as if the story selected them, whereas if they emerge and the coverage latches on to them, it tends to feel as if they are self-selecting through their active display of agency.
- We can explore Settings completely independent of character mediation, but if we experience a Setting through a character's experience, their responses become more important than any intrinsic qualities of the Setting.
- Settings are important for control of pacing, to compress time, or more importantly, to provide the audience with time for emotional resonance and reverberation after some particularly intense or meaningful events that change the protagonist in a profound way.

What you can do . . .

Fast-forward through some of your favorite movies and look for Settings.

- Are there any scenes where prolonged coverage of Settings is used? If so, when in the movie is this used? Is that Setting something that has a big impact on characters in terms of opportunities and constraints? Did you understand that from the coverage?
- Are there any scenes where Settings were used to provide some time away from the pressure of constant story progress? If so, how did the coverage assist your understanding of the story or characters?
- Are there Settings that are social and not purely physical? How did you know? What effect did your understanding of the social setting have on your judgment of character actions?
- Are there Settings shown in a single shot at the start of a scene? Did the story need a chapter marker at that point?
- Are there Settings that are only in the background, with no dedicated coverage? What effect did that have on your understanding of character actions?
- Do you find anywhere in the movie, the use of Settings at the end of a scene, section, act, or entire movie? If so, how did they feel, and how did they affect your understanding of the story or characters?

Notes

1 *American Beauty*. Directed by Sam Mendes, Cinematography by Conrad Hall. DreamWorks Pictures, released 1999. DVD: Dreamworks Home Entertainment (2000, USA). Start time: 00:26:27.
2 *No Country for Old Men*. Directed by Ethan Coen & Joel Coen, Cinematography by Roger Deakins. Paramount Vantage, Miramax, Scott Rudin Productions, released 2007. DVD: Buena Vista Home Entertainment (2008, USA). Start time: 00:20:52.

3 *The Silence of the Lambs*. Directed by Jonathan Demme, Cinematography by Tak Fujimoto. Orion Pictures, Strong Heart Demme Production, released 1991. DVD: Criterion Collection (2018, USA). Start time: 01:38:17.

4 *Alien*. Directed by Ridley Scott, Cinematography by Derek Vanlint. Brandywine Productions, Twentieth Century Fox, released 1979. DVD: Director's Cut, Twentieth Century Fox Home Entertainment (2004, USA). Start time: 00:02:00.

5 *Leave No Trace*. Directed by Debra Granik, Cinematography by Michael McDonough. BRON Studios, Creative Wealth Media Finance, Harrison Productions, released 2018. DVD: Universal Studios (2018, USA). Start time: 00:01:23.

6 *The Shawshank Redemption*. Directed by Frank Darabont, Cinematography by Roger Deakins. Castle Rock Entertainment, released 1994. DVD: Warner Bros. Entertainment (2007, USA). Start time: 00:08:43.

7 *Parasite*. Directed by Bong Joon Ho, Cinematography by Kyung-pyo Hong. Barunson E&A, CJ E&M Film Financing & Investment Entertainment & Comics, CJ Entertainment, released 2019. DVD: Universal Studios (2020, USA). Start time: 00:12:44.

8 *Parasite*. Ibid. Start time: 01:32:08.

9 *Saving Private Ryan*. Directed by Steven Spielberg, Cinematography by Janusz Kaminski. DreamWorks, Paramount Pictures, Amblin Entertainment, released 1998. DVD: DreamWorks (1999, USA). Start time: 00:45:54.

10 *Children of Men*. Directed by Alfonso Cuarón, Cinematography by Emmanuel Lubezki. Universal Pictures, Strike Entertainment, Hit & Run Productions, released 2006. DVD: Universal Studios (2007, USA). Start time: 00:58:59.

11 *Gladiator*. Directed by Ridley Scott, Cinematography by John Mathieson. DreamWorks, Universal Pictures, Scott Free Productions, 2000. DVD: Signature Selection, DreamWorks (2000, USA). Start time: 01:11:45.

Chapter 10
Patterns for objects

Objects have either functional or intrinsic significance

Objects are declarative story information. In terms of their value in the storytelling, we can categorize them as being either functional – characters use them to accomplish goals – or with intrinsic story significance – acting with a feeling of story agency that makes them almost like characters, or intrinsically significant Settings. That usually means there is a need for more extensive coverage of that Object.

An example from Chapter 5 shows us a common approach to handling coverage of functional objects – in this case, the gun in the fight scene from *Out of Time*[1] (Figure 5.7). In the final frame from the first section of the fight, we see the gun prominently in the foreground, with Matt desperately reaching for it. The functional Object is only important through character use, and thus is seen in the same frame as the character or handled by the character, or through a Look/See pattern that tells us the object is the focus of the character's subjective attention.

In the second part of the fight, a broken balcony railing, seven floors above concrete, is an Object with more intrinsic significance (Figure 5.8). The railing is rusted and breaking. We do not know when it will break, and neither do the characters. It has its own contribution to the action, independent of character agency. As a result, in the full scene there are many CUs of the rusted posts as they bend, buckle, and start to give way. The railing, about to plunge one or both combatants to certain death, is the third party in the fight.

Functional objects are within the scope of character agency

In a scene from the movie *The English Patient*[2] (Figure 10.1), we see a number of functional objects, all within the scope of character agency. There is a bomb, detonator wires, and the wire cutter. Most are seen through Kip's subjective attention. The first Look/See pattern provides our first view of the detonator and wire cutters in alignment with Kip's eyeline, for clarity that this is his action. The second Look/See pattern shows us the defined

DOI: 10.4324/9781003080657-10

Figure 10.1

Kip defuses a huge bomb. The bomb and wire cutters are objects with functional significance. In the first Look/See pair, we are aligned with his eyeline and POV.

Kip picks a wire to cut. We observe the act in extreme detail, at the clearest possible angle.

Hardy looks down. We see his perspective and reaction to certain death if it goes wrong. We see the wire cut – no explosion. Kip and Hardy exchange reciprocal looks of relief in non-verbal dialogue.

focus of his attention in the best and clearest angle. Even though it deviates from his eyeline, we understand that this is indicating Kip's intense focus on choosing the right wire before he and Hardy are blown to smithereens. Stretching out the action to create additional tension, we see Hardy's reactions. As always, the bystander's reactions give us a way to calibrate our reactions to a situation. We see Kip's vulnerable position in the pit. The moment of clipping the wire is clearly seen, giving us the chain of C&E – which in this case means no explosion. The appropriately asymmetrical, non-verbal exchange of relief is shared between Kip and Hardy.

This entire scene is filled with the importance of functional objects in this risky operation, as wire cutters fall into muddy water and other small events add to the tension. Functional objects are always presented in the context of character actions.

Establishing functional objects before critical action

We've seen the concept of ***establishing*** used for Objects in a chase scene, such as in the example in Chapter 5 from the movie *Jurassic Park*[3] (Figure 5.12, Figure 5.13). If we didn't know that the Jeep had a big, easily-hit stick shift, we wouldn't comprehend what happens when Ian knocks the vehicle out of gear. The reason to establish a functional Object prior to the action is that we don't have time to introduce new story information in the middle of dynamic actions, which would interrupt the rapid chain of C&E. We may wonder why we are being shown that Object, but once it becomes a significant part of rapidly unfolding events, we are able to fit it into the flow.

In like manner, a weapon is usually established before it comes into play in a rapid chain of C&E. If a character has a weapon, the audience will anticipate its use. If you don't establish a weapon, its use will jolt the audience for a moment as they wonder how it got there. They might lose the thread for an instant as they test its credibility. Establishing facilitates clear C&E – the gear shift or the bomb. Not establishing disrupts clear C&E to create surprise – Grandma's got a gun!

Objects can have their own story agency

In the movie *The Lord of the Rings: The Fellowship of the Ring*[4] (Figure 10.2), we see the One Ring of Power as having its own active story agency. It is the subject of much coverage, focused on the feeling of possession that is actually mutual possession. No functional object can have this effect.

The Ring isn't physically active; it is psychologically active, and so its effect is only visible in the reactions of those who possess or covet it. When possession of the Ring changes hands – such as when Isildur is killed – we follow the Ring itself as the important story Object. Before Bilbo finds the Ring, we see it in its own frame. The variability of the Ring's size is shown through special effects that shrink it to Isildur's size in the first

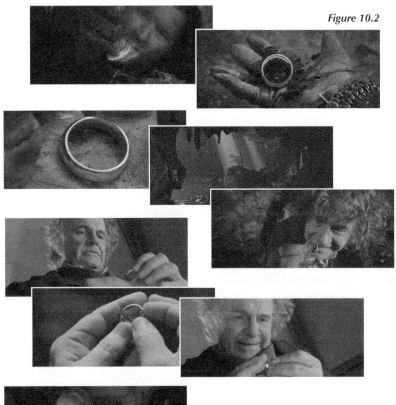

Figure 10.2

The One Ring is definitely an object with intrinsic story significance. Those who confuse it with a functional object would be doomed. Each stage of Ring ownership involves the intensely focused Look and a shot of the Ring. There is a strong sense of possession – holding it in your hand. You could even see the Ring as having asymmetrical dialogue with its holder – Isildur and Bilbo are seen within its context, but it is seen alone. With Frodo, both have individual frames and their own autonomous goals. Frodo recognizes an adversary, not a magic trinket or weapon.

instance. Its unusual weight is seen in each character's reaction to holding it for the first time.

An Object with its own will and agency is rare, but this example shows the types of coverage needed to convey this to the audience, so that we feel it and are not simply shown it.

Forces can be objectified

Active forces within the storytelling might not be physical objects but are instead things or situations with blind story agency. A deadly contagious disease is such a thing and might be represented as a physical object, like a vial with a warning label, or as a presence suggested by the way characters use protective clothing or respirators.

Extreme storms would be another example. The wind is not visible, but we can see its effects and the reactions of characters. Sometimes weather is seen from an objectified vantage point, as in a satellite observation of a hurricane – making it a discrete Object.

Pervasive psychological forces might similarly be seen through character actions and reactions. When all the characters in a team are facing certain death or destruction, we may see the reaction play out in each character, as a kind of polling of their individual responses to an overall situation. This is common before entering physical or emotional battle.

Objectifying characters

The patterns for presenting Objects give us the means to objectify characters for storytelling purposes. This can be done through Look/See patterns that often support the presentation of Objects. Whenever a character sees another character and they look back, this creates the Dialogue pair of shot-and-reverse. When there is a Look/See pattern and the other character does not look back, this can be felt as objectification. Objects don't look back. People do.

In Chapter 6, we saw such an exchange in the movie *Altered States*[5] (Figure 6.1). Emily sees Eddie as the object of her desire. He does not look back at her, and a dynamic push-in on Emily emphasizes that seeing him has emotional impact. Objects of desire, Objects of affection, Objects of derision – there are many ways this can serve storytelling.

This objectification of characters through one-sided perspective is rather common. In war movies, we have characters on "our side" Look and See the enemy, but there is no subjective perspective from the other side. They don't get Look/See coverage from their perspective. Being objectified has an aspect of being dehumanized.

In a less dire situation, the presence of a character may affect the action, such as when a parent arrives to stifle a pillow fight. If we follow the storytelling through the kids' perspective, it would be normal for them to see the parents and react but not see the parents' perspective or their Looks or view of the scene.

Objects with intrinsic significance as symbols

There are times when an Object has intrinsic significance as a symbol. Common examples are pictures of loved ones, a piece of jewelry that represents a relationship, a treasured fountain pen, or a lock of hair from a loved one.

Although not illustrated here, the pocket watch in *Cast Away*[6] shows how an Object can start out as functional and develop intrinsic significance as a symbol. At Christmas, Kelly gives Chuck a working pocket watch – a family heirloom – with her picture inside. Chuck gives her an engagement ring – an Object with intrinsic significance as a symbol. He sets the watch to the local time zone – "Kelly time" – as a functional way to be in touch with her day. But during the plane crash sequence, the watch saves his life when he leaves his seat to grab it and narrowly avoids being crushed. Long after the pocket watch has stopped functioning, he hangs on to it as a symbol of life and love. The way the watch is valued has changed – from functional to intrinsic significance. This is the same way that Chuck himself must change in order to survive.

Other examples might be socially understood symbols of religious or cultural affiliation. Their inclusion in coverage would be scripted moments of a character's self-reminder of affiliations. These Objects will typically be seen through a character's subjective attention, either through handling or Look/See patterns.

On some occasions, a symbolic Object will be seen, independent of character perspective, as a reminder of some affiliation, belief, or oath that a character has neglected or rejected, bringing that into our judgment of their actions.

Summary

- The only Objects that demand coverage are those that have either functional or intrinsic significance to the storytelling, seen through their presentation in the script.
- Functional Objects are used by characters to achieve goals and are usually seen through use or through Look/See patterns.
- If Objects are part of a chain of dynamic C&E, they may need to be established prior to playing their role in the action, so that the audience is not taken out of the flow.
- Objects can have their own story agency, whether it is impersonal or part of what we perceive as supernatural powers. These may be seen independently from character perspective and their power seen through character reactions.
- Forces of nature or psychology can be objectified through representative objects or through character reactions.
- Using the patterns for Objects, characters can be objectified to suit storytelling purposes.

- Objects with symbolic significance are a visible shorthand that reveals a character's inner state, remembering an important affiliation or story force. Occasionally, these are seen outside of character perspective, for us to judge the neglect of this affiliation.

What you can do . . .

Fast-forward through any of your favorite movies and look for Objects.

- Do we see them through the character? Is it in a Look/See pattern? Is it in a shot that shows their functional use by a character?
- How do you understand the Object? Does it have functional story significance? How do you know? Does it have intrinsic story significance? How do you know? Does it have symbolic story significance? How do you know?
- Are any Objects shown (not part of the background, but foreground) that don't have any story significance? Why do you think they were included in the coverage?

Notes

1 *Out of Time*. Directed by Carl Franklin, Cinematography by Theo van de Sande. MGM, Original Film, Monarch Pictures, released 2003. DVD: MGM Home Entertainment (2006, USA). Start time: 01:10:06.
2 *The English Patient*. Directed by Anthony Minghella, Cinematography by John Seale. Miramax, Tiger Moth Productions, released 1996. DVD: Buena Vista Home Video (2005, USA). Start time: 01:55:35.
3 *Jurassic Park*. Directed by Steven Spielberg, Cinematography by Dean Cundey. Universal Pictures, Amblin Entertainment, released 1993. DVD: Universal Studios (2000, USA). Start time: 01:20:04.
4 *The Lord of the Rings: The Fellowship of the Ring*. Directed by Peter Jackson, Cinematography by Andrew Lesnie. New Line Cinema, WingNut Films, released 2001. DVD: Special Extended Edition, New Line Home Entertainment (2002, USA).
5 *Altered States*. Directed by Ken Russell, Cinematography by Jordan Cronenweth. Warner Bros., released 1980. DVD: Warner Bros. Home Video (1998, USA). Start time: 00:06:36.
6 *Cast Away*. Directed by Robert Zemeckis, Cinematography by Don Burgess. Twentieth Century Fox, Dreamworks, released 2000. DVD: Twentieth Century Fox Home Entertainment (2001, USA).

Chapter 11
Patterns for evocative imagery

Evocative imagery puts emotions in the foreground

The vast majority of stories and films will only have those concrete elements that are easy to categorize: Character Actions, Looks, and Dialogue; Settings and story-significant Objects. This neglects one additional element that is less concrete: Evocative Imagery, which is the utilization of aesthetic or emotionally charged imagery within the storytelling, purely for the feelings it evokes and not to convey any specific story information.

Think of things like a beautiful sunset or the mesmerizing patterns of moving water. Their value in storytelling is the feelings they evoke, not any objective or concrete meaning. When Evocative Imagery is written into a script, these feelings are the focus. Evocative Imagery contributes to the storytelling at the level of pure feeling. The visible element in the script – the declarative information – is different from all the other categories in that it has no purpose beyond the feeling evoked. That feeling is lent to the story, coloring it without attributing any specific or concrete information. Of all the visible elements, Evocative Imagery is the most like music in a soundtrack.

In typical storytelling, Evocative Imagery is used to serve mood, tone, and compression of time, usually through Settings presented mostly for their emotional resonance and less for any objective information. Sometimes, though, we will see Evocative Imagery as a pervasive aspect of stories with philosophical, spiritual, or existential content.

We may see Evocative Imagery play a role in the experience of characters undergoing some alteration of their perceptions or psychology. This bundle of character, plot, and thematic reasons may exist in a single story, such as when a character is a seeker of truths beyond everyday existence. In another common usage, a character may have deeply subjective experiences that break from our normal reality and need to be presented through Evocative Imagery in order to put us in their shoes.

In all cases where Evocative Imagery is called for explicitly in the script or deemed necessary in the interpretation of the filmmakers, we are asking the audience to place meaning in their perceptual and aesthetic response.

DOI: 10.4324/9781003080657-11

The feeling evoked takes precedence over any additional story information that might be inferred.

Mood and tone in the compression of time

We've discussed how Evocative Imagery, used within Settings, can convey the passage of time while also conveying changes in mood and tone.

In our example in Chapter 5 from the movie *Saving Private Ryan*[1] (Figure 5.4), the moments of Evocative Imagery are used to compress time and shift the mood, helping us empathize with the troops marching through the night in drenching rain. When the storytelling resumes with an ECU of combat boots stepping in a muddy puddle, we can almost feel how tired and miserable the soldiers must be.

Another example, from Chapter 9, is the opening of the movie *Leave No Trace*[2] (Figure 9.2). Evocative images of blowing leaves, shifting shadows, and glistening spiderwebs evoke an aesthetic response to the timeless beauty of benevolent nature. We have no idea if these represent moments or days, months or years. It may not even matter, because the poetic quality could attach to any reading of the time represented and still be true.

This aesthetic experience aligns us with the characters and their subjective experience. It allows for a real mood change in the audience, as we transition from our lives in modern society to this life immersed in the natural world. We are enchanted with the beauty and rapturous dissolving of puny self-importance in the grander experience of the natural world. When the characters' place in this world is threatened, we feel and understand what they stand to lose.

Characterization through evocative imagery

Evocative Imagery can deliver an aesthetic experience that feels like dislocation and distortion, to serve characterization. In a prior example from *Altered States*[3] (Figure 3.2), we begin the movie with an inexplicable shot of the main character, Eddie, that distorts his image, blanks out his eyes, and is glowing and liquid. The exciting and prolonged pull back makes sense of this image – he is in an isolation tank in a basement lab. But the feeling sticks with us that this character is on some internal adventure and can't be reached, and the strangeness of it all is central to his character.

This is the story of a mad scientist who learns meaning in love and connection after a destructive and selfish journey seeking ultimate truth. The introduction encapsulates much of the core of Eddie's character and much of the thematic content of the story. The poetic power of Evocative Imagery is able to carry multiple levels of meaning, while stimulating our aesthetic responses and bringing those to the characters and story.

This is also why Evocative Imagery is often used in the opening of movies, to indelibly set a mood and tone that colors our entire sense of the story's meaning from its first moments.

Providing time for processing strong emotions

In Chapter 9, we discussed how Evocative Imagery of a Setting can be used to provide time for emotional reverberation. In the example cited from *Children of Men*[4] (Figure 9.7), we see how the poetic quality of Evocative Imagery suits the need for time to process intensely emotional events. Evocative Imagery can be used to great effect at life-changing moments for the main character. The imagery can feel drenched with character emotions or simply pause the relentless story progress to give us emotionally neutral time to process what just happened. This can give events the magnitude they deserve in our understanding of the story and of irrevocable change for the main character.

Evocative imagery in relation to montage

You could say that a conventional montage, or a set of sequential images, falls within the category of Evocative Imagery when it is devoted more to feeling and less to concrete story information. To help differentiate, a montage that is used to provide salient story information – such as a character learning to fight – is being employed to compress time. It is like a high-speed time-lapse of story information. In contrast, a montage that is used to immerse the audience in feeling or mood is being employed to suspend time. It is like a breather from the pressures of relentless story progress.

Separating experience from consensus reality

Now let's look at an entirely new example, from the movie *Arrival*[5] (Figure 11.1). This is a scene where Louise enters the spaceship of the alien heptapods – remarkable creatures who can control gravity and experience time as a circle. It is the first and only time we see anyone actually with them, without being separated by glass from their misty atmosphere.

Under the influence of Louise's encounter with the aliens, we enter a setting that is pure Evocative Imagery. We stay with Louise and her experience. When the effects of gravity are felt, we need to see her full body to feel the sensation ourselves. When her thoughts, feelings, and intentions are understood through connection to her expressions, we have CUs. Look/ See pairs link us to sightings of the alien and then to reciprocal dialogue pairs. Her inner look, eyes shut, connects us to the child, Hannah. This is how we know that this is happening in her mind as a subjective experience, outside of the normal flow of time.

The poetic quality of dimensionless space translates well for a story where time is treated like another dimension to travel through – not the irrevocable straight arrow we understand from real life but more like a landscape of experience.

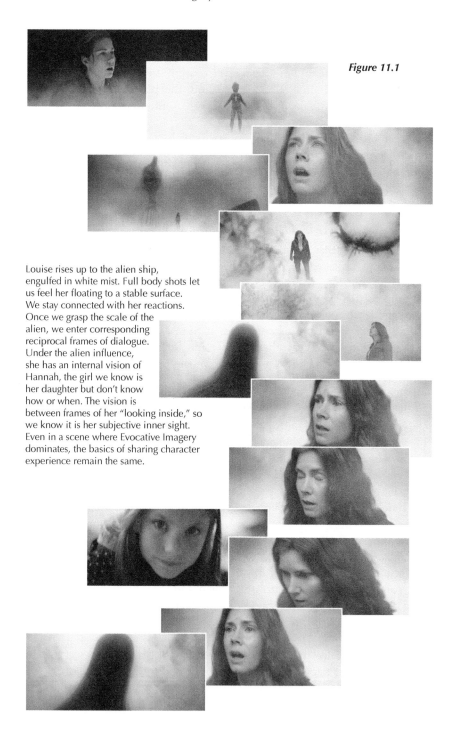

Figure 11.1

Louise rises up to the alien ship, engulfed in white mist. Full body shots let us feel her floating to a stable surface. We stay connected with her reactions. Once we grasp the scale of the alien, we enter corresponding reciprocal frames of dialogue. Under the alien influence, she has an internal vision of Hannah, the girl we know is her daughter but don't know how or when. The vision is between frames of her "looking inside," so we know it is her subjective inner sight. Even in a scene where Evocative Imagery dominates, the basics of sharing character experience remain the same.

Signaling departure from conventional narrative

Painters have always known that imagery can speak to the heart in a direct way. Some movies use imagery for the evocative sensations that come from reflection and feeling, rather than action and feeling. In these cases, the poetic imagery is replacing conventional narrative sequence-of-events storytelling. The storytelling might be considered closer to poetic philosophical musings than any linear story and character arc.

In the movie *The Tree of Life*[6](Figure 11.2), we see an example of an unconventional narrative, using the patterns of Action and Dialogue but dialed away from a presentation of reality into a presentation of a kind of dance performance with speaking characters. This example is from a section of the movie that is poetically sensible but not possible in reality. Constantly evolving frames house surreal imagery. The frame swings out of level, feeling unstable but fluid, like riding a wave. The fluid and graceful instability is in sync with the gestural acting. The physicality of the camera's movement through space gives a strong sense of vicarious presence, as if our independent perspective was included in this dance.

In the three frames of Mrs. O'Brien walking toward the horizon at sunset, the camera sweeps over the ground toward her at a rapid pace, feeling like the story situation – in this case of a philosophical nature – is dynamically amplifying the significance of her gestures. The full body framing gives us the expressiveness of full movement and gestures. When facial expressions are conveying inner states, we are in closer proximity. When the flow of story energy flows along hands, we see hands.

The same kinds of concerns that influence cinematic decisions about conventional narratives are at play here. What is the appropriate perspective – observing, participating, connecting? All three are seen. What is the appropriate proximity? All three basic framings are seen: expressive (usually a face but here, sometimes, hands); social presentation or medium shots where social relationship is central; and full body expressiveness and physicality. The priority of the Evocative Imagery, its aesthetic and feeling, seems appropriate, as this storytelling is a kind of abstract performance of poetic content.

Summary

- Evocative Imagery is appropriate when the storytelling moment puts an aesthetic or sensory response as the main goal. If written into the script, the feeling and aesthetic is the declarative story information to be conveyed.
- Small moments of Evocative Imagery can be used for compression of time, enabling shifts in mood and tone, almost like time-lapse photography of the emotional transitions.

Figure 11.2

A dreamlike place lets loved
ones – living or dead, at any stage
of life – share moments bathed in natural
beauty. This storytelling is more like
a ballet than a conventional narrative
movie, with expressive visual beauty
evoking a very subjective experience.

This example deliberately separates the
experience from objective reality, with
unusual, destabilizing angles and
story-not-character–motivated
moves. Surreal settings take it
into metaphoric realms.

Evocative imagery comes into play
any time that an aesthetic response
is a storytelling priority. Evocative
imagery takes cinematic storytelling
beyond contextual support
functions, making the feeling of the
imagery central to the storytelling.

- Settings are often used to bring us to characters. When Evocative Imagery is used, the associated feelings can become part of their characterization.
- When Settings are used to provide time for the audience to process strong emotional moments, it is common to use Evocative Imagery to momentarily break free of the relentless drive of story progress and just feel what has happened.
- Series of images, or montage, using Evocative Imagery allow the audience to bathe in moments of feeling or mood without the pressures of story progress.
- Signaling a strong aesthetic response with Evocative Imagery can suit the presentation of character experiences that are unreal, not of this world, or expressively subjective.
- Movies that seek to convey spiritual or philosophical content can employ Evocative Imagery to function as both metaphor and direct simulant of strong emotional responses without the need for conventional narrative constructs.

What you can do . . .

Fast-forward through some of your favorite movies and look for what you consider Evocative Imagery, where the aesthetic or feeling of the images takes precedence over their objective informational value.

- What aesthetic response or feeling do you have from the Evocative Imagery, and how does that relate to the storytelling?
- Were these employing Settings as the source material? What about Actions or Dialogue?
- Does the Evocative Imagery relate to your understanding of characters? Mood? Theme?

Notes

1 *Saving Private Ryan*. Directed by Steven Spielberg, Cinematography by Janusz Kaminski. DreamWorks, Paramount Pictures, Amblin Entertainment, released 1998. DVD: DreamWorks (1999, USA). Start time: 00:41:42.
2 *Leave No Trace*. Directed by Debra Granik, Cinematography by Michael McDonough. BRON Studios, Creative Wealth Media Finance, Harrison Productions, released 2018. DVD: Universal Studios (2018, USA). Start time: 00:01:23.
3 *Altered States*. Directed by Ken Russell, Cinematography by Jordan Cronenweth. Warner Bros., released 1980. DVD: Warner Bros. Home Video (1998, USA). Start time: 00:00:16.
4 *Children of Men*. Directed by Alfonso Cuarón, Cinematography by Emmanuel Lubezki. Universal Pictures, Strike Entertainment, Hit & Run Productions, released 2006. DVD: Universal Studios (2007, USA). Start time: 00:58:59.

5 *Arrival.* Directed by Denis Villeneuve, Cinematography by Bradford Young. Lava Bear Films, FilmNation Entertainment, 21 Laps Entertainment, Xenolinguistics, released 2016. DVD: Paramount Pictures (2017, USA). Start time: 01:26:37.
6 *The Tree of Life.* Directed by Terrence Malick, Cinematography by Emmanuel Lubeski. Cottonwood Pictures, River Road Entertainment, Fox Searchlight Pictures, Brace Cover Productions, Plan B Entertainment, Summit Entertainment, 2011. DVD: Criterion Collection (2018, USA). Start time: 02:10:08.

Chapter 12
Patterns and movement

Movement is the last piece of the puzzle

We've gone over the patterns that connect the scripted storytelling to the cinematic presentation. The plainly visible elements present the declarative story information. The qualities of representative keyframes, developed into patterns, help the audience feel the physical and emotional meanings by pointing toward the inferential story information. These are employed to create a temporal context that supports audience assessment and understanding using conventions understood by movie-watchers, adjusted to suit story specifics and track story progress.

Perspectives and proximity shape story attention through spatial relationships between the audience and the characters in the storyworld. Movement is the last ingredient that puts spatial relationships into a temporal – time-based – experience.

Cameras can move in almost any imaginable way. Framing can stay attached to characters who are on the move. Our vantage point can fly through the air to find subjects of story significance. We can suddenly get closer to characters as the story situation hits them hard. Even stock-still and locked-off, movement in front of the camera makes the frame come alive. Now we can tie movement to the employment of patterns, so it can play its part in cinematic presentation of both declarative and inferential story information.

Movement is the energy of cinematic storytelling. Let's put it to use.

Movement within the frame

The locked-off shot, such as in the slideshow pattern for Settings, could be considered like a "living" photograph or like a real window into the imaginary storyworld. What moves inside the frame? Anything from leaves in the wind, to birds on the wing, to balls being tossed, to planes crash-landing. A lot can happen looking "through the window" of a stationary frame. Most important would be the movement of characters.

DOI: 10.4324/9781003080657-12

Characters move through the frame

It is fairly common to have characters enter the frame, do something or talk for a bit, then exit the frame (Figure 12.1, A). It helps with the feeling of story progress, with compression of the time and distance between scenes or segments understood as insignificant to the story. It is common with traveling and with walk & talks.

There are two ways that characters move through frames. When it is on their own volition – walking, riding, or flying – it feels like they are on the move, coping with whatever story situation they are in, taking action toward their goals. The patrol scene in *Saving Private Ryan*[1] (Figure 5.3) has characters enter the frame, go through a segment of the story, then move past us and away before we pick them up again, coming toward us in the next phase.

In *The Lord of the Rings: The Fellowship of the Ring*[2] (Figure 12.3), the main character goes on a great journey in a team of nine fellows. We observe them from a distance, in settings that visibly change. This indicates passage of time and travel distance, compressing it into moments on screen. We touch base with them as they pass through a natural gateway of rock, giving us a glimpse of their individual states of mind as they enter frame, pass by us, and move onward. The camera sweeps away, and they become tiny dots merging into the wilderness. This is also an example of using Settings to connect with and disconnect from characters. When we pick up with them at their next camp, we understand the long and grueling nature of the trek, and their comradery makes sense in light of the time and efforts endured together.

In violent or drastic physical action, characters may get knocked through the frame, or blown or scattered – this is involuntary movement. Consider how lacking in energy the scene between Harry Potter and the dragon[3] (Figure 5.5) would be if it didn't start out with him getting knocked around. The camera tries to hold him in frame, but he's at the mercy of the dragon. Having him at the mercy of the situation is an essential contrast to the triumphant feeling of him getting his magic together and starting to control the frame.

The sense of being at the mercy of the story situation is multiplied in an example from Chapter 1 (Figure 1.4). In *Gravity*,[4] Astronaut Stone is shot into space after debris destroys the space shuttle. If we lacked the observational vantage point that shows violent motions through the frame, we could not share her terror when we connect with her perspective. Movement within the frame informs her subjective experience and POV.

Character movement alters proximity and frame size

Character movements can also alter proximity and frame size, creating a very different effect than a change in camera position (Figure 12.1, B). In some ways, it is more like real life, where people can come closer or move

Movement *within* the Frame

Figure 12.1[1]

A. Character passing through Observation

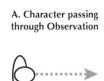

If voluntary, this tends to feel like coping with "the situation." When characters enter and exit frame, it support passage of time and distance.

If involuntary, it tends to feel like they are at the mercy of "the situation."

B. Character altering Proximity

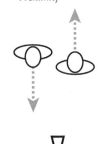

For emerging from, or merging into, the Setting.

For setting up L/S or for starting Dialogue pair.

C. Character altering perspective angle

Useful for modulation within a story phase or signaling new phase.

Movement *of* the Frame – Independent of Character

D. Tour/Survey of Setting

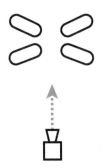

Audience experience independent of character. Can foster sense of shared experience or suspense.

E. Observe beyond Character

Objective story information exceeds character knowledge. We have the bomb brought to our attention, to generate suspense.

F. Hand-off

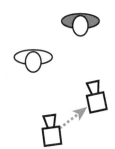

To fluidly shift attention to a different character, maintaining the flow.

Movement *of* the Frame – Dependent on Character

Figure 12.2

A. Frame instability with subject fixation

Minimal – for sense of presence or witnessing.

Maximal – for sense of externalizing strong feelings or physical effects.

B. Simultaneous reset for Staging change

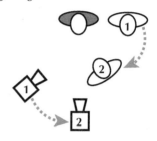

Character move unlocks camera movement. Here, one character moves from side-by-side to diagonal staging, while the camera moves from a two-shot to over-the-shoulder. Moving at the same time retains the sense of motivation and character agency. Any staging change handled this way is a powerful signal of a new story phase.

C. Subject fixation and Following

From Observation, Participation, or Connection – following character sustains framing perspective while the setting goes by.

When the camera is stationary and only pan and tilt are used, it is called "following action."

D. Injection of Dynamism

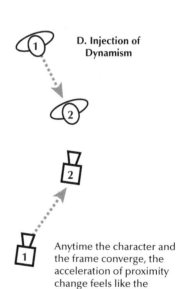

Anytime the character and the frame converge, the acceleration of proximity change feels like the injection of energy.

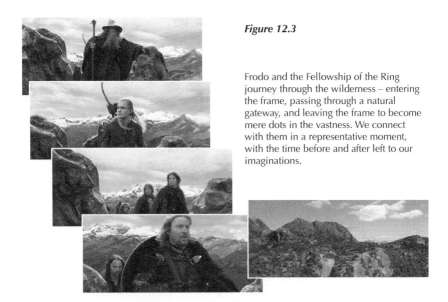

Figure 12.3

Frodo and the Fellowship of the Ring journey through the wilderness – entering the frame, passing through a natural gateway, and leaving the frame to become mere dots in the vastness. We connect with them in a representative moment, with the time before and after left to our imaginations.

farther away, and we feel the social and psychological effect of these changes in proximity. These feelings can be aligned with story specifics and put to use in helping us feel the emotions.

We see the effect of characters coming closer to the camera and moving away in the end of the ball scene in *Harry Potter and the Goblet of Fire*[5] (Figure 12.4). Hermione started the evening on a high pitch of positive emotions. Ron's callous actions have ruined the night for her, and she gives him an education in human feelings. She and Ron emerge from the emptying dance floor, starting to control the frame and moving into a walk & talk. Signaling a new phase, she turns, and this fluidly converts to a dialogue pair. Hermione's emotions are at the center of this scene and we are closer to her than to Ron, in asymmetrical frames. We pivot with her, remaining connected to her subjective experience as Harry walks past. We participate with her, as she lumps Harry's attitudes in with those of Ron. Feeling unfairly targeted, Harry walks away with Ron and we see them go – staying with Hermione. She walks to the stairs, changing the proximity from access to her facial expressions to the heartbreaking expressions conveyed through her full body.

This example illustrates the power of social and psychological feeling conveyed by character movement within the framing to achieve different proximities. There is movement of the frame to stay with them and movement within the frame to reset staging and patterns.

Figure 12.4

At the end of the ball, Hermione and Ron emerge from the setting. The first phase of the scene is presented as action from in front – a walk & talk – to following from behind. The next phase is when Hermione stops and the framing transitions to reciprocal Dialogue pairs. Action pattern converts to Dialogue pattern.

Hermione pivots, and now Harry is seen over her shoulder as she gives him a dressing down.

We are with her, watching the boys leave. She moves to the middle distance to cry and rub her aching feet. We leave her, feeling how she will have to cope with this alone.

Character altering angle and perspective

Whether in a single character action/activity scene or a dialogue scene, the social and psychological feelings of resetting relative angle will give us a sense of story progress (Figure 12.1, C). Whenever we see a new angle, we will tend to feel that we are getting a new angle on the story. Combine this with stopping and starting, and we get a sense of scene shape following the inferential story information. For example, in *Midsommar*,[6] after Dani responds to a troubling email and before she calls her boyfriend, she swivels her chair and faces in a different direction. This severs her connection to her laptop, giving us a new angle (Figure 1.3). In a scene from *Se7en*[7] (Figure 8.1), we see how the basic idea of altering angle also works in a walk & talk, where different staging configurations happen through movement within the frame.

Movement within the frame doesn't require stationary camera

Movement within the frame and of the camera can occur in any number of ways and combinations. Like all the various components of patterns, the basic functional uses of movement can be mixed and matched with all other cinematic options, working together to create the desired effect to suit the story moment.

Movement of the frame – independent of character

A **motivated** move is done in conjunction with a subject moving on screen. This might be smoothly tracking the subject or moving simultaneously with the subject. All motivated movement can be accomplished below the radar of audience notice, because our attention is caught by movement within frame and we have the urge to track it. Whenever we stay with characters or follow action with them as the fixation of the frame, we are using motivated movement.

The other general category of movement is **unmotivated**, meaning that we have nothing in frame to trigger or spur motion. The unmotivated move is noticed and felt and becomes part of the foreground of our attention. In the vast majority of cases, the unmotivated move is bringing our attention to something or someone with story significance. Let's start there.

Tour and survey of settings

Unless presented through the subjective experience of characters, any significant Setting will be seen through some extended pattern of slideshow – stationary and immobile frames – and tour or survey. These are explicitly unmotivated movements through or across the setting. The feeling is of exploration and leading toward something of story significance.

We saw this in the opening to the movie *Alien*[8] (Figure 9.1), where the movement of the framing is totally independent of the presence of characters. We arrive at subjects with story significance – first on the bridge with computers and the alert, then back on the move to arrive at the pods, which open up to reveal characters awakening from stasis. These pods are in the diagram (Figure 12.1, D) showing Tour/Survey of Setting.

In the example from the opening of *Altered States*[9] (Figure 3.2), the unmotivated camera move creates a feeling of suspense as it slowly provides the information that will make the scene comprehensible.

A third example is from the scene in *Saving Private Ryan*[10] (Figure 6.5), where Captain Miller's inner Look brings us to a slideshow of the carnage on the beach. Then the attention shifts – the camera lifts off and flies over the beach to search for and find one particular body, one of the last Ryan brothers. We know that we've found something with story significance, creating anticipation to find out exactly what it means.

Observation beyond characters

The example in our diagram of camera movements (Figure 12.1, E) shows the classic idea of a bomb in the room that the characters don't know about. We know it's there, and that is the root of the suspense – audience knowledge exceeding that of the characters. An unmotivated move signals us that we are moving to something with story significance. The very idea that the frame breaks away from a character to do so provides the feeling that we need that information now, because it will have immediate significance.

A more subtle movement is seen in our example from *The Shawshank Redemption*,[11] of Red looking in the pawn shop window (Figure 6.6). From inside the pawn shop, we follow Red's gaze to the gun. The camera doesn't fixate on the gun but instead drifts up to the compass on the higher shelf. Is this drift to the compass motivated by Red's attention? Or is it unmotivated and brought to our attention directly? This tension in fuzzy meaning helps to raise questions. We are held in suspense until the next scene plays out, and we find out Red's choice of a hopeful direction instead of suicide. This simple shot works in the grey area between motivated and unmotivated moves, effective in making us suspend judgement and wait for answers.

Hand-off brings us to the next character

The hand-off, or an unmotivated move from one character or subject to the next, just feels like we are following the story, as if we followed a bouncing ball (Figure 12.1, F).

We see that in the patrol and conversation scene from *Saving Private Ryan*[12] (Figure 5.3). You won't get a true sense of it just from a collection of still images, but there are a number of hand-offs in that scene. One character speaks, then the camera "slips" off of them and on to the next soldier with something to say. It's fluid and effective in sustaining attention, and in supporting the very classroom-like feeling of each person getting a chance to say their piece on the topic at hand. When we find out that Captain Miller, the brave and stalwart warrior leader, was actually a high school teacher before the war, it all makes sense. These hand-offs are functioning as very subtle support for characterization. This explains his deft touch with the young people under his command.

Movement of the frame – dependent on character

Let's discuss the classic uses of motivated camera movement. Attention is trained on the subject, and any movement of that subject will be tracked by the camera. In real life, we will immediately and automatically track a ball thrown to us. Even babies will track something moving with their eyes, long before they are coordinated enough to play catch. When framing attaches to the subject, we get that same natural feeling.

Let's go over the main ways that this happens and the potential feelings that can result, in support of the story specifics.

Frame instability with subject fixation

In real life, it is extremely rare to notice any instability in our visual field, no matter what we are doing. We can be running and still our vision is smooth and stable. Our minds do this for us. If we are turning somersaults, our vision may be blurred and smeared, but there are no "frame edges" to our natural vision. This is something that motion picture cameras can do, that we can't. It is like lens flares – things that our eyes don't do but cameras can do for creative interest.

The photographic image, especially and particularly because it has exact and rectangular frame edges, can be unstable while still fixating on a subject. The usual way this happens is through a handheld camera or similar means. Even the most stable and smooth camera operator, using the widest-angle lens, will have some slight variations in frame edges over the course of time, even if it is just the effect of their own breathing. A camera operator who is intentionally agitating the frame, especially with longer lenses, can make this very noticeable. The frame edge instability can be a main feature of the shot (Figure 12.2, A). This can be a useful thing to employ for story support.

For example, the use of handheld camera and the slight unsteadiness of frame edges in the movie *The Wrestler* (Figure 8.8) makes it feel like watching a documentary, with all the associated sense of entering and observing "real" events.

The superb handheld work maintains the verticals of the world – trees and houses – that keep us from feeling like we are woozy or otherwise in a totally subjective experience. Instead, the instability is minimal and not distracting, for a sense of witnessing and presence, entering the world of this troubled character.

When frame instability is maximized and becomes a major feature of the coverage, we will have more of a feeling of externalizing strong emotions and reaction to physical effects. We have referenced scenes from the movie

Saving Private Ryan.[13] One of the most famous scenes in that movie shows the landing on the beaches in the first waves of the invasion. The visceral nature of that scene is completely supported by the constant and sometimes extreme frame instability. From being rocked by explosions, to a constant state of extreme anxiety under mortal peril, the framing instability is central to the sense of shared subjective experience.

In the movie *If Beale Street Could Talk*[14] (Figure 12.5), we see young people in love. Strong emotions become externalized in the framing, providing a sense of giddy exuberance. This instability rises with their moment of peak emotion and settles down as they connect and move on to the next moments, filled with joy in their hearts. This is hugely important in the storytelling. It's very effective in setting a high point to contrast with tragic unfairness in the characters' lives. Frame instability offers a means to externalize strong emotions, whatever their nature.

In a scene from the movie *Midsommar*[15] (Figure 12.6), we get a very different and radical use of frame instability combined with subject fixation. Dani has gone through trauma, bad drug trips, and more. She is completely freaking out. Women villagers join with her in a seething, howling, synchronized mass of bodies linked together in anguish. The camera becomes detached from everything but their breathing, their motions, their ragged inhalations followed by howls. It is like one massive creature, led by and feeding off Dani's subjective emotional state. The shifting of frame edges loses significance in the total rocking and movement of the frames in powerful synchrony with the action, bringing us into vicarious sharing of the experience.

The movements of the frame have no fixation but the characters and their deeply subjective experience. The intersubjective nature of the experience is emphasized by the Dialogue pairs of Dani and the woman holding her face, mirroring her state. We become part of a pulsing human mass of feeling.

Subject fixation and following

Many times in this book, you have seen and read of examples where the framing follows characters on the move. We have seen it when the character Michael Clayton climbs a hill to be with mysteriously peaceful horses[16] (Figure 6.7). We stay with him, whether participating by following behind, connecting by staying in front, or following action as we observe him from more of a side angle.

We have seen how a character can stand out from the crowd, emerging from a social setting to capture the frame and have it follow them as they move. Refer back to the example from *The Shawshank Redemption*[17] (Figure 9.3), where Andy is passively, involuntarily arriving on the prison bus, while Red is revealed to be an important person behind bars.

When there is no competition for attention, we think nothing of following and sustaining attention on the sole character in frame. It fulfills our expectations of staying with a character.

Figure 12.5

Tish and Fonny are madly in love. Fluid handheld camera dances with them in a giddy moment. They stabilize around each other. Actively destabilized framing is often used for tension and anxiety. It works just as well to support exuberant emotions.

As a technical note, the term "following action" is sometimes reserved for a stationary camera panning and tilting to maintain a frame on a character. But the storytelling sense of staying with any character on the move extends to all perspectives and moving camera. This includes participating angles, following from behind, staying in front of a character in a connecting angle, or maintaining pace with a character when seen from an observational side angle. The net effect is that story attention is fixated on them and is sustained while they move (Figure 12.2, C).

Another very interesting example of camera movement that stays with a character is from a scene in *Midsommar*,[18] where Dani is given psilocybin mushrooms and has an intense and destabilizing trip. In the first part of the example (Figure 12.7), we observe her drinking the hallucinogenic tea, then watch her and her dazed friends drift off. Once we see her hallucination, in a Look/See pattern showing grass growing out of her hand, we know

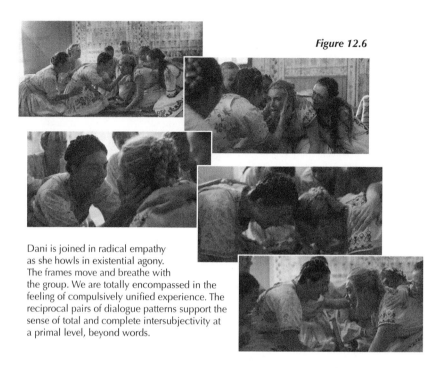

Figure 12.6

Dani is joined in radical empathy
as she howls in existential agony.
The frames move and breathe with
the group. We are totally encompassed in the
feeling of compulsively unified experience. The
reciprocal pairs of dialogue patterns support the
sense of total and complete intersubjectivity at
a primal level, beyond words.

that we are inside her subjective experience. When we observe her, close-up but from a slightly detached lower angle, we can see that the drugs have unhinged her. She rises, and we are with her. Her erratic motions continually switch the perspective of the following camera from participating, to connecting, to observing angles, as the story attention is as floating and loopy as she feels.

Interestingly, after that first, initially peaceful Look/See pattern of her hallucination, we never leave her to go to her POV. Even more interesting and significant to the story is her walking up to and talking to Ingemar, brother of their mutual friend from home, Pelle (Figure 12.8). Even though he tries to calm her down, we never enter the reciprocal pairs of dialogue. We do not enter dialogue – there is no intersubjective and mutual attention. We stay with her while he talks at her, not with her. It lets us share her isolated subjectivity.

Her intense anxiety as she departs indicates her inner state and reaction to her totally subjective experience.

Simultaneous reset for staging change

Any prolonged dialogue scene is going to need some dramatic shape to sustain the feeling of story progress and support the performances. An

Figure 12.7

In the first part of Dani's mushroom trip, action patterns of observation lead to connection with her dazed state. This flows into a Look/See that follows her gaze to the grass growing from her hand. From slightly below, we have a keener observation of her inner state. We follow her, participating in her walk. She sees others laughing and thinks it's directed at her. We stick with her experience.

Figure 12.8

In the second part of Dani's trip,
we follow her to meeting Ingemar.
This never becomes a reciprocal
shot pair of dialogue. Dani is too alienated.
We are on her side as he talks at her. We
reconnect with her seething state. She runs
toward the hut, leaving us behind. We never
leave her exclusive subjective experience.

effective way to do this is to restage or change the staging or physical arrangement of the characters (Figure 12.2, B). This could be any manner of alteration of the staging pattern, or simply going from standing to sitting.

We see a variation on this in a scene from the movie *The Girl with the Dragon Tattoo*[19] (Figure 12.9). Main character Mikael calls on expert hacker Lisbeth. She hacked his financial and personal records earlier in the movie, and he is willing to return the favor and intrude on her personal space for the sake of her help in tracking down a killer of women. Adding to the tension between them, Lisbeth has a traumatic relationship with abusive male authority, and she is understandably wary. They start near the entryway, in a set of asymmetrical dialogue pairs. She is an autonomous, singular subject. He is in a compound subject frame, past Lisbeth, putting him in her context. They physically move across the room to the table, so that he can put out some breakfast sandwiches. We follow them, and this becomes a new dialogue pair set.

The feeling of evolving through movement both sustains the momentum and gives us clear cues that we are moving on to a new phase. In this

Figure 12.9

Mikael needs help from Lisbeth, the expert hacker. He knocks on her door. She is extremely wary, for good reasons. The dialogue pairs in the entry are asymmetrical. He is over her shoulder; she is a singular subject. They move to the table, restaging for the next phase. Their shot pairs are now mutual OTS frames but still imbalanced. When he offers her a chance to help catch a killer of women, they get on the same page.

The shot pairs are closer and more equal. Their mutual framing shows a partnership starting.

A slideshow of clues begins the next scene, seen over the same shoulder. Pattern continuation sustains the story thread.

example, the change is not in the staging – they remain across from each other. It is not in the 180° Line of Continuity. The camera follows and lands in a new OTS shot of Mikael, keeping the same orientation of Mikael frame right and Lisbeth frame left. It is in the movement.

The movement of people and camera brings us to the table, where social presentation is not as exposed – the table in between them makes it safer. The social significance of sharing food makes trust-building possible. Their mutual OTS shots are now much more aligned, with less imbalance. We feel that. When he piques her interest in catching the murderer, the frames get closer, indicating increasing intimacy and intensity. They also become close to mirror-image frames, helping us feel a shared subjectivity, an intersubjectivity. This starts an effective partnership.

The scene is shaped by asymmetry becoming symmetry. Movement helps it evolve to another level. Closer proximity puts inner states at the forefront. Aligned and reciprocal, these help us feel their connection and willingness to share an important purpose.

The scene ends with us registering her intense reaction to the hunt for the killer. When Mikael shows her the first clue, it feels simply like a Look/ See pattern over her shoulder. In a very interesting continuation of story thread across scene boundaries, we next see a series of clues in articles on paper and on computer screens. When we finally emerge from that slide-show, we are actually in a different place and time – at a coffee table in the living room. There really is no sense of time passage. It feels as if the pattern of clues was so engrossing that we lost track of time. The scene at the table poses the question of whether she will help. Continuation with the clues at the coffee table answers that question.

A five-minute argument in the movie *Altered States*[20] (Figure 12.10) demonstrates the use of movement for restaging, to create the shape that matches the various phases of this prolonged dialogue scene. When filmmakers are faced with the prospect of many pages of dialogue, the need for scene shaping becomes paramount. Movement and restaging are the usual mechanisms. This allows the performances to go through numerous peaks and valleys without feeling flat or random. Here, Emily and Eddie have been separated for a long time while each followed their intellectual pursuits. As they engage in mutual comparison of scientific notes, she is unpacking in the new house she's rented for her and the kids. She moves around; he stays still. The reciprocal shot pairs are generally asymmetrical.

When she hits a nerve that frightens and upsets them both, a major restaging happens. She sits next to him, in diagonal staging. They are now on equal ground, and their fierce argument happens with matched reciprocal CUs. Eddie jumps up, moves around, and they end up in a new configuration in a widely separated diagonal. When he joins her, staged across, he urges her to consider the scientific possibilities and to join his efforts. Now they are on the same level, and the reciprocal pairs are evenly matched. This scene continues with Emily becoming distant and Eddie becoming aggressive. Escaping the house, they end up outdoors on the porch, airing out

Figure 12.10

Restaging through movement
shapes an extended dialogue
scene, to support story progress and
performances. When discussing
scientific findings, Emily and Eddie
are distant.

When arguing about the safety of his
experiments, they are restaged on a
close diagonal.

As Eddie urges her to help him, they
reset across from each other.

These restagings happen two more times,
finally ending outdoors on their porch,
where he gets her agreement.

their argument. Eventually, and with misgivings, Emily realizes she can't stop him, so she agrees to look at his findings.

This scene uses the power of restaging through movement to break this very long argument into discrete and comprehensible phases. It lets the buildup and dissipation of intensity happen in a way that supports the sense of emotional C&E and helps us feel story progress driven by character needs, elevating the performances.

There are a huge number of possible ways to restage in order to signal a new story phase. Using moving camera to flow from one to the next is a very powerful way to build and channel energy. This is particularly true with motivated moves that enhance the sense of character agency. These methods let us feel how the story is evolving and not simply moving forward incrementally.

Injection of dynamism

There are many ways that the energy of camera movement can contribute to a scene. When a dynamic or exciting camera movement lands on characters, it can have a powerful effect (Figure 12.2, D).

In the movie *The Silence of the Lambs*[21] (Figure 12.11), Agent Starling has been dismissed by Hannibal "The Cannibal" Lecter. But when another prisoner is abusive to her, Lecter calls Starling back to give her a critical clue that begins to unlock a terrible murder case. Lecter calls out to her. Simultaneous with her run back to his cell, the camera converges on Lecter. It continues to push in to a close two-shot while he gives her information in the form of a riddle. The powerful net effect is a combination of the shouting, the running, and the simultaneous camera move toward Starling and Lecter, with a dramatic shift in proximity to the characters.

Whenever you need to fuel an acceleration in energy level, converging moves of camera and character can give it a rapid and dynamic boost.

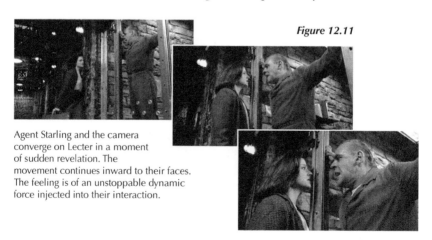

Figure 12.11

Agent Starling and the camera converge on Lecter in a moment of sudden revelation. The movement continues inward to their faces. The feeling is of an unstoppable dynamic force injected into their interaction.

Summary

- Movement is the energy of cinematic storytelling.
- Movement facilitates and expands the potential for pattern applications, putting the spatial elements of angle and proximity into a fluid and dynamic total package.
- Movement within the frame expands the expressive potential of Observation, Participation, or Connection by having characters enact changes in angle relative to camera.
- Movement of the frame is intrinsic to the Tour/Survey pattern for Settings.
- Movement of the frame gives filmmakers the chance to clearly shift attention to story information that characters do not see.
- Movement of the frame gives the opportunity for fluid hand-offs between characters without interrupting the flow.
- Frame instability, typically handheld, can be used to provide a sense of presence and witnessing when it is mild or minimal. When it is obvious or maximized, it can provide a sense of agitation, the externalizing of strong emotions, or the physical consequences of events like explosions or storms.
- Movement of the frame can work hand in hand with character restaging to create fluid and evolving shaping of scenes.
- Movement of the frame, evolving from keyframe to keyframe, creates the sense of evolving story progress, in contrast to the sense of incremental progress from using single shots per keyframe, edited together through cuts.
- Movement works to enable the audience to stay with the characters – following from behind, staying in front, or moving along with them from the side.
- Movement can be used to inject dynamism through trajectories that converge with characters. This is especially dramatic when the character is also moving and converging with the camera.

What you can do . . .

Fast-forward through a few of your favorite movies and look for movements. Watch your selections in real time (not fast-forwarded) so that you can feel the movement at the speed intended.

- Find movement within the frame. Who or what was moving, and what relationship did that have to the storytelling? Did it lead us to some other framing? What about leading us to another pattern, such as Action becoming Dialogue?

- Find movement of the frame. Was the frame fixated on and tracking a subject? If so, how did it feel? Was it independent of any subject? If so, how did it feel, and what did it lead to?
- Find movement that resets some portion of a longer dialogue scene. Was it constant or just at moments? Did it assist in any reset of the scene? If so, did that fall on or support some sense of the dialogue moving on to a new story phase?
- Find movement that is purely physically exciting. Is it attached to characters, and if so, what sort of proximity or frame size is used? How does it feel? Is there a sense of kinesthesia or bodily movement? Do you feel it in your own body?
- Find movement that feels dynamic. Is the camera following with characters, maintaining a constant framing? Is the camera movement converging with the character, or characters moving toward the camera simultaneously?
- Find two or three push-ins. How do they feel? When do they happen in the scene? Is there any time when it feels like the dramatic situation is having an impact on the character in the moment?

Notes

1 *Saving Private Ryan*. Directed by Steven Spielberg, Cinematography by Janusz Kaminski. DreamWorks, Paramount Pictures, Amblin Entertainment, released 1998. DVD: DreamWorks (1999, USA). Start time: 00:42:40.
2 *The Lord of the Rings: The Fellowship of the Ring*. Directed by Peter Jackson, Cinematography by Andrew Lesnie. New Line Cinema, WingNut Films, released 2001. DVD: Special Extended Edition, New Line Home Entertainment (2002, USA). Start time: 01:50:07.
3 *Harry Potter and the Goblet of Fire*. Directed by Mike Newell, Cinematography by Roger Pratt. Warner Bros., Heyday Films, Patalex IV Productions Ltd., released 2005. DVD: Warner Bros Home Video (2005, USA). Start time: 00:57:50.
4 *Gravity*. Directed by Alfonso Cuarón, Cinematography by Emmanuel Lubezki. Warner Bros., Esperanto Filmo, released 2013. DVD: Warner Bros Home Entertainment (2017, USA). Start time: 00:12:20.
5 *Harry Potter and the Goblet of Fire*. Ibid. Start time: 01:21:28.
6 *Midsommar*. Directed by Ari Aster, Cinematography by Pawel Pogorzelski. A24, B-Reel Films, Nordisk Film, Square Peg, released 2019. DVD: A24 Films, LLC, Lions Gate Entertainment (2020, USA). Start time: 00:02:38.
7 *Se7en*. Directed by David Fincher, Cinematography by Darius Khondji. Cecchi Gori Pictures, Juno Pix, New Line Cinema, released 1995. DVD: New Line Home Video (2000, USA). Start time: 00:01:58.
8 *Alien*. Directed by Ridley Scott, Cinematography by Derek Vanlint. Brandywine Productions, Twentieth Century Fox, released 1979. DVD: Director's Cut, Twentieth Century Fox Home Entertainment (2004, USA). Start time: 00:02:00.
9 *Altered States*. Directed by Ken Russell, Cinematography by Jordan Cronenweth. Warner Bros., released 1980. DVD: Warner Bros. Home Video (1998, USA). Start time: 00:00:16.
10 *Saving Private Ryan*. Ibid. Start time: 00:27:08.

11 *The Shawshank Redemption*. Directed by Frank Darabont, Cinematography by Roger Deakins. Castle Rock Entertainment, released 1994. DVD: Warner Bros. Entertainment (2007, USA). Start time: 02:10:02.

12 *Saving Private Ryan*. Ibid.

13 *Saving Private Ryan*. Ibid. Reference start time: 00:04:30 until 00:22:00.

14 *If Beale Street Could Talk*. Directed by Barry Jenkins, Cinematography by James Laxton. Annapurna Pictures, Plan B Entertainment, PASTEL, released 2018. DVD: Twentieth Century Studios (2019, USA). Start time: 01:09:00.

15 *Midsommar*. Directed by Ari Aster, Cinematography by Pawel Pogorzelski. A24, B-Reel Films, Nordisk Film, Square Peg, released 2019. DVD: A24 Films, LLC, Lions Gate Entertainment (2020, USA). Start time: 02:04:30.

16 *Michael Clayton*. Directed by Tony Gilroy, Cinematography by Robert Elswit. Samuels Media, Castle Rock Entertainment, Mirage Enterprises, released 2007. DVD: Warner Bros. Home Video (2008, USA). Start time: 00:13:25.

17 *The Shawshank Redemption*. Ibid. Start time: 00:08:43.

18 *Midsommar*. Ibid. Start time: 00:28:52.

19 *The Girl with the Dragon Tattoo*. Directed by David Fincher, Cinematography by Darius Khondji. Columbia Pictures, MGM, Scott Rudin Productions, released 2011. DVD: Sony Pictures Home Entertainment (2012, USA). Start time: 01:16:39.

20 *Altered States*. Ibid. Start time: 00:57:01.

21 *The Silence of the Lambs*. Ibid. Start time: 00:19:18.

Chapter 13
Scene shaping and interconnections

Scene shaping through cinematic means

We've gone over the six underlying patterns associated with the visible elements in the script: Character Actions, Looks, Dialogue, Settings, Objects, and Evocative Imagery. Everything in the script that can be seen by the audience will fall into one of these categories. That's what we point the camera at. The way we point it – the qualities of the framing – provides contextual cues that help the audience understand and assess what they see. Each visible element is associated with framing patterns that the audience responds to unconsciously. That's what helps the audience *feel* the story and its progression.

We've also discussed how movement works with framing and patterns to add another layer of contextual depth. Framing qualities and patterns, combined with movement, provide the cinematic context for the storytelling. Like riding the current of a river around the bend, through the rapids, and into calm waters, the audience rides this cinematic context through time.

Creative control of this cinematic context will help the audience build story meaning in their own minds, tapping into their mostly unconscious understanding of the film "language" they've known since childhood. Importantly, context-sensitive framing and movement supports nuanced performances. Like the sense of leaning into a curve, the cinematic context leans into strong and complex emotions, amplifying attention without competing or distracting.

Metaphorically, this is like communicating with words, using preexisting components, rules, and guidelines to convey new ideas. Or like music, where we don't need new notes to create a new melody. We just need to make appropriate selections, adjustments, and combinations of the elements to create exciting and entirely new creative expressions.

Consistency, modulation, and change shape our experience

Let's think about music for a moment and how we feel the shape of a song, going from verse to chorus. Repetition – consistency – lets us know that we are in one phase of the song. Adjustments and modulations – smaller

DOI: 10.4324/9781003080657-13

changes in repetitive patterns – give us the sense of impending change and anticipation. Major changes, such as from verse to chorus, tell us we have broken through into a new phase. Energy rises and falls (just like story action). We are aware of beginning, middle, and end. Cinematic storytelling is like music. **Consistency, modulation, and change shape the cinematic storytelling.**

Framing equals story attention. Cinematic storytelling is shaping that attention – through the framing across time – so that the audience is taken along for the ride. Framing tells us who or what has story importance from moment to moment. Common underlying patterns of framing and movement give us the context needed to understand and assess what we see.

Consistency: The basic employment of patterns shapes audience understanding. The Look/See pattern tells us that the character sees the waterfall. The shot-and-reverse pattern tells us that characters are talking to each other. Careful and selective application of patterns allows the audience to instantly understand things such as non-verbal communication between characters.

Modulation: Variables within patterns fine-tune and adjust this context through time. Modulations of the pattern variables and qualities give subtle support that shapes audience understanding. When a character's inner turmoil is paramount, we pay attention to facial expressions without distraction – a close-up. When one character hurts another character's feelings, their sudden emotional distance can be felt by going to more distant shot pairs.

Change: Complete alterations of framing qualities and patterns contextually alert the audience to story progress. We feel changes in patterns and major alterations in framing qualities or movement. When these changes are in synch with the storytelling, we feel story progress more vividly. This type of major change can happen incrementally – from one shot to the next – or through evolving change of the framing qualities using movement.

Scene shaping depends on only three patterns

The patterns for Settings, Actions, and Dialogue form the backbone of cinematic structure. Those are the patterns that carry story progress across time, and therefore become the patterns we will rely on to shape a scene through consistency, modulation, and change.

The other elements provide moments – a Look, an Object, or Evocative Imagery. Moments are important in the storytelling, but they are nested within the overall structure and the unstoppable flow of time. The structuring patterns for Settings, Actions, and Dialogue are like the cookie dough, and the nested patterns are like raisins or chocolate chips.

Because most of the time on screen is devoted to characters and their story, the majority of scene shaping employs just the patterns for Action and Dialogue.

Cinematic shaping across multiple scenes

To examine the questions of scene shaping, let's look at three scenes in a sequence from *His Dark Materials*,[1] a long-form, multi-episode narrative. This extended example is from the third episode of season one.

Our examples up until now have come from feature films. I see no functional difference to the cinematic storytelling within short films, feature films, or long-form multi-episode stories. Our job is to help tell the story with pictures. The script will account for whether there are many acts or just one; whether there are multiple, intertwined stories or just one; and so on. By following the script, the same cinematic storytelling approach works across the board.

We will be looking at how the use of keyframe patterns and movement present story information in context, so that the audience feels and grasps the flow of story progress. When the story is in one phase, the cinematic context remains consistent. As the action rises and falls, contextual cues are modulated. When a story change happens, pushing the scene forward into a new phase, the patterns and framing qualities change. Because these are contiguous scenes, we can examine how that same process works from scene to scene, shaping how the audience feels storytelling connections from one scene to the next.

Within this example, the orphaned and hunted Lyra is being protected by Ma Costa. She is keeping Lyra hidden from authorities and the evil Mrs. Coulter, who heads a kidnapping ring.

Scene interconnection through sustained action pattern

The first part of our example (Figure 13.1) begins with two keyframes from a scene where Lyra is forced into hiding from the authorities. When the coast is clear, Ma Costa releases her, and Lyra bolts. This is handled as sequential action from one scene to the next. Lyra exits the frame, moving from left to right. Respecting an imaginary 180° Line, we follow Lyra outside, entering frame left, heading to the right. This continuation of pattern and character creates a hard connection from one scene to the next.

This makes the action feel continuous. It blows past the time and space needed for Lyra to exit her hiding place, go up on deck, leave the boat, etc. The story action follows her impulse directly, across an ellipsis of time and space. Despite the change in setting, we understand that she bolts from her hiding place to get out into the free air. Ignoring the moments that we do not see, we know that her emotional state is continuous.

Emphasizing the emotional force behind Lyra's movement, the stable frames in the hiding place are replaced by handheld camera that externalizes her agitation. The visible story information is the declarative part – Lyra running away. By sustaining attention on the subject and using left-to-right movement from hiding place to open air, it feels as if there were no scene boundary at all. This continuity of context makes it emotionally continuous. The modulations from stable to shifting frames, and from close to farther distant, help us feel rising tension, supporting the performances.

Figure 13.1

Action takes us from Lyra's hiding place to her escape. Ma Costa chases her, and they argue across a well-placed divide.

When Lyra learns the identity of her real mother, she runs. Action leads us in and out of Dialogue.

Throughout, handheld framing externalizes Lyra's sense of her destabilizing self.

Shaping the first phase of a big dialogue scene

We follow behind Lyra as she runs across a rickety plank bridging a creek. Looking back, we find Ma Costa chasing her. The changes in proximity to Ma Costa let us know she's catching up, but she stops on the other side of this divide, signaling the end of the chase.

From an observational perspective, we see the gulf between them, enabling us to grasp their physical proximity and its influence on how we understand the dynamic between them. We see each character in frames that connect them in classic shot-and-reverse reciprocal frames. Action has become Dialogue. They share keyframe characteristics, mirror-imaged. Social presentation proximity permits important gestures to be seen. We feel this shifting from action to interaction − inferential story information supported through change in keyframes and patterns.

We can know, through observation, that characters are physically distant, but their Dialogue keyframes suggest closer emotional proximity. The conflict is intimate and intense. We accept and blend the dueling inferences of distance and closeness, helping us feel this complicated relationship. The cinematic storytelling gives us the declarative information − they're talking now − while supporting a complicated understanding of their fraying relationship.

Respecting the 180° Line keeps Ma Costa frame left and Lyra frame right. This sustained orientation allows us to concentrate on their interaction. The continued use of handheld camera sustains the underlying emotional agitation. In the actual clip, we are reminded of the gulf between them through return to that wide two-shot between the Dialogue frame pairs. Consistency in the keyframes and contextual cues sustain a phase of the storytelling.

Ma Costa decides to tell the truth to a distraught and mistrustful Lyra − the evil Mrs. Coulter is Lyra's birth mother. Lyra, stunned and disbelieving, runs away. We are back into Action patterns and we feel that the story has progressed to a new phase, precisely because we have changed the pattern.

The second phase brings pattern and movement change

After Lyra turns and runs from the truth, Ma Costa crosses the bridge dividing them and catches up (Figure 13.2). In a classic move that converts Action to Dialogue pattern, she steps in front of Lyra and into OTS framing. This reverses their relative screen positions, firmly establishing this as a new phase of the scene, which helps us feel the story progress.

There is a metaphoric sense to Ma Costa approaching Lyra from a different angle. That helps to explain how it works cinematically. But more important than any metaphor is the plain sensory fact of the images being different, and the characters being oriented toward each other differently. We don't need to provide visual metaphors − we need to provide visual change that will be apprehended without thought, just as it is in real life. The audience feels the difference, and that supports the inferences within the story. The cinematic storytelling does not and cannot provide one

Figure 13.2

The next phase begins with Ma Costa crossing the bridge to reach Lyra. We are also on the other side of their Dialogue pairs. Frames continuously evolve. Realizations of betrayal, love, and destiny are supported by the fluid and shifting perspectives. Action flows in and out of Dialogue, to track the storytelling.

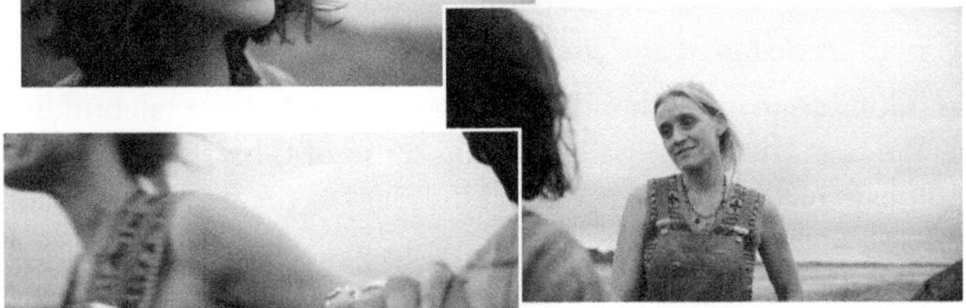

Lyra is left to sort out her feelings. Her nemesis is her mother. Lyra's internal Look leads to Mrs. Coulter.

specific inference – it provides visual cues that support the feeling that story inferences are happening. The story itself provides the meaning of the inferences. The camera just says, "Look here – feel how something has changed."

The framing is reciprocated to form shot-and-reverse Dialogue pairs. Not only have the characters swapped sides of the frame, but there are differences in movement that continuously shift both perspective and proximity. These fluid changes in keyframe qualities feel like we can't land somewhere stable, just like Lyra.

More active camera usage plays a role in feeling the degree to which Lyra's world and identity are completely destabilized. We are now connecting more closely and deeply with her internal state and subjective experience by moving past social presentation to closer framing. Gestures take a back seat to Lyra's realizations. The framing features multiple shifts from single to compound subject, from observing to connecting, as Ma Costa delivers a massive load of story information. Framing anchored on Lyra is continuously changing, helping the audience to absorb a ton of story exposition from inside Lyra's subjective experience. Intense emotions coupled with the moving target of unstable framing provide a dramatic context. This makes the tale of Lyra's birth and upbringing both more meaningful and easier to swallow.

This second phase of the scene ends with Ma Costa's loving hand on Lyra's shoulder, supportive but giving her the space to sort out her emotions. Lyra turns, and we push in to fully register her thoughts, feelings, and emotions as the situation drives in on her. Lyra's gaze becomes internal. We know she is thinking of her mother, the evil Mrs. Coulter, and this provides us with a "soft" connection to the next scene, different from the hard connection of continuous action at the start of the scene. Lyra's internal gaze leads us to Mrs. Coulter, in an emotional chain of C&E.

Witnessing gives us distance and judgment

We see Mrs. Coulter, drink in hand, walking on the edge of a tall building (Figure 13.3). We start the scene with a strong sense of Observation from a high angle and relatively distant proximity. This gives us the bodily sensation of great height and fear of falling.

In this fantasy world, characters have a "daemon" – an animal that is inseparable from them, representing their inner self. In this scene, Mrs. Coulter's daemon anxiously watches her precarious act. Death for Mrs. Coulter means death for the daemon, too.

Even when we are in front of Mrs. Coulter, it is from a distance to see the bodily effect of momentary losses of balance. The net effect of all the observation – the witnessing – is for us to judge the risk of flirting with self-destruction and condemn it.

This is an Action/activity scene that uses a subset of perspectives – mostly Observation – to provide a context that supports the inferences of the actions. Initially, it is supporting a sense of judgment of foolish and potentially catastrophic risk.

Figure 13.3

Mrs. Coulter teeters on the edge of a building and a moral choice. Her daemon watches anxiously. So do we.

We feel the height. See her lose balance. We judge the foolish risk.

She sits on the edge, opens a locked box. We see the focus of her attention – spy flies.

We see her intent gaze, then follow the chain of C&E as she puts the evil devices on Lyra's dress.

Here we have witnessed her disregarding consequences. We have seen the reaction of the bystander – her own inner self, or daemon – to this foolhardy behavior. The daemon's Look provides its reaction, in effect a self-condemnation. We bring that judgment to her eventual CU, where we see greed and fascination.

In addition to the Look of her daemon anxiously watching Mrs. Coulter walk the edge, we have Mrs. Coulter's Look that introduces story-significant Objects – spy flies. The detailed and close coverage aligns with Mrs. Coulter's fascination and obsession with these forbidden Objects. Seated precariously on the edge, we see her place the spy fly tracking devices on Lyra's party dress. We just experienced an emotionally devastating scene with Lyra, and now we know that she is in more danger. We have emotionally connected with Lyra, and we have observed Mrs. Coulter's madness. We know whose side we're on. We have not just empathized with Lyra's situation, but we have felt the connection that binds her to Mrs. Coulter through the cinematic storytelling.

Mrs. Coulter balancing on the edge functions well as a metaphor. The framing qualities help us feel it, supporting the metaphorical inferences. The encouragement of vertigo through framing gives us vicarious unease. The cinematic storytelling encourages judgment through observation, distance, and the Looks of her daemon. We share her fascination with the spy fly Objects. This all brings strong support to the characterization of Mrs. Coulter as someone whose actions we must assess and judge.

Without the initial restraint of distant witnessing, the scene would not feel this way. Without the kinesthetic component of physical danger, we wouldn't feel the consequences. Without the detailed CUs of the spy flies, we wouldn't note their significance to her and subsequently their place in the story as the plot unfolds. All of this is executed through stable and controlled framing. This is in direct contrast to the externalization of Lyra's agitation.

Progress within this scene is incremental, with one piece of information building on the next. This is in contrast to the previous scene, where fluid and evolving framing intermingles with the incremental nature of shot-and-reverse Dialogue pairs, giving us a sense of growing and ratcheting realizations.

In this three-scene example, the cinematic storytelling shapes each scene and provides important contextual cues that lead the audience to feel that one scene connects to the next. We feel the first and second scenes as one block of continuous action, with hard connections through subject, pattern, and movement. Between the second and third scene, we feel the soft connection of the inner Look by Lyra to seeing Mrs. Coulter.

Handling settings in our three-scene example

Throughout this three-scene example, the Settings have been functional background. The first Setting is Lyra's claustrophobic hiding place. The second Setting is the empty marshland, with derelict and rotting boats littering the channel beyond. It serves to "air out" the intense emotions and provides space for her to reach the truth about her past. The third Setting is Mrs. Coulter's high balcony. It provides a precarious perch of splendid isolation and danger and characterization of Mrs. Coulter as someone who toys with life.

All three Settings serve the emotions and structure how we understand story inferences. None demand specific coverage in order to understand their contribution to the story. Because each scene flows into the next, through hard and then soft continuations, it would be counterproductive to interrupt the flow with establishing shots as chapter markers.

Moving from example to general usage

In our three-part example, we have seen cinematic storytelling with free and creative usage of keyframe patterns and movement. These are used to shape individual scenes for dramatic purpose and to form meaningful interconnections between adjacent scenes. This is the framework of cinematic storytelling.

Consistency of patterns and movement allows the audience to "keep their place" in the story. Modulations or subtle variations in the coverage provide nuance and support movement toward the central dramatic beats of a scene. Changes in the coverage signal story progress to a new phase and new dramatic beat of the scene.

The visible story elements and patterns that enable scene shaping are Action, Dialogue, and Settings, with Settings only used as needed. Action patterns seamlessly lead into and out of Dialogue. Modulations of the shot-and-reverse reciprocal pairs of Dialogue will support rising and falling action within the scene. Looks and Objects nest within these overall structuring patterns.

The boundaries between scenes can be considered in terms of hard or soft continuation or in terms of reset or disconnection. A hard continuation feels like continuous action and is accomplished through continuity of pattern, movement, and character. A soft continuation feels like an answer to a character's internal state in the chain of emotional C&E or like a continuation of undercurrents that exist in new form in the next scene.

There could also be discontinuations between adjacent scenes, which we did not see in the three-scene example. A simple chapter marker of Settings – the conventional establishing shot – can serve as a reset and reorienting to move from one story thread to the next. An extensive break in the action through Settings coverage or Evocative Imagery will signal big story changes like Act breaks or serve as the emotional reverberation chamber for a life-changing story event.

The next step will be process oriented

Chapter 14 will look at how to analyze a scripted scene, identify elements, and work out a coverage plan that describes cinematic storytelling intentions. It is from the coverage plan that we will finally emerge with a shot list. It will be a resilient shot list, because it will be backed up by the coverage plan. With that process in hand, you will be equipped to tackle projects of any length.

Summary

- Consistency, modulation, and change in patterns and movement shape the context and help the audience follow story progress and meaning.
- The patterns associated with Action, Dialogue, and Settings provide the extensible structure to enable scene shaping. The patterns for Looks, Objects, and Evocative Imagery nest inside or between these three structuring patterns.
- Action patterns provide the means to flow into and out of Dialogue patterns at will.
- The visible, physical chain of C&E is central to shaping physical Action.
- The felt chain of emotional C&E is central to shaping interactions and the connections between scenes.
- In Action scenes, the 180° Line of Continuity becomes a matter of consistent presentation from one side of the action, plus the front (Connection) for reactions and behind (Participation) for shared experience. Switching sides can effectively segment the action.
- Sometimes it can serve the story best to use only a subset of perspectives and angles, proximity, and shot size.
- The feeling of incremental story progression comes from individual shots intended to be cut together in editing. The feeling of evolving story progress comes from using movement of and within the frame to create a continuous shot from a series of keyframes strung together.
- Shaping Dialogue scenes will likely focus on just a few variables to avoid competing with or undermining performances. One major variable relates to choices between symmetrical or asymmetrical shot pairs, through selective angle and proximity. The other major variable is the incorporation of movement, which can compete with interactions if not fully integrated with the emotional content of the scene or externalization of character state.
- Shot-and-reverse pairs can use the same keyframe qualities, mirror-imaged, or variations that provide nuanced contextual support of inter-action dynamics.
- Movement of the frame or within the frame is a fluid way to feel flow, trajectory, and rising energy within a scene. Cessation of movement can drop the energy level. Unstable framing can provide a more subjective experience and a way to convey emotional intensity.
- The tools of cinematic storytelling lend their weight – the shaping of visual attention – to whatever is within the story. All of the specific meanings come from the script and performance. Cinematic storytelling

is providing a context-rich presentation, the specific content and meaning of which is derived from the script. This is why it works for different stories.

- The strength of the emotional arc of a scene, and between scenes, can be amplified or dampened by cinematic choices. Sensitive cinematic choices can boost the intensity of emotional performance, bringing the audience to tears. Clinical cinematic choices can emotionally distance the audience from characters and events to be judged.

What you can do . . .

Take a new look at one of your favorite movies . . .

- Fast-forward to scene boundaries and look at a series of connections. Find places where scenes disconnect, have soft connections that feel emotive, or have hard connections where action feels continuous.
- What cinematic storytelling mechanisms were used on either side of the scene boundary?
- Examine one longer scene with intense Dialogue that contains important story points. What cinematic storytelling mechanisms were used to shape the scene? Could you tell when the interaction was in a new phase? How?
- Did that long Dialogue scene begin with Dialogue patterns? If not, how did they enter the shot-and-reverse pairs central to Dialogue? Did the patterns modulate, getting tighter or wider, or shift angle? Was movement used at any point, either for modulation or for a complete change in patterns? Did characters shift screen location at any time, or swap left and right sides of the frame? How was that accomplished? Did the shifts tie to your feeling of story progress, of moving on to a new phase?
- Find an Action scene or sequence. Were all three perspectives used (Observation, Participation, and Connection)? Or was a subset used? If so, what was the effect? Were there any phases to this scene that you felt made the story progress? How were those accomplished cinematically?

Note

1 *His Dark Materials*, S1E3. Directed by Dawn Shadforth, Cinematography by Suzie Lavelle. Bad Wolf, British Broadcasting Corporation (BBC), Home Box Office (HBO), Warner Bros., released on streaming, 2019. DVD: Warner Bros. Home Entertainment (2020, USA). Start time: 00:25:50.

Chapter 14
Developing the coverage plan

The process of coverage plan development

Through analyzing existing films, we get a sense of how cinematic means support and shape the visual presentation of unique and individual stories. Keyframes and patterns direct audience attention to story significance in a context-rich presentation. Cinematic storytelling synchronizes with performances as each scene unfolds and as one scene interconnects with the next.

Our next step is to model the process of going from a script, to a coverage plan, to a shot list. We'll use a scripted example of modest length for practicality but will extend and generalize the process and decision making, so that it can be applied to complete stories.

Breakdowns identify story structure at three levels

Each filmmaking role has its own specialized ways of extracting information from a script to do their art and craft. This extraction of information, inference, and consequences of the script is called a **breakdown**. Directors will make numerous breakdowns for all the different concerns and layers of storytelling, performance, and production. It is their interpretation of the script that guides the process. They are responsible for the storytelling. Cinematographers will also break down the script for the concerns of lighting, camera, and lenses that will mold and support the storytelling in a compelling manner. They are responsible for the pictures. A successful outcome depends on their collaboration in the cinematic storytelling. Standard breakdowns are preliminary steps that will inform the development of a coverage plan.

Total arc of the story

A breakdown of the total story arc will inform all scene-to-scene interconnections so that the cinematic storytelling can match and strengthen the broad strokes. Knowing the big arcs of the story will give you confidence in your scene entries and exits. When a script has an explicit act structure with clear segmentation of the storytelling, it is relatively easy to know where major resets and reorientation occur. But many scripts will not have such handy bright-line segmentation. You may need to do this yourself.

DOI: 10.4324/9781003080657-14

Most short scripts will be one continuous rush to conclusion – a single segment. Feature films may be in three or more acts. Some may feel like a continuous flow of events without subdivision. Long-form storytelling may have an arc within each episode, tying to a longer arc across a season. Some stories may have a stately, novelistic quality of chapters in sequence, adding up to the total arc. Others may split at some midway point of no return. There is no need to impose an artificial segmentation, only to discern how the audience will experience the storytelling at its ideal best.

Cinematic storytelling must respect the big story arc and support it. If the coverage and scene-to-scene transitions are not aligned with this, the picture can feel flat and the dynamic of the performances can be squashed.

The broad shape of each scene

The breakdown of each scene for dramatic beats – the inflection points of the story – will be your guide for scene shaping through cinematic means. There may be one, two, three, or more major beats within the scene depending on its length and ambition.

Coverage decisions will be organized around a clear idea of how the scene is segmented into phases, to support these major scene beats. Targeting the cinematic needs for each phase will productively limit the number of options, keeping the process manageable while serving the storytelling. Consistency of keyframes and pattern is what visually sustains a phase. Modulation of keyframes and patterns supports the move toward the next phase. Changes in these help the audience feel that the story has moved into a new phase – story progress. This story progress has to exist in the script. You can't conjure it up with the cinematic storytelling, but you can definitely support it.

The point-by-point beats within the scene

There will likely be more performance beats than scene beats. There could be one with every line of the script. This granular level of analysis will inform decisions on the nuanced modulations and variations of patterns within an overall phase of the scene. You might choose sustained and steady keyframe patterns, so that the performances have undivided attention. Or you may choose to amplify attention to understated or psychologically interior performances, or to support conventional subtext within Dialogue. This is akin to helping the audience listen carefully. Cinematic tracking of the performance beats can feel very organic if used with restraint. Like soundtrack, if the camera work becomes intrusive or excessively leading of emotions, it can undermine performance.

A cinematic approach divides the visible from all else

The visible elements and subject matter are declarative. Everything else conveyed through perspective or angle, proximity or shot size, stasis or movement, assists in conveying inferential story information. Cinematic mechanisms point toward interpretations of meaning within the script.

Filmmakers contemplating performances and the dramatic arts might think in terms of surface action and subtext. Switching gears to a cinematic storytelling mode, that same kind of thinking applies but in a purely visual sense. The six visible elements within a script – the basis of our coverage patterns – are all conveying declarative story information. These elements are literally what can be seen, arranged into story-information categories.

The benefit of keeping standard dramatic analysis and cinematic analysis in separate lanes, using different terms, is so that we don't confuse or conflate the cinematic means with the story meaning. A character's Look is declarative, because we can plainly see it. If it's part of a Look/See pair with a car accident, you might say it points toward the surface action of physical C&E. But if it's part of an inner Look/See pair that connects their feelings to a future love interest, you might say it points toward the subtext of emotional C&E. The derived meaning of everything realized in the audience's imagination – C&E in the plot, conventional subtext, inducement of kinesthesia, etc. – is all inferential from a cinematic viewpoint. The cinematic storytelling is at the service of dramatic interpretation, not a substitute for it.

The declarative and inferential story information add together, through a context-rich presentation that delivers both. This helps the audience to feel the storytelling, without any need for conscious thought or interruption to the flow of emotional responses.

The coverage plan is central to principal photography

The coverage plan is like an electric wire. One end plugs into the script, and the other end plugs into what will be seen. The story energy flows through it. This makes the coverage plan – even more than the resulting shot list – the central organizing plan for principal photography.

The coverage plan is the "origin story" of cinematic intention. The keyframe qualities lie beneath the exact specifics of composition and lighting. A shot list is derived from it. If and when some shot isn't feasible during production, it will be through a return to the coverage plan that new shots can be invented that sustain the cinematic storytelling intent. This provides resilience on set, when pressures can be intense. This is what prevents the arbitrary or mechanical from creeping into the coverage.

Working through the process at the scene level

We are going to work through an eight-step process with a scene example. The first steps employ the fruits of standard script breakdowns and dramatic analysis. Then we transition from all that is defined by the script, or interpreted from the script, to the cinematic decision making of a coverage plan. We will follow the process of making keyframe decisions, planning camera work to troubleshoot execution, and arriving at a shot list. After that, we will summarize these steps as a general process for working scene by scene, and through scene-to-scene interconnections.

Let's bring this approach to an example of a scripted scene.

```
INT. FARMHOUSE OF KATHLEEN & BRENDAN - NIGHT

Urgent BANGING on the sturdy wooden plank door.

KATHLEEN (51), in her nightdress, runs to open it. She
is a wiry and plain woman, with a thin face hardened by
years of work and worry.

Her husband, BRENDAN (53), follows close on her heels.
Balding and jowly, his aging body is fleshy on top of the
muscles of a farmer.

Kathleen opens the door and sees Rose on the threshold, cloak
wrapped around her shivering eight-year-old girl, SIOBHÁN.

                        KATHLEEN
            Great Mother! Come in, come in.

As soon as Rose and Siobhán enter, Brendan goes to the
door and looks out. Nothing.

A small part of tension leaves his body, and he closes
the door, putting a little-used crossbar in place.

                        ROSE
            We've been burnt. Legacies.
            They got my workshop.

Brendan lights a lantern.

                        BRENDAN
            The house?

                        ROSE
            No. I don't know. We ran.

Kathleen drops to Siobhán's level and strokes her hair.

                        KATHLEEN
            You're safe here.
                (to Brendan)
            They can stay in Fergus's room.

                        BRENDAN
            Of course.
                (to Rose)
            I'll go back with you tomorrow.

                        ROSE
            Thank you, both. I miss my Donal.

                        BRENDAN
            We all do. Rest now. We'll keep watch.

Rose kisses her daughter on the top of the head and
leads her to the stairs.
Brendan sits heavily at the table. Kathleen joins him,
watching until the child disappears up the stairs.
```

                    KATHLEEN
                 (to Brendan)
              Those bastards.

                    BRENDAN
          They're just fools. Probably drunk.

        Kathleen gives him a sharp look.

                    BRENDAN (cont'd)
              Justice will be done.

                    KATHLEEN
          So you say. What's the damn point
          of our son joining the Guard, if he
          sits on cushions in the Capital? He
          should be here.

        Brendan stiffens.

                    BRENDAN
          I'm sure he's engaged in important
          work.
                                   DISSOLVE TO:

Step 1: Segmenting the scene into phases

The first step in breaking down a script for cinematic storytelling is to mark the major beats and demarcate the major phases of the scene. That defines the general shape. We will use the segmentation into phases as a way to reach two goals. The first is to understand the scene in broad strokes. The second is to break the task into manageable segments.

This scene works in three phases. Draw a line in the margins at the end of each phase.

- The first phase is the sudden waking to the arrival of neighbors in crisis. It lasts until Brendan bars the door.
- The second phase is the confirmation of what happened, with implications about the rural reliance on distant neighbors, the shared understanding of the threat, and the household of Kathleen and Brendan. It lasts until the guests go upstairs.
- The third phase is Kathleen and Brendan talking about events and implications. This links these troubles and threats to their son, whose absence provides the empty room for Rose. It reveals a rift between them about the choices made by their son. This closes out the scene.

Step 2: What the audience needs to know

In order to reduce the scene to a list of what the audience needs to know, conclude, and question, we need to do some story and character analysis. We will gloss over some of the dramatic analysis in order to focus on the main points in regard to cinematic storytelling.

Overall impressions

In terms of character, the scene feels aligned with Kathleen. This has implications in terms of who may be most prominent and in terms of story agency that may motivate movement. Brendan is more cautious and reactive. They work together as a rule, assuming separate roles that reflect their personalities, and only disagree in private. They come across as an old married couple. This means that they have a solid relationship that could be at stake.

In terms of plot, we pick up the chain of C&E from the last scene of the arson. Rose's arrival brings knowledge of this violence to Kathleen and Brendan. We learn of Rose's status as a widow. We infer the shared understanding of threat from Legacies as one axis of story conflict. The second axis of story conflict is implied as a rural/urban split. This comes home to roost with Kathleen and Brendan, whose grown son is in the city, presumably protecting city folk, and not at home. This is a bone of contention in the household.

Storytelling in Phase 1

We begin with an image of the door, the source of the BANGING that wakes the owners. We are meeting Kathleen and Brendan for the first time, known by the ALL CAPS names and first visual impression of the characters. Character introductions are always a consideration in designing coverage. Kathleen is in the lead.

Circle the Look when Kathleen sees who is at the door and registers their physical and emotional state. Her reaction is clear through her words, so we may not need to see her Look. Brendan checks that the coast is clear. Circle his Look. His reaction would provide us with the clarification that no impending danger is close at hand, which might not be crystal clear otherwise. The crossbar for the door is an Object, so underline that. But it is purely functional, so it could be seen in use by Brendan and not demand any special, additional coverage.

We are identifying visible elements that may play a role in the coverage, not yet deciding what to do with them. If audience story comprehension depends on Looks and Objects, they may need to be part of the coverage plan. If the implications are clear without special attention, they can be part of the overall action.

The prior scene introduced Rose, so the audience will recognize her. The daughter, Siobhán, is seen for the first time. Her current function is to personify what needs protecting.

Storytelling in Phase 2

The second phase of the scene is interaction that delivers exposition and raises useful story questions. The prior scene showed the thugs committing arson, so Rose is recapping the events for Kathleen and Brendan, not for us. Their comprehension leads us to conclude that they share common knowledge. It implies that this is not an isolated incident.

Kathleen, Rose, and the child are the center of the interaction. Brendan takes part while busying himself along the periphery. Brendan is using fire to light a lantern when Rose talks of arson. That may be useful resonance or simply background.

When Kathleen drops down to reassure Siobhán, she is also reassuring Rose.

Rose and her daughter are offered refuge by Kathleen, who informs rather than asks Brendan. This is both taking control and indicative of tacit understanding between them. She offers an empty room, raising initial questions about Fergus and why he is not there.

Rose provides backstory references that let us picture her circumstances and infer a chain of C&E. Loss of a partner makes Rose vulnerable, leading to victimization and to this moment. This phase demonstrates that these rural folks look out for each other.

Brendan's promise of returning with Rose to her homestead raises the question of what will be found. As with all story questions, the need for answers pulls us along, providing anticipation.

Rose's kiss on her daughter's head feels incidental. On the page, it reminds us of maternal care, but actually seeing mother and child together will be more emotionally powerful.

Brendan sits at the table, which is described in terms of his physical reaction. This punctuates the end of activity. Rose and Siobhán's move to the stairs is a social cue that closes out this second phase.

Storytelling in Phase 3

The third phase gives us characterization and exposition and raises useful questions.

With the child out of earshot, Kathleen can vent. Brendan is right that the thugs were drunken fools. We saw it in the prior scene. That lends credibility.

We learn that their son, Fergus, moved away to the big city to join some type of police force. Kathleen implies that the events of the night could have been prevented by force, while Brendan believes in the letter of the law.

When Kathleen attacks the choice Fergus made, Brendan is defensive. This implies that the family plays out a rural/urban split through their son, which is a wedge between them.

This is all conveyed through interpersonal interaction and conventional use of subtext.

Point-by-point summary of the storytelling

- Banging on the door wakes KATHLEEN and BRENDAN.
- Kathleen opens the door to see Rose, the victim of arson from the prior scene. She arrives with a young child, SIOBHÁN. Kathleen urges them in.
- Brendan confirms the coast is clear and bars the door for good measure. END PHASE 1.

- Rose recaps the attack. The death of Rose's husband is established. The bonds of rural life are demonstrated. An available empty room is established.
- Kathleen waits for Rose and Siobhán to go upstairs. END PHASE 2.
- Kathleen vents to Brendan about the attackers. Brendan pushes back that they are bad apples and will be subject to the rule of law. Kathleen scoffs.
- Kathleen gives us the pieces to figure out that their son, Fergus, is in the city, having joined the equivalent of a police force. This is clearly against her wishes.
- Brendan presumes, or hopes, that Fergus made a good decision. As we have been given proof of Brendan's accurate assessment of the arsonists, we may give him the benefit of the doubt. END PHASE 3.

Step 3: What is actually seen

The story analysis helps us understand overall scene shape, impressions of character and plot, and the point-by-point identification of what the audience needs to know. Now we can make the transformational step of determining what is actually seen – the declarative storytelling. This will target the visible elements by category, so we can provisionally assign patterns.

By the process of elimination, this will clarify how much story information is inferential. This includes the chains of physical and emotional C&E, all the indicators of characterization, and the subtext underneath the spoken words, plus all the story questions that fuel anticipation.

Point-by-point summary of what is seen in the script

These are numbered so that you can trace the correspondence of visible elements to the keyframes in the next step of the process.

1 The door. Object. Could be part of reverse Look/See.
2 Kathleen in front, Brendan behind. Action.
3 At the door, Rose and Siobhán. Action. Line of dialogue could be functional and not demand Dialogue pattern. Or Dialogue pattern could stem from Action for shot-and-reverse, from Kathleen's Look out the door.
4 Everyone inside. Action.
5 Brendan checks for threat. Look.
6 Door is barred. Action and Object.
7 Three-way interaction with Kathleen, Brendan, and Rose. Siobhán is glued to Rose. Dialogue, with functional 2 + 1 of Kathleen and Rose, Brendan peripheral. Kathleen drops to child's level. Action, which could lead to Dialogue shot-and-reverse pair with Siobhán.
8 Brendan lights the lantern. Action, Object. Could be background.
9 Rose and Siobhán exit. Action. Kathleen watches. Look, but inferences are not related to Rose, and so any special Look might interrupt the flow.

10   Brendan sits. Action. Kathleen joins. Action.
11   Kathleen and Brendan talk. Dialogue.

Now we have our distillation of what is actually visible and seen in the script. We also have the list of subject matter for planning on singular, compound, or plural framing.

We can begin to make some cinematic decisions.

Step 4: Keyframe qualities to align declarative and inferential

Let's consider what is off the table, so that we can focus on the decisions to be made.

We see nothing that demands Settings coverage. There is the door. It is like a bell being rung in alarm, so it functions like an Object. We need to decide if this door will be part of a Look/See pair with Kathleen.

There is no mention of the exterior of this isolated farmhouse, and no extensive descriptions of the interior. The Setting is purely functional and will work as background. We do not need Settings patterns.

There are numerous character Actions. We will consider those in terms of storytelling perspective and proximity. We will also consider subject as singular, compound, or plural.

There are Looks, which may or may not need to be brought to audience attention. If they are needed for story comprehension, they should be included.

There are two main sections of Dialogue. Phase 2 of the scene is a three-way Dialogue, and the application of a 2 + 1 scheme for pattern use is suggested by the way Kathleen is close to Rose, while Brendan moves about.

There is also Kathleen at Siobhán's level, which is not described as reciprocal – it could be an Action pattern – but we might want to see the emotions of the child. That suggests Dialogue.

The third and last phase of the scene is clearly Dialogue. If handled in shot-and-reverse pairs, we need to decide if they are mirror-image keyframe qualities, resulting in symmetrical pairs. We may decide that the storytelling is better served by shot pairs that are asymmetrical and thus need to make decisions on how they are imbalanced.

There is no imagery in the script, described purely for the mood or feeling conveyed. We do not need the Evocative Imagery pattern.

This clarifies what parts of our toolkit of patterns will be in use and what we can set aside. It is all Action, Dialogue, and perhaps one Look.

Next, we will consider a "wish list" of all keyframes that could fit our cinematic storytelling intentions, along with their qualities. After that, we will boil the list down to what is essential for the cinematic storytelling. We have limited time on screen to accomplish the storytelling while sustaining appropriate pacing.

The following is the end product of these types of decisions. The parts of a total wish list that don't merit keyframe coverage planning are noted, so you can track the correspondence of the point-by-point list from Step 3 to the chosen keyframe coverage plan. Everything written is seen, if only within the total action. The main points deserve keyframe status, organizing the coverage through story focus.

Keyframes of the coverage plan

The point-by-point summary is translated into representative frames, keeping the same numbering so you can follow their path. The highlight moments will form our keyframes. The less important actions that can be in the background are left out. Keyframes carry the essential story information.

A rough storyboard shows most of these frames (Figure 14.1). Each image has a reference to the keyframe number (KF#) corresponding to those listed next. Each image also has a reference to the camera position (CP) from the overhead diagram, described later on in Step 7.

Normally, I don't storyboard scenes, except when fellow filmmakers have trouble envisioning a frame. That is because I can understand these frames from the overhead diagrams, from extensive practice. If you want to storyboard your keyframes, include that in this step of the process. Even stick figures can be fine as a way to keep track of camera positions. If you do more complete renderings, as shown here, make sure that you or your storyboard artist has practical knowledge of lenses, so that you don't end up with "impossible" frames.

1) **Story:** Banging on the door. **Pattern:** Object. Start of reverse Look/ See.

2) **Story:** Household wakes in alarm, Kathleen in the lead. **Pattern:** Action. **Perspectives:** Observation, Connection. **Proximity:** Social for Kathleen, full body for Brendan. **Subject:** Singular on Kathleen, becomes compound with Brendan.

3) **Story:** Kathleen finds neighbors at the door, in distress. **Pattern:** Action. **Perspective:** Participate with Kathleen, becomes Connect to Rose and Siobhán past Kathleen. **Proximity:** Landing on Rose, Siobhán in full body/social presentation. **Subject:** Kathleen as singular becomes compound with revealing Rose, Siobhán past Kathleen.

   LEFT OUT: Kathleen's reaction at the door. It might slow down the action.

4) **Story:** Everyone inside. Brendan enters what was Kathleen's participation/ OTS frame, leans out to check for threat. **Pattern:** Action. **Perspective:** Participate. **Proximity:** Social/expressive. **Subject:** Plural of Rose, Siobhán, Kathleen exiting frame into house, becomes singular with Brendan.

5) **Story:** Brendan checks for threat. **Pattern:** Looks. **Subject:** Singular.

   LEFT OUT: Door is barred. If they were under active attack, this would be important. This can be background, as it signifies a lowering of prior tensions.

7) **Story:** Three-way interaction, with Kathleen, Brendan, and Rose. Siobhán is glued to Rose, making them an ongoing compound subject.

Figure 14.1

The first phase is Action, with Kathleen and Brendan being woken by baging and finding Rose and Siobhán. Brendan checks outside, then bars the door.

The second phase is three-way Dialogue with Kathleen, Siobhán, and Rose in a group, and Brendan off to the side.

The third phase is Dialogue, Kathleen and Brendan at the table.

Pattern: Dialogue, employing 2 + 1 of Kathleen and Rose, Brendan peripheral.

7a) **Story:** Kathleen drops to child's level. **Pattern:** Action. **Perspective:** Connect. Becomes Dialogue shot-and-reverse pair with Siobhán, and with Brendan. **Subject:** Compound, Kathleen OTS Siobhán.

7b) **Story:** Siobhán reassured. **Pattern:** Dialogue, other side of pair. **Subject:** Compound, Siobhán alongside Rose, OTS Kathleen.

7c) **Story:** Brendan's part of three-way interaction. **Pattern:** Dialogue to work as part of 2 + 1 strategy. **Subject:** Singular or compound. Let staging and blocking determine.

7d) **Story:** Rose's part of three-way interaction. **Pattern:** Dialogue to work as part of 2 + 1 strategy. **Subject:** Singular or compound. Let staging and blocking determine.

LEFT OUT: Brendan lights the lantern. Giving it special attention would interrupt the flow.

9) **Story:** Rose and Siobhán go upstairs. **Pattern:** Action. **Perspective:** Participate with Kathleen. **Subject:** Compound, Rose and Siobhán, OTS Kathleen.

LEFT OUT: Kathleen watches them go upstairs. She is simply waiting for them to leave.

LEFT OUT: Brendan sits. Doesn't merit special attention.

LEFT OUT: Kathleen joins him to sit at the table. We can see this in the flow of coverage.

11) **Story:** Kathleen and Brendan talk. **Pattern:** Dialogue, shot-and-reverse pair. Likely symmetrical, sharing one set of keyframe qualities. **Subject:** Singular/compound on Kathleen.

11a) **Story:** Kathleen and Brendan talk. **Pattern:** Dialogue, shot-and-reverse pair. Same keyframe qualities as Kathleen's. **Subject:** Singular/compound on Brendan.

Step 5: Decide qualities of movement

From this coverage plan, we have 13 individual keyframes. This is the foundation of the cinematic storytelling. Depending on choices of evolving versus incremental storytelling, this may result in fewer actual shots. Let's consider issues of movement in these terms.

The first phase of the scene feels like it should be evolving rather than incremental. The second phase of the scene is mostly interaction, and Dialogue is usually incremental unless you choose to avoid shot-and-reverse pairs.

The second phase should evolve into the third phase through Action, so it drops into the final Dialogue pairs. That will keep it part of a flow.

Kathleen is the character who demonstrates central story agency. When we follow action, or stay with a character on the move, it likely will be to stay with her. When we use movement to reframe on the total group, it likely will hinge on her movement. Brendan is the secondary choice for following action, if seen alone in frame.

Externalization of strong emotions or agitation would confuse the sense of finding refuge, so we will use some form of stabilization of the frame. This will likely be with a conventional dolly, as there are no stairs or other physical barriers that would demand some form of stabilization arm or servo-based camera mount.

Step 6: Scene-to-scene interconnections

The scene prior to our example ended with Rose yelling for her daughter to escape the fire. The sense of urgency is carried forward with the banging on the door. It is a straight chain of C&E. Therefore, a conventional establishing shot of the exterior would drop the energy level between these scenes, which would be detrimental. The script has accounted for the transition, which might not always be the case.

This scene is leading up to the introduction of the main character, Fergus. The audience will be putting together the pieces of exposition that lead to this: the empty room, Fergus's name, and Kathleen and Brendan's disagreement.

The last person talked about in this scene – Fergus – is the first person we see in the next. This is a standard script device. We may want to emphasize it through cinematic means. A push-in on Brendan feels too emphatic. We could simply have Brendan break his gaze from Kathleen at the end, to provide the sense of interior thought. That would be enough to register an internal Look/See pattern. This type of soft connection preserves the sense of story and emotion crossing the scene boundary.

The next scene will start with Fergus, as he rouses himself from the bed of his patrician lover. This will make Brendan's convictions ironic and let us know that Kathleen has a point. The scene-to-scene interconnection cinematically supports this inferred storytelling.

Step 7: Mapping out camera positions for keyframes

We can make plan view diagrams that identify the camera positions according to keyframes. These are commonly called overheads. Working out this type of overhead diagram is a good way to problem solve.

This coverage plan is designed for a conventional single-camera production process. One shot is executed at a time, so each can be the full focus of production efforts. Every camera position you see listed in Figure 14.2 is a different angle. Arrows show camera movements, when a continuous shot is moving through multiple keyframes, as from CP-1, to CP-2, to CP-3. The storyboard frames correlate to the camera positions on these overhead diagrams.

The four overhead diagrams (Figure 14.2, Figure 14.3) present the phases of the scene and make the camera position choices clear. Each camera position is abbreviated as CP. As this scene takes place in one contained location, it is practical to have a Master-CP that will capture all of the action. This is especially important in the second phase of the scene, when a three-way interaction is the central component, and for connecting to the third phase.

The Master-CP position is not significant for the first and third phases, but in any short- to medium-length scene it is prudent to have that overarching coverage, to permit the editor to smooth over unforeseen problems. As with any Master shot, this is primarily observation or witnessing the action, which is the initial level of audience vicarious engagement. We will describe the coverage from the Master-CP when we get to the second phase of the scene.

The dominant coverage for the first phase is based on active engagement with Kathleen, entering her subjective experience of the action, then handing off to Brendan. The first diagram (Phase 1.1) shows an unmotivated move that meets Kathleen after she comes down the stairs and pauses to see the door. This moment of arrival happens at CP-1. This will energize her action, through the rapid move from full body to a medium shot. Her introduction is dynamic. Brendan will land in the middle distance of this shot, instantly informing us of his role in the relationship. (This gives us keyframe #2.)

When she moves to the door, this becomes a motivated move, attached to Kathleen and participating with her experience. This ends on CP-2 in the overhead plan. When she opens the door to find Rose and Siobhán shivering on the threshold, we will be looking past her. (This gives us keyframe #3.) The dynamic move to Kathleen in CP-1, then from CP-1 to CP-2, provides an evolving sense of story progress to open the first phase of the scene, vicariously attached to her experience.

When Kathleen and the neighbors move into the house (Phase 1.2), they will clear that frame and Brendan will enter it. This is a hand-off through movement within the frame. He looks out to check that the coast is clear (giving us keyframe #4). The plan is also to include his Look so that we can connect with his reaction, lowering the tension and shaping the scene. It is listed as CP-9 on the diagram. Even though it is important, it is a lower priority, being the only shot from outside (providing keyframe #5). From the CP-2 camera, we will be able to cover the action of barring the door, and also see it from the Master-CP.

Sticking with this moving camera, we will stay with Brendan when he moves to a side table to light a lantern. This will dolly from CP-2 (Figure 14.2) to CP-3 (Figure 14.3), which is a social presentation framing of Brendan for the three-way Dialogue (providing keyframe #7c).

Backing up a bit in time, we will start to make substantial use of the Master-CP, moving into the room with Kathleen, Rose, and Siobhán (Phase 2.1). Now it is an active Master shot, and would include the door being shut and barred in the background (providing keyframe #7).

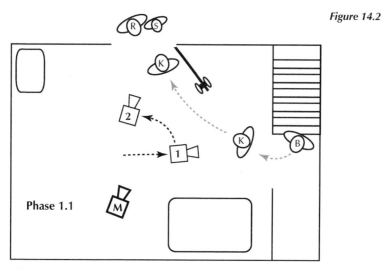

Figure 14.2

Phase 1.1: Kathleen and Brendan are woken. A Master-CP establishes a main axis. Camera pushes in on Kathleen to meet her at CP-1, then follow to the door as OTS at CP-2. Opening the door reveals Rose and Siobhán.

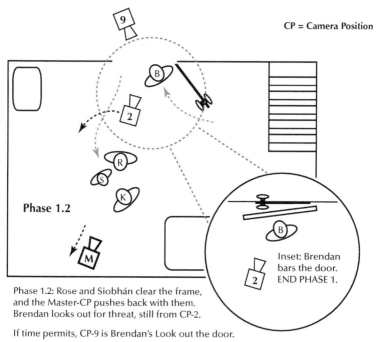

CP = Camera Position

Phase 1.2: Rose and Siobhán clear the frame, and the Master-CP pushes back with them. Brendan looks out for threat, still from CP-2.

If time permits, CP-9 is Brendan's Look out the door.

Inset: Brendan bars the door. END PHASE 1.

Figure 14.3

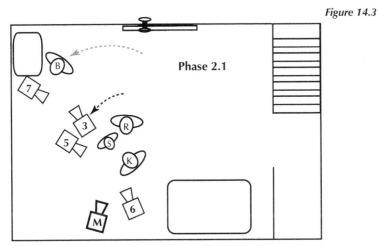

Phase 2.1: Three-way interaction, the Master-CP adjusts with Brendan's move. Coverage includes OTS shots of Kathleen from CP-5, and Siobhán from CP-6.

Brendan moves to light the lamp, followed with moving camera from the door at CP-2 to CP-3.

CP = Camera Position

Rose's dialogue to Brendan has reciprocal framing, CP-7.

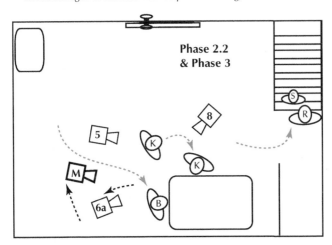

Phase 2.2: Rose and Siobhán go up the stairs OTS Kathleen from CP-5. Master-CP shifts with them, following Kathleen to the table. END PHASE 2.

Phase 3: CP-5 becomes two-shot. Brendan sits into frame. Camera pull back to re-set CP-6a, which becomes Kathleen OTS Brendan when she sits. CP-8 is Brendan OTS Kathleen.

Kathleen will drop down to enter the frame of CP-5, OTS Siobhán. (providing keyframe #7a). When she turns her head to address Brendan, we can read the shift in gaze clearly from this position. The shot-and-reverse pair is from CP-6, on Siobhán (providing keyframe #7b, not shown on the storyboard). Finishing up this interaction is CP-7 on Rose (providing keyframe #7d). This will be more distant social framing, as we want to keep more active engagement with the subjective experiences of Kathleen and Brendan.

When Rose and Siobhán go upstairs (Phase 2.2), we will cover it from CP-5. (This is keyframe #9, not in the storyboard.) We participate with Kathleen's experience by sharing the view past her, as she waits for them to be out of earshot. The Master-CP will also follow the pull of Rose and Siobhán to the stairs but stay anchored on Kathleen, then follow her to the table. This helps with the sense that the household pivots around her. It also gives the editor a choice of shots for transitioning from the guests going upstairs back to Kathleen and Brendan.

Now the Master-CP can follow Kathleen sitting (Phase 3). CP-5 camera will also pan over with Kathleen, sustaining our engagement with her. Brendan sits into these frames. This sets up the third phase of the scene, and clearly establishes the 180° Line for their Dialogue. What was CP-6 will dolly back to provide the angle on Kathleen, OTS Brendan (providing keyframe #11). Its mirror-image shot-and-reverse pair is CP-8 on Brendan, OTS Kathleen (providing keyframe #11a).

This diagonal staging keeps them from being directly oppositional. From that angle, we can clearly read Brendan's look away for his last line, shown in the last storyboard frame. That will help to emphasize the scene-to-scene connection that we wanted.

The only thing that is not on our overhead diagrams is the very opening shot of the door. This shot doesn't need the cast. Any member of the crew can bang on the door, from either CP-2 or CP-1. As long as the need for keyframe #1 is not forgotten, it is the easiest part of the coverage. We may also see it from the Master-CP, but it won't have the impact of a closer shot. With many ways to work around this, it seems safe to make it the last item.

These diagrams keep the action facing toward the door until we get into the shot-and-reverse pairs of Dialogue. This helps define the 180° Line and keeps the audience oriented.

Three-way Dialogue is always tricky, but we have it anchored by the 2 + 1 approach. The balanced and mirrored shot-and-reverse at the end helps to solidify the sense that Kathleen and Brendan are equal partners in their private life.

With the keyframes listed, and check-listed against our overhead diagram, we are ready to put the shot list down on paper. The shot list has more of a record-keeping function than being the center of creative efforts.

Step 8: From overhead diagram to the shot list

The shot list is the document that is used on set to check-list the coverage, making sure that everything necessary is completed. It is also arranged in order of priority. That way, if you run out of time, it is the lowest-priority coverage that is left over, to execute later or simply drop.

Shot list

1   Master of the whole scene, critical for the second phase, from Master-CP, covering all four characters. NOTES: This dollies back from the door with Kathleen, Rose, and Siobhán. Another small dolly move can keep it useful through the end of the scene. We only depend on it for the second phase, so there is no need for retakes if that section is good.

2   Entire first phase of the scene, from Kathleen and Brendan entering through arrival of Rose and Siobhán, to Brendan checking for threat and barring the door. CP-1 to CP-2. This continues through the second phase of the scene and Brendan's part in the three-way Dialogue, from CP-3. NOTES: This must be usable from the start until Brendan shuts the door. It doesn't need to be perfect through to CP-3, so any retakes on that section can start from the door.

3   Siobhán, OTS the kneeling Kathleen, from CP-6, for the second phase of the scene. This moves to CP-6a to become Kathleen OTS Brendan for the last phase of the scene at the table. NOTES: If it's not possible to light the whole room at once, CP-6a can be a separate shot.

4   Kathleen, OTS Siobhán from CP-5, for the second phase of the scene, continuing through to the scene's end. This is primarily for the three-way Dialogue, and for the exit up the stairs by Rose and Siobhán OTS Kathleen. NOTES: This will let us share her view and make the switch to sitting with Brendan clear and performance based.

5   Rose, for her lines to Brendan of the three-way Dialogue from CP-7.
     NOTE on SHOT ORDER: If we need to keep CP-6 and CP-6a as separate shots, we could shoot CP-6a here, before Brendan, OTS Kathleen.

6   Brendan, OTS Kathleen from CP-8, from him sitting into frame until he breaks her gaze at the end of the scene. NOTES: This is the first time we see this part of the room, so it is best to leave until the rest is complete. If CP-6a is a separate shot, this becomes shot #7.

7   Brendan's Look outside, from CP-9. NOTES: This is potentially a different lighting setup, only needing one character, so leaving it until the end is practical. If CP-6a is a separate shot, this becomes shot #8.

8   The door, as it is banged on from outside. NOTES: Whatever angle looks best. If we need to break CP-6a into its own shot, this would be shot #9.

Evolving story flow turns keyframes into beads on a string

Our overhead diagram and shot list contain shots that include multiple keyframes. There is the dynamic move to Kathleen in CP-1 with Brendan in the background, then with Kathleen from CP-1 to CP-2 to find Rose and Siobhán. This becomes Brendan's OTS shot, looking outside. This is what we mean by saying that keyframes can be like beads on a string. A single shot can pass through them, like a series of gates. This works well on set. Camera crews are all familiar with going from Position #1 to #2 to #3, etc. Using keyframes makes this transition from context-focus to shot-focus quite functional for moving camera shots, whether on a stabilized mount or handheld. In a shot list, static shots are very clear. Moving shots can be difficult to convey. Talking in keyframes provides clarity when communicating about moving camera shots.

Incremental story flow turns keyframes into individual shots

We've seen how Dialogue, with its shot-and-reverse patterning, provides story information in increments. Anytime you choose to have story progress tracked and modulated through the editing process, without movements that change framing qualities, you are providing story information incrementally. This turns individual keyframes into individual shots.

Scene by scene, you design the coverage plan in keyframes

This is the process. You go through a scene, first through analysis of the story, then thinking of coverage in terms of keyframes. You take into account how and why you want to employ movement of the frame and within the frame. You consider the scene-to-scene interconnections and any effect they would have on your intentions for the start and finish of the scene. This is translated into an overhead diagram, from which you derive a conventional shot list. Then you move on to the next scene and do it again.

The resilient shot list comes from a coverage plan

The entire shot list for this scene could be different in a hundred ways and still meet the creative intentions of the coverage plan. You have great freedom for creative or stylistic interpretation. This flexibility in the derivation of a shot list from the coverage plan also gives you resilience going into production.

Because the coverage plan has a very general and story-based keyframe approach, you can execute changes to the shots without fear of disrupting the cinematic storytelling. If things go wrong on set for any reason, you can retreat to the coverage plan and keyframes, throw out the overhead diagram and shot list, and still meet your creative intent. It's not fun or easy. But it's better than making up shots on the fly that have an arbitrary relationship to the storytelling.

Not only that, the work of deep analysis that is needed to take this approach will make you able to solve problems flexibly. You will have confidence in your story knowledge and clarity in your creative intentions, enabling you to deliver it through cinematic storytelling.

Summary

Here is a summary of the process we followed for this scene example. You can follow this process step by step until you've internalized it. Then you can adapt it to your own filmmaking style.

Resist the urge to commit to shots before you've figured out the storytelling, point by point, and derived a coverage plan. Simply assigning patterns to sections of the script will give you a good foundation. But it is in the choice of keyframe qualities and the use of movement that you can really bring the feeling of the storytelling to the audience through cinematic means.

1   Break down the scene into major beats and mark the major phases of the storytelling.
2   Outline the storytelling, point by point, according to what the audience needs to know, conclude, understand, or question. This is a functional retelling, blunt and transparent.
    NOTE: These first two steps would be part and parcel of normal storytelling preparation.
3   Determine or decide what is actually seen at each point. This identifies the visible element pattern and the subject of framing.
4   Decide what keyframe qualities or attributes would help to align the visible, declarative story information and the inferential story information. These keyframes will be the foundation of the coverage plan. If you choose to storyboard, here is when you would do a first rough storyboard, to be adjusted as you finalize plans.
5   Decide what qualities of movement of the frame, or within the frame, would best communicate the inferential story information. Consider incremental or evolving story progress, story agency, externalization of strong emotion or physical effect, and flow or dynamism of the moment.
6   Identify scene-to-scene interconnections, so that the open and close of the scene assist the total arc of the story. There may be the need for continuous action. There may be the need for a soft connection that carries forward into the next scene. There may be the need for a chapter marker to indicate a new story thread. There may be a disconnection and reset of the story, for major segmentation of the story arc or to resonate with major emotional moments.
7   Map out camera positions to suit the keyframes. This will point out practical issues of staging and blocking. It will show how moving camera can connect keyframes like beads on a string. It will show which camera positions will serve incremental needs, with a single keyframe per shot.

8   Derive the shot list from the coverage plan and overhead diagram. This
tracks the keyframes and decisions on movement. Multiple versions of
a shot list are usually generated, taking into account the need for econ-
omy, practicality, and stylistic concerns. This is then prioritized to suit
production needs.

What you can do . . .

Work through this process with your own scenes and scripts. Start simply
and work your way up to more complex challenges. For each exercise on
the list, block, light, and shoot the results, then edit to see how your choices
function in a flow of storytelling. If you want to work on just the framing
concepts, use overall lighting.

•   Start with a simple Action scene. Figure out your perspectives, proximity, and movement. Design the coverage plan. In Action scenes, you
can decide to use one, two, or all three perspectives and just follow the
characters.
•   Try a Dialogue scene. Consider how to enter the shot-and-reverse
patterns. Try symmetrical balanced pairs with mirror-image keyframe
qualities. Try asymmetrical pairs with dissimilar keyframe qualities and
see how they feel.
•   Try a three-scene sequence. Make sure that two out of the three scenes
are continuous action and that the third scene is either a soft connection
or a new story thread. Work through each scene, then figure out how
to make the connections between them.
•   Then try a short film script. Work through the coverage plan for each
scene, for all the interconnections, and assess the way it supports the
total story arc. If it feels like there is no rising in energy, consider holding back on any dynamic movement and tight CUs until the energy is
building. If it's flat, add evolving shots that use movement. If individual
scenes lack shape, consider how to switch staging to put characters in
different sides of the frame.
•   Then try a feature film or long-form story . . . and make great cinematic
storytelling that excites and enthralls us.

Reference materials

Overview

This chapter is a compilation of addenda: reference materials, additional notes, and guides. It is separate from the main text and not intended to be read through from start to finish. Use this material to look up specific concerns you may have when planning to execute your own scripts. You can read sections in isolation, as you need the information. Each section is standalone information.

This includes:

- A comprehensive guide to the conversion and cross-application of basic patterns, referencing examples within this book.
- Additional notes are provided on scene-to-scene considerations, beyond what is covered in the main text. This includes:
  - Beginnings and endings
  - Major story points and act breaks
  - The life-changing moment for the main character
  - Production considerations and planning for sequences of continuous action
  - Planned intercutting between scenes
  - Use of chapter markers
  - Soft interconnections between scenes
  - Implications of scripted transitions
- Pitfalls for new filmmakers to avoid when going into production.

Reference: Conversion and cross-application of patterns

This a comprehensive reference guide explaining how patterns convert from one to the next or are used in a cross-application manner. This includes

DOI: 10.4324/9781003080657-15

references back to examples in the book, so that you can see those examples with fresh eyes.

This is based on the structuring patterns of Action, Dialogue, and Settings. It shows how each can convert to the next. It also shows how each might be cross-applied – by which I mean used for presenting story information when the pattern does not match the scripted format. The nested patterns of Looks, Objects, and Evocative Imagery are considered within the structuring patterns.

Use this as a reference while you figure out what works best for your story and your creative interpretation of the script you are making into a cinematic masterpiece.

Action pattern conversions . . .

1) To Dialogue with the addition of another character in frame, and the development of reciprocal shot pairs.

   a) Refer to the example: *Out of Time*[1] (Figure 8.5).

2) To Look/See with focused gaze followed by any POV or focus of character attention.

   a) Refer to the examples: *No Country for Old Men*[2] (Figure 5.10, Figure 5.11).

3) To Object with Look/See pattern.

   a) Refer to the examples: *Cape Fear*[3] (Figure 6.3), *The English Patient*[4] (Figure 10.1).

4) To Object through shared framing indicating functional relationship.

   a) Refer to the example: *Out of Time*[5] (Figure 5.7).

5) To straight interpersonal Look with shared eyeline, overlaid on social situation.

   a) Refer to the example: *Out of Time*[6] (Figure 6.2).

6) To Settings with exit of character or increased distance to "lose" character in Setting, or through Look/See to Setting.

   a) Refer to the example: *The Lord of the Rings: The Fellowship of the Ring*[7] (Figure 12.3).

7) To Evocative Imagery through any means that displaces declarative with aesthetic concerns in handling of subject matter.

   a) Refer to the examples: *Children of Men*[8] (Figure 9.7), *Arrival*[9] (Figure 11.1).

Action cross-application . . .

8) Walk & talk or any Dialogue interaction without using reciprocal pairs, including functional Dialogue for Action or process (operating a spaceship).

   a) Refer to the examples: *Se7en*[10] (Figure 8.1), *The Right Stuff*[11] (Figure 8.2), *Saving Private Ryan*[12] (Figure 5.3).

9) Setting through subjective character experience, usually connected through Look/See but also possible simply through character entry into frame.

   a) Refer to the example: *Parasite*[13] (Figure 9.4, Figure 9.5).

Dialogue pattern conversion . . .

1) To Action with exit of other character or with characters on the move, walk & talk.

   a) Refer to the examples: *Harry Potter and the Goblet of Fire*[14] (Figure 12.4).

2) To Settings with exit of characters or move back to "lose" characters in Setting, or through Look/See to Settings.

   a) Refer to the example: *Gladiator*[15] (Figure 9.8)

3) To Look/See with averted (away from Dialogue partner) gaze and any POV or appropriate angle on the subject of attention, replacing inter-subjective with single-character subjective experience.

   a) Refer to the example: *The Lord of the Rings: The Fellowship of the Ring*[16] (Figure 10.2). The third segment of the illustration shows Bilbo with the ring. Before that, he was arguing with Gandalf. He turns away and enters an intimate Look/See with the ring.

4) To Object with Look/See or with exit of characters to CU on Object.

   a) Refer to the example: *The Lord of the Rings: The Fellowship of the Ring*[17] (Figure 10.2). The last segment of the illustration shows Gandalf holding out the ring to Frodo with tongs.

5) To Evocative Imagery through any means that displaces declarative with aesthetic concerns in handling of subject matter.

   a) I have not included an illustration of this. However, in *The Girl with the Dragon Tattoo*,[18] there is a scene with Lisbeth at a dance club. Dialogue pairs are shown in the stroboscopic light of the club. The non-verbal dialogue is handled as Evocative Imagery to suit the all-encompassing vibe of the club and the night.

Dialogue cross-application . . .

6) Non-verbal reciprocal pairs within action or subsumed within overall Dialogue.

    a) Refer to the examples: *Cast Away*[19] (Figure 1.2), *Michael Clayton*[20] (Figure 6.7).

7) Mimicking reciprocal pairs in Look/See with Object having intrinsic significance.

    a) Refer to the example: *The Lord of the Rings: The Fellowship of the Ring*[21] (Figure 10.2). The third segment shows Bilbo obsessing over the ring in what could be felt as an asymmetrical dialogue pair.

Settings pattern conversion . . .

1) To Action with the arrival, finding, or emergence of character.

    a) Refer to the examples: *Leave No Trace*[22] (Figure 9.2), *The Shawshank Redemption*[23] (Figure 9.3).

2) To Dialogue with arrival/finding/emerging of characters.

    a) I have not included a screenshot illustration of this. Typically through exterior establishing shot, followed by interior dialogue scene. But also possible with characters entering Settings frame while in conversation.

3) To Look/See through reverse Look/See, resulting in shared experience.

    a) Refer to the example: *Saving Private Ryan*[24] (Figure 6.5).

4) To Object through slideshow or tour/survey with Object as frame subject.

    a) Refer to the example: *Saving Private Ryan*[25] (Figure 6.5).

5) To Evocative Imagery through any means that displaces informational intent with aesthetic or mood and tone concerns.

    a) Refer to the example: *Saving Private Ryan*[26] (Figure 5.4).

Settings cross-applications . . .

6) Distant observation of dialogue within physical or social settings.

    a) Refer to distant Dialogue two-shot within the example: *His Dark Materials*[27] (Figure 13.1).

7) Settings as Evocative imagery for temporal ellipsis, or emotional reverberation.

    a) Refer to the example: *Children of Men*[28] (Figure 9.7).

Reference: Scene-to-scene considerations

The following are general considerations regarding scene-to-scene connections or disconnections. These are ways to think about these issues if you get stuck making a coverage plan for any reason.

Beginnings and endings

Only two scenes in a movie lack scene-to-scene boundaries – the first and last scene. Consider that boundary to be between the everyday life of the audience and the immersion in your storyworld. You can be reasonably assured that your audience wants to get immersed in the storyworld. Immediately offer them something that showcases the overall experience and satisfactions of your story. How could you cinematically tell the opening moments of your scripted story, in a way that aligns with expectations for the movie?

Consider vicarious engagement and perspective. Does the totality of your story take you far into the subjective experience of one character? Try your opening scene through their experience, participating or connecting with them, using their Look to introduce the storyworld and situation. Does your movie invite judgment of the characters or situations? Try opening with prolonged observation, with the sense of witnessing, before you align closely with character experience.

Some movies may start in the middle of action, throwing us in the thick of it and forcing us to figure it out on the fly. But many movies start with prolonged coverage of Settings, leading to characters. This coverage allows the audience to shift gears and enter the storyworld.

The end of the movie has the reverse concerns, equally critical. We say goodbye to the characters, leaving them in the storyworld, and we return to our own temporal flow. How are we released? Will it resonate properly? The screenwriter has certainly considered these issues, and so, as filmmakers, we need to grasp the inferences on entering and leaving the storyworld.

Does the story seek full resolution of all major story issues? Tensions can be resolved, and we can say goodbye to the story and characters through progressively pulling back from their location until they or their community are simply the details of a broader picture. Or are loose ends and lack of resolution part of the feeling of the story's finish? Consider how patterns are felt to be complete when all the components are finished, like a Look/See pair or shot-and-reverse. What happens if you start a pattern and end the film without finishing it? Would that align with the sense of unresolved story questions? If the action demands knowing how the main character feels, and you deny the audience the connection that gives them access to expressions, would that feel unresolved? Use what you know of patterns to suit the desired experience.

Major story points and act breaks

Any major segmentation of the story will need to be felt and understood by the audience. These are endings and beginnings within the total arc.

Consider a story in three acts. Act One is set in the past, Act Two in the present, Act Three in the future. You can treat the coverage the same in all three, relying on costumes, language, settings, and the look of the cinematography to make each act its own unique segment.

You could also consider coverage style – choosing a subset of approaches and leaving others off the table – as a means to feel the difference. For example, in the past, all the coverage is incremental and movement of the frame is minimal. In the present, incremental and evolving framing intermix for scene shaping and to feel a sense of energy. In the future, there is nothing but evolving, moving framing that's very dynamic. As we've seen in horror and suspense, restricting perspectives can provide a payoff. The same is true with entire styles of coverage.

Consider a change of pace. Exploration of Settings through Evocative Imagery can feel like a moment when plot pressures give way to pure feeling and aesthetics. That can feel like a change of pace. If the last scene of a major segment ends on a contemplative note, you might consider leaping into the middle of Action at the start of the next, precisely to have a change of pace.

Clarity of presentation is essential for those moments. You can afford questions and uncertainty in many places in a story – or even encourage it. But clarity is key when some critical story point happens, just as it is key when some major clue is provided in a mystery or some major decision is made that affects the plot. Even if the scene involves misdirection – with the character's goal being a phantom or waste of time – you need to have it presented clearly or the misdirection won't happen.

The life-changing moment for the main character

There is typically only one life-changing moment for a character, which alters or even blows up their prior belief system and leaves them searching for new ways to cope. Please refer to the examples from *Children of Men*[29] (Figure 9.7), and *Gladiator*[30] (Figure 9.8).

It is the singularity of a life-changing moment that makes it special and central to the total story arc. Keep something in reserve for that moment. It could be the one ECU on the main character, or the use of Evocative Imagery for registering that moment.

Production considerations in planning for sequences

Sequences are collections of scenes that function as continuous action. The action must cross scene boundaries with hard connections, as in chase sequences that move through a series of locations.

The component scenes may be shot on different days or even weeks apart. Make notes so that you have consistency of pattern and character. Make sure you maintain screen direction. Make sure that it is covered as if it were one scene. **Continuity of pattern and character turn a collection of scenes into one sequence.**

Without notes for each scene within a continuous action sequence, you can make simple mistakes that confuse the audience. This is where coverage from directly in front (Connection) and following directly behind (Participation) can be immensely useful. These are "neutral" positions, and so could work with Observational perspectives from either side.

If you have predetermined a direction of flow and trajectory, clearly note it and stick with it. Perhaps your action goes from frame left to frame right. If there isn't a reason to change that, stick with it. Change sides if you want a phase change, or jump around if you want a sense of chaotic action or of characters being lost or confused, or turned in circles.

Coverage for planned intercutting between scenes

Whenever the script calls for intercutting between scenes, it will be specially formatted on the page. Your job will be to make the coverage between the two scenes match in whatever way is appropriate to the storytelling. A common example is a phone call. When you see the movie, it feels like one scene. No problem, right? When you look at the script, you will see that each end of the phone call is in a different location. That's only sensible. But that means you may shoot those scenes days or weeks apart. That means you might forget.

Please refer to a phone call intercutting example from *The Right Stuff*[31] (Figure 8.3). You will see how important the mirror-image framing is, with the matched angles and shot size, and implied shared eyeline. That scene would not work without that coverage planning. Many phone calls are not such tight and intimate connections between characters. They may need asymmetrical or unbalanced shot pairs, mismatched eyelines, or even facing in different directions.

Other common intercutting scenes are when sets of characters are engaged in parallel preparation for some later action that joins them in the same scene. You must set them up with parallel coverage, matching perspective and proximity, so the intention of the storytelling is carried across.

Use of chapter markers

Some scenes need to be set apart from the scene before, so the audience understands that they have moved on to something new. This is not a major story segmentation, like an act break. Perhaps the same character is in both scenes but time has passed, and they have moved on to whatever is next. The scene boundary is clear. This is a job for a chapter marker that signals "turning the page" and going to the next event, time, or place.

The most common chapter marker is the conventional establishing shot of the location's exterior. Usually the action is inside that location. The conventional, single-shot establishing of a location is reorienting the audience to a new physical location (see Figure 8.4, *No Country for Old Men*[32]). Or we see a building and tilt up to higher floors. We cut to the inside of an apartment. We see a car whiz by, and we cut to inside the car and join the characters (see Figure 8.9, *American Beauty*[33]).

Soft interconnections between scenes

Some scene boundaries will need major breaks and others will need minor breaks. Most will have a sense of flow between scenes – not continuous action but the sense that mood, or emotions, or a story thread is connecting them, even if it isn't entirely obvious. Most often, it is just felt. That is inferential story information, and cinematic means are well suited to providing those feelings of subtle, loose, or soft continuations of the story thread, character actions, or even just the mood or tone.

Here is a short list of how that can be accomplished:

1) If you have continuity of character, very little planning is needed.

    a) Refer to the examples: *Midsommar*[34] (Figure 12.7), from drinking mushroom tea to hallucinating, staying with Dani. *Out of Time*[35] (Figure 8.5), from police station, to outside house, to meeting Ann, staying with Matt.

2) If you have continuity of pattern, then you must make notes at the boundaries of both scenes so that the consideration of keyframe matching is executed. Otherwise, it is very easy to forget, and you won't have the pattern continuation you are counting on.

    a) I have not included a screenshot illustration, but in *Sleepless in Seattle*,[36] there is a scene that ends with Annie exiting one door on the East Coast, and we see Sam coming through a door on the West Coast. These are planned and matched. The Action pattern continues, but with a different character and location, giving us the sense of their connection.

3) If you have continuity of trajectory or flow, intended to loosely connect one scene to the next, you must make notes for the boundaries of both scenes. Is it left-to-right? Fast or slow? Whichever is shot first, make notes about the camera work so that it can be continued when you shoot the adjoining scene.

    a) If you intend a graphic match between scenes, once again, make notes for the boundaries of both scenes involved. Take a still image of the frame to match from the one you shoot first. Use that to match the exact composition in the adjoining scene.

5) If you are using an inner Look/See pattern, forward or reverse, you don't need to make many notes. The only exception is if the eyeline

must match to reinforce the sense that the character is actually seeing it, not just seeing it in their imagination.

a)   Refer to the example: *Saving Private Ryan*[37] (Figure 6.5).

6)   If you plan to use sound or soundtrack to loosely join scenes, you need to discuss the implication with your sound technicians and include those notes in your production documents. Sound plays a huge role in the continuation of emotion and the adjustment or resetting of emotion. That is outside our purview, but every filmmaker should fully investigate the role of sound in the audience's sense of movie context. Music and soundtrack are almost entirely contextual, and the same type of thinking we are using for cinematic storytelling also applies to sound.

Implications of scripted transitions

Many modern scripts contain few, if any, scripted transitions beyond "FADE IN" at the open and "FADE TO BLACK" at the end. Some scripted transitions are conventions for signaling changes in time for things like flashbacks, or the introduction of montage segments. Some are simply punctuation between scenes or automatically added by scriptwriting software.

The transition "CUT TO:" can usually be ignored if it appears after every scene. If it is an anomaly, check if this means that the scenes have hard or soft connection, or disconnection.

The transition "DISSOLVE TO:" is a convention in some types of screenwriting. It is usually not an actual instruction to use a dissolve in the editing; it is instead telling the reader that a non-standard scene is coming up. These are usually soft connections, analogous to the visual dissolve of overlapping images in editing. This could be a flashback, montage, series of images, or intercutting. It could be a new location, never seen before but carrying forward some aspect of the prior scene. In all cases, there is a connection between the scenes that could be reinforced.

Any transition that includes "FADE", outside of the first and last scene, usually means a disconnection between scenes for some major story segmentation. This goes beyond a simple chapter marker and usually signifies the need for some extended reorienting time, usually using Settings patterns or Evocative Imagery.

Reference: Pitfalls for new filmmakers to avoid

There are many things that experienced filmmakers learn through painful mistakes. Here is a list that can save you from repeating some of those mistakes.

a)   Never rely on just one angle. Do a second angle, even for simple scenes.
b)   Always have any motions by actors completed in any shot. The only way to "cut on action" is to have the in-frame movements overlap. That

is only possible if every character action is complete from every angle that it is covered.

c) Any planned character Looks should be held longer than might feel natural for the actors. The audience needs to register them before they can be used in a planned Look/See pair. Like a pair of pants, too long is okay because you can tailor them; too short is useless.

d) The same is true for any shots of Objects. Too long is okay; too short is useless.

e) If characters can enter frame at the start (head of the scene), and/or exit frame at the end (tail of the scene), make it happen. If you don't use it, no big deal. But if you need it, it's there for the editor to use.

f) If any scene ends on strong emotions, especially reactions, don't cut the camera the instant the actor conveys that emotion. Wait for the actor to leave that moment before you cut. We are talking about a few seconds of time. That won't affect your schedule but could be brilliant.

g) Try not to be too rigid with framing or staging, or anything that multiple people will be involved with (actors plus director plus cinematographer, etc.) Stick to your context-creation plans but consider letting the exact details be a combined effort. Otherwise, you may destroy the mood on set and probably won't get that "perfect" shot you want. As long as it feels the way it needs to feel, it will function for your coverage.

h) Don't lose sight of continuity or 180° Line issues related to the coverage. Make notes so you can refer to them on set. You can always switch sides through a "neutral" front or back position. Make any switch in the Line on purpose, not by accident.

i) If in doubt about how any camera moves will edit, include buffer shots to save the coverage. A buffer shot is an insert that allows the editor to cut between long takes. This is the only time I recommend shooting anything without central story significance.

  1) Do this if a complex shot will evolve through movement to another staging. The buffer shot lets the editor select the best take without messing up the flow.

  2) Do this when a complex and lengthy scene has only a single angle for one phase. The buffer shot will let the editor mix and match the best takes for start and finish.

j) When you do initial blocking before lighting, do the entire blocking all the way to the end. It is easy for filmmakers to get through the "hard part" and forget to block the ending of the scene. This will be a disaster. Block from the first to the very last instant. Then your shot list will function, performances will be supported, and the producer won't want to fire all of you.

k) The shot list may include "insert" shots that may be considered sacrificial in the heat of the moment. These may actually be critical storytelling elements. Do not neglect the "little shots." because the whole storytelling may depend on them. Your coverage plan and list of key-frames should tell you their significance, in case you forget for any reason.

l)   ALWAYS BE POLITE. Some days you may love each other, and some days you may not. As long as you always practice courtesy on set, you can keep working productively, no matter the circumstances or mood on set.

Notes

1   *Out of Time*. Directed by Carl Franklin, Cinematography by Theo van de Sande. MGM, Original Film, Monarch Pictures, released 2003. DVD: MGM Home Entertainment (2006, USA). Start time: 00:02:04.

2   *No Country for Old Men*. Directed by Ethan Coen & Joel Coen, Cinematography by Roger Deakins. Paramount Vantage, Miramax, Scott Rudin Productions, released 2007. DVD: Buena Vista Home Entertainment (2008, USA). Start time: 00:05:12.

3   *Cape Fear*. Directed by Martin Scorsese, Cinematography by Freddie Francis. Amblin Entertainment, Cappa Films, Tribeca Productions, released 1991. DVD: Universal Studios (2005, USA).

4   *The English Patient*. Directed by Anthony Minghella, Cinematography by John Seale. Miramax, Tiger Moth Productions, released 1996. DVD: Buena Vista Home Video (2005, USA). Start time: 01:55:35.

5   *Out of Time*. Ibid. Start time: 01:10:06.

6   *Out of Time*. Ibid. Start time: 00:56:48.

7   *The Lord of the Rings: The Fellowship of the Ring*. Directed by Peter Jackson, Cinematography by Andrew Lesnie. New Line Cinema, WingNut Films, released 2001. DVD: Special Extended Edition, New Line Home Entertainment (2002, USA). Start time: 01:50:07.

8   *Children of Men*. Directed by Alfonso Cuarón, Cinematography by Emmanuel Lubezki. Universal Pictures, Strike Entertainment, Hit & Run Productions, released 2006. DVD: Universal Studios (2007, USA). Start time: 00:58:59.

9   *Arrival*. Directed by Denis Villeneuve, Cinematography by Bradford Young. Lava Bear ilms, FilmNation Entertainment, 21 Laps Entertainment, Xenolinguistics, released 016. DVD: Paramount Pictures (2017, USA). Start time: 01:26:37.

10   *Se7en*. Directed by David Fincher, Cinematography by Darius Khondji. Cecchi Gori Pictures, Juno Pix, New Line Cinema, released 1995. DVD: New Line Home Video (2000, USA). Start time: 00:01:58.

11   *The Right Stuff*. Directed by Phillip Kaufman, Cinematography by Caleb Deschanel. The Ladd Company, released 1983. DVD: Warner Home Video (1997, USA). Start time: 02:09:04.

12   *Saving Private Ryan*. Directed by Steven Spielberg, Cinematography by Janusz Kaminski. DreamWorks, Paramount Pictures, Amblin Entertainment, released 1998. DVD: DreamWorks (1999, USA). Start time: 00:42:40.

13   *Parasite*. Directed by Bong Joon Ho, Cinematography by Kyung-pyo Hong. Barunson E&A, CJ E&M Film Financing & Investment Entertainment & Comics, CJ Entertainment, released 2019. DVD: Universal Studios (2020, USA). Start time: 00:12:44. Start time: 01:32:08.

14   *Harry Potter and the Goblet of Fire*. Directed by Mike Newell, Cinematography by Roger Pratt. Warner Bros., Heyday Films, Patalex IV Productions Ltd., released 2005. DVD: Warner Bros Home Video (2005, USA). Start time: 01:21:28.

15 *Gladiator.* Directed by Ridley Scott, Cinematography by John Mathieson. Dream-Works, Universal Pictures, Scott Free Productions, 2000. DVD: Signature Selection, DreamWorks (2000, USA). Start time: 01:11:45.

16 *The Lord of the Rings: The Fellowship of the Ring.* Ibid.

17 *The Lord of the Rings: The Fellowship of the Ring.* Ibid.

18 *The Girl with the Dragon Tattoo.* Directed by David Fincher, Cinematography by Darius Khondji. Columbia Pictures, MGM, Scott Rudin Productions, released 2011. DVD: Sony Pictures Home Entertainment (2012, USA). Start time: 01:15:48.

19 *Cast Away.* Directed by Robert Zemeckis, Cinematography by Don Burgess. Twentieth Century Fox, Dreamworks, released 2000. DVD: Twentieth Century Fox Home Entertainment (2001, USA). Start time: 00:14:06.

20 *Michael Clayton.* Directed by Tony Gilroy, Cinematography by Robert Elswit. Samuels Media, Castle Rock Entertainment, Mirage Enterprises, released 2007. DVD: Warner Bros. Home Video (2008, USA). Start time: 00:13:25.

21 *The Lord of the Rings: The Fellowship of the Ring.* Ibid.

22 *Leave No Trace.* Directed by Debra Granik, Cinematography by Michael McDonough. BRON Studios, Creative Wealth Media Finance, Harrison Productions, released 2018. DVD: Universal Studios (2018, USA). Start time: 00:01:23.

23 *The Shawshank Redemption.* Directed by Frank Darabont, Cinematography by Roger Deakins. Castle Rock Entertainment, released 1994. DVD: Warner Bros. Entertainment (2007, USA). Start time: 00:08:43.

24 *Saving Private Ryan.* Ibid. Start time: 00:27:08.

25 *Saving Private Ryan.* Ibid. Start time: 00:27:08.

26 *Saving Private Ryan.* Ibid. Start time: 00:42:40.

27 *His Dark Materials*, S1E3. Directed by Dawn Shadforth, Cinematography by Suzie Lavelle. Bad Wolf, British Broadcasting Corporation (BBC), Home Box Office (HBO), Warner Bros., released on streaming, 2019. DVD: Warner Bros. Home Entertainment (2020, USA). Start time: 00:25:50.

28 *Children of Men.* ibid. Start time: 00:58:59.

29 *Children of Men.* Ibid. Start time: 00:58:59.

30 *Gladiator.* Ibid. Start time: 01:11:45.

31 *The Right Stuff.* Ibid. Start time: 02:22:04.

32 *No Country for Old Men.* Ibid. Start time: 00:20:52.

33 *American Beauty.* Directed by Sam Mendes, Cinematography by Conrad Hall. DreamWorks Pictures, released 1999. DVD: Dreamworks Home Entertainment (2000, USA). Start time: 00:25:29.

34 *Midsommar.* Directed by Ari Aster, Cinematography by Pawel Pogorzelski. A24, B-Reel Films, Nordisk Film, Square Peg, released 2019. DVD: A24 Films, LLC, Lions Gate Entertainment (2020, USA). Start time: 00:28:52.

35 *Out of Time.* Ibid. Start time: 00:02:04.

36 *Sleepless in Seattle.* Directed by Nora Ephron, Cinematography by Sven Nykvist. TriStar Pictures, released 1993. DVD: 10th Anniversary Edition, Columbia TriStar (2003, USA). Start time: 00:38:42.

37 *Saving Private Ryan.* Ibid. Start time: 00:27:08.

Index

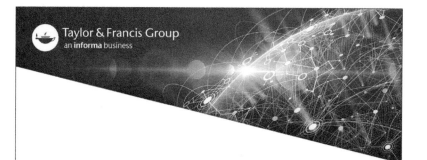